PRAISE for COMING HOME
by Brandon Houston

"Brandon Houston's *Coming Home* is a powerful antidote to the poison of mainstream psychiatric thinking. We need more accounts like this: deeply personal and heartfelt, infused with spiritual reflection, and pointing the way towards new responses to madness."

—Will Hall, host of Madness Radio and author of *The Harm Reduction Guide to Coming Off Psychiatric Drugs*

"*Coming Home* offers an important contribution to our understanding of madness along with profound implications for supporting the recovery process. The author invites the reader to step outside the narrow and battered box of medical reductionism and onto a broad tapestry composed of an intriguing weave of biology, psychology, spirituality and lived experience. This is one adventure you don't want to miss!"

—Paris Williams, Ph.D., clinical psychologist, author of *Rethinking Madness*

"Houston compassionately invites us into his, and potentially everyone's, opening, coming apart and re-integrating, as a sacred unfolding to befriend and be expanded by an intimate vision of a psychotic break and a challenge to mainstream models of pathology, shared with love, straightforward candor and zen perspective."

—Adam Jogen Salzberg, Zen teacher, spiritual counselor

"Madness is a topic that's ill-treated in both the Western and Eastern psychological traditions. We need more well-written and engaging books like this to help normalize, soothe, and support the most sensitively attuned among us. Although Brandon is describing an outlying experience (very few have such incredibly destabilizing psychedelic experiences) I think we can assess the wisdom of society, in part, by seeing how it treats its outliers. If you find yourself living in an unwise society, as many of us do, count yourself lucky to have access to the wisdom of *Coming Home*."

—Vince Fakhoury Horn, BuddhistGeeks.org

"In his seminal book, *Recovering Sanity*, Ed Podvoll quoted Charles Darwin, who asked in his journals, 'Why don't the psychologists ever talk about courage?' Here we have the very example of courage in Brandon Houston's excellent memoir-manual of losing and regaining mind. He is honest, intelligent and lionhearted in his challenge of the reductionist medical 'best practices' used to treat psychosis, and offers a personal journey of recovery that embodies the age-old Windhorse principles of synchronizing body, mind and environment. This is an important contribution to the literature and body of work in the 'contemplative psychotherapy' field. I would recommend this book to interested clinicians and anyone with lived experience."

—Blake Baily, MA LPC, Windhorse Legacy Project

COMING HOME

www.BrandonHouston.info

COMING HOME

A Psychotherapist's Reflections on Madness and the State of Western Psychosis

Brandon Houston

SKYHORSE
PRESS

SKYHORSE
PRESS

Published by Houston Press
Westhaven, California

A Guide for Families written by Constance Packard, MSW; Sally Clay; and Harold Raush, courtesy of Windhorse Integrative Medicine
www.WindhorseIMH.org

For information about special discounts for bulk purchases or author interviews, appearances, and speaking engagements please contact:

www.BrandonHouston.info

First Edition

Edited by Christina DeBusk
Cover design by Lisa Cline
Interior design & production by Rodney Miles

"We wish that all this medical materialism could be made to hold its tongue."

William James

The Varieties of Religious Experience

For the dragons.

Contents

Introduction 1

Section One: Lived Experience 7

Moving Box 8

No Return 13

Rhythm and Routine 23

Thank You Jesus for Being Here 27

East-West 32

The List 38

Unfathomable 46

Finding Rhythm and Routine Again 54

Zen 58

Paul 64

How Do You Not Be Crazy? 71

Pulled to Madness 79

Traveling 99

An Interlude 115

Catastrophic Mental Health Crisis 116

Section Two: Expertise by Training 123

Where's My Training? 125

Human to Human 131

Basic Attendance 137

Asylum Awareness 143

The Cocktail 149
Power 156
History of Sanity 160
Islands of Clarity 165
Synchronizing Body, Mind, and Environment 170
Another Reality 176
Section Three: Expertise by Experience 183
Diagnosis 185
Sensitivity 200
Making Meaning of Experience 212
Madness-Based Ego 227
The Body of Activity 242
Conclusion 253
Acknowledgments 267
About the Author 269
Appendix: A Guide for Families 273
Contents 274
About Windhorse and this Guide 274
Introduction: Family Guidelines 275
Attitude: Cultivate Acceptance And Raise Respect 277
Orientation: Choose Happiness 281
Boundaries: Set Limits, Give Space 282
Full Expression: Show Appreciation, Be Honest 283
Social Environment: Find Community 284
Conclusion 285

Introduction

IN THE FALL of 2008, at the age of 23, I experienced a devastating psychedelic-induced acute psychotic break. I was lost to another world of overwhelm beyond anything I had experienced before. I quickly became homeless, stranded in a state of heightened intensity and confusion for months, finally "coming down" only after my father took me in.

Following the intensity of my break, I experienced a period of severe social isolation and withdrawal. I hardly spoke to another person for a year and a half. I also gave up almost all expressions of being human. I did not brush my teeth, rarely bathed, and completely gave up on "having a life." I was trapped in an in-between state, not quite human and not able to find the thread of my life again.

During this time of isolation, I experienced a severe and punishing depression — a near-constant state of suicidal shame. On repeat, I would tell myself to kill myself. Every moment of every day, my thoughts were a continual reminder to end my life. I saw it as a fitting punishment for having "lost" or "given up" my life so fully during my psychotic break. My only reprieve from the torment of my mind was to watch television. Which I did, almost continuously for a year and a half.

Amidst this punishing depression and isolation, I somehow found the energy and enough reprieve from the relentless self-hate to re-enter the human condition. Once again attending to the basics of being human. And rather quickly moving into working, living, and finding meaningful engagement with the world again.

At the same time, while putting my life back together again, I was in a near-constant state of underlying fear. I did not know at the time it was possible to recover from a psychotic break and go on to live a full, meaningful life. I felt as though I was cheating in some way by pretending to be normal again.

I assumed, as many do, that I had a long-term "mental illness" excluding me from living a full life. Most likely, it was schizophrenia. This thought terrified me. While rebuilding myself post-break, the fear of having a lifelong defining mental illness was my greatest barrier to rebuilding and maintaining the new life I was creating.

Somewhere along the way, I decided I would not be defined by the Western medical model's understanding of psychosis, "mental illness," or brain-based mental health disorders. Instead, I chose to go my own way, committed to living a full life and honoring my unique way of experiencing myself and the world.

From my previous contemplative training in Zen monasteries and my undergraduate studies in transpersonal psychology, I knew it was possible to work with my mind and move from more "open" expansive states of consciousness to more mundane everyday states of consciousness with ease and fluidity. It was this training that gave me the confidence to forgo defining myself as "ill" and instead see myself in need of training and healing.

During this time, I was fortunate to meet a dear friend who experienced seven years of madness in the 1970s. By the time I met Paul, he was approaching 80 and had lived a full and vibrant life. He became the foundation from which I knew it was possible to experience a devastating psychotic break and continue to go on living, full-heartedly. He was a beacon of possibility at a time when I desperately needed to know it was possible to go on living after what I had been through.

One of my biggest fears was I would not be able to lead a spiritual life following my period of madness. Prior to my break, I was a committed Zen student studying many of the various transformative offerings now available in the modern West. I even contributed to a book, *Living Deeply: The Art and Science of Everyday Transformation.*

I met Paul through a Zen community I became connected with following my period of madness. It was through Paul's example and the support of my Zen teacher that I was able to integrate the grounded, functional aspects of living with my deeper spiritual calling to awaken and be of service.

This book is meant to be an offering. A continuation of what Paul offered me. A template in a way. Not a template for how to heal from or even understand psychosis. I hope my ambitions are more basic and humble. All I want to convey to you is that it *is* possible to experience a psychotic break and go on to live a full and meaningful life. And maybe I can provide a few tips and perspectives to support the unique healing journey that is madness.

Unfortunately, our current understanding of psychosis and schizophrenia does not leave much room for the possibility of living a full life post-psychosis. Now that I am a trained therapist and have attempted to understand some of the root causes of my original fear of not being able to "come back" to living a full life, I see the Western medical model is deeply confused about the nature of psychosis.

It does not understand the basics of how to treat and support people in navigating a psychotic break. Instead, the Western medical model defines people who've had a break as having a brain-based chemical imbalance, a life-defining illness. This "story" of madness does not account for any possibility of healing from and moving beyond a psychotic break.

The Western model offers a maintenance-based treatment approach, placing individuals on antipsychotic medications proven to damage brains in the long run, causing increased symptoms, increased hospitalization, and negatively impacting a person's ability to fully recover from their initial psychotic break. This maintenance-based approach essentially tells people to expect to be struggling with their "illness" for the rest of their lives and, with medication, they can live a life resembling a "normal" life.

I would like to offer a different view on madness, psychosis, and even schizophrenia. One that is not rooted in "science" as we currently understand it but is more rooted in a contemplative understanding of learning to work with our unique experiences. At my core, I am a contemplative trained in a Western Zen tradition. I do not see the mind or human experience as psychologists or scientists view the human condition. For me, this life is a mysterious gift playing out. It is in living into the mystery and surrendering our desire to control and define our lives that life begins to share some of its beautiful secrets with us.

As a contemplative, I am not here to explain what psychosis is, create a new treatment, or even really understand psychosis. I only want to honor a basic human truth. Psychosis is a human condition and people have recovered from it for millennia. We do not need to "understand" or discover the "root cause" of madness to help people heal and return to functioning vibrant lives.

This book is broken down into three sections. The first section, **Lived Experience**, shares some of what I lived through both in my descent into madness and my return journey. In a way, this lends some credibility to my voice, letting you know I've been there. And I still struggle to "understand" what I went through.

The second section, **Expertise by Training**, looks at my training as a psychotherapist, offering some of what I've learned in how to work with extreme states of mind. I wish I could say my graduate training as a therapist prepared me for working with madness. It did not. It only helped me more fully understand the depths of confusion and denial the Western medical model has in working with psychosis.

My real training by expertise occurred after graduating, when I began working as a clinician at a contemplative mental health organization called Windhorse. The Windhorse Approach of working with extreme states was first developed in the 1980s. It is one of the few active "alternative" treatments to psychosis in the United States and an integration of Western psychology and Tibetan Buddhism.

The Windhorse model provides clients with the possibility of fully recovering from serious mental health crises. It is rooted in the power of healing relationships. I will share some of what I feel is relevant from the Windhorse Approach in supporting the recovery process.

The final section of this book, **Expertise by Experience**, is an alternative perspective on psychotic breaks. While my view is informed by Western scientific understanding, it is not a brain-based view of madness. Conversely, I explore what it means to be a sensitive individual in the modern world, amidst the lack of training we provide to people who experience "reality" differently than others. I look at my own return from madness and what I found helpful in finding my way back to functional, engaged living while honoring my unique sensitivity and the different ways I experience myself and the world around me.

May this book be of support to you on your journey. May you find the healing and guidance you need to live a full, wholehearted life. May we as a culture move beyond our current limited understandings of madness and psychosis, finally embracing what we've known for millennia: madness is part of the human condition and, with the right support, madness can be a healing and growth-driven experience for those on their recovery journey and for the world at large.

For all those who did not receive the support they needed to find their way back, I am sorry. And I hope we can do better for those in the future who've lost their footing and need some support in finding their way home.

Section One:

Lived Experience

IN THIS SECTION, I share my lived experience of madness and recovery. I explore the mind-bendingly confusing nature of madness. Of both being more open and connected to the world at large while, at the same time, losing complete touch with your life and the structure of rhythm and routine that makes you who you are.

I make the case that madness is not something to be understood or even cured. Instead, madness is a process that needs support, and the right healing ingredients to help someone find their way.

Moving Box

I am walking up the stairs to my apartment. To my right, on the banister, is a moving box. It is glowing. Radiant with benevolent energy. Weighted with some type of spiritual density.

As I look at it, I "know" it is time to move out of my apartment. I proceed to give away almost everything I own. There are free boxes in the college town I am living in. I bring load after load to the boxes. Letting go of almost everything that has defined me.

I watch Pirate, a fixture in the homeless community, walk the bike I gave him to the bike shop and sell it for beer money. I only keep a few items, some clothing and items from my altar, making a type of "travel altar" I bring with me everywhere I go.

I don't know at this moment if I will end up homeless in the same community as Pirate, sleeping in parks, wandering up and down the West Coast, lost to a psychedelic-like otherworldly reality, a constantly bending, overwhelming, dream-like landscape.

A reality where I don't know the rules of engagement. Where I don't know how to navigate. How to make sense of the new experiences I am having? I am constantly adjusting. Trying to make sense of this new "other world" I am living in. Trying to find my way home. Back to myself.

It will take me years to find my way back, to once again be able to live, to engage, to function, to maintain a continuous existence.

When I was in my early twenties, I had the fortunate misfortune of losing my mind. I was the homeless kid you see in the streets, lost, living in his own reality. No longer able to function, assumed by many to never find my way back again.

I am the story you've probably heard of, someone who took a psychedelic in the wrong set and setting and didn't "come back." The kid who went too far. Icarus falling into the ocean.

In modern medical thinking, which is sometimes referred to as the Western medical model, I am predisposed due to my genetic make-up to have schizophrenia or another equally serious mental health disorder that is irreversible. The night I ingested psychedelics with friends at a house party brought out my latent psychotic tendencies. I am now destined to manage my illness for the rest of my life, medicated, always aware that at any moment I might have another psychotic episode. Trained by the medical establishment to see my different ways of perceiving reality as "wrong," "broken" or, more simply, "symptoms."

Luckily for me, this is not my story. I am not saying this story is wrong, although I believe it is. I am saying that I choose to not use this story of latent "brokenness" to define my recovery from psychosis.

I choose another story, a story I didn't know existed when I started my journey of recovery. I choose the story of living fully, of healing and learning to work with my unique experiences. Learning to not always pathologize my altered state experiences as "broken." It was not easy to find my way home. Back into living, growing, loving, connecting, helping others, and being helped by others. Being a part of this human story.

I wish to tell *this* story. Not my story of madness. But my story of finding my way back from madness. Back into living. This book is meant to hold two purposes.

Firstly, to let anyone who needs to hear it know, you can recover from psychosis. It is totally normal to recover from psychosis. It is as human as recovering from depression, from moving past grief, from mending a broken bone, from a wound closing.

Psychosis is a human experience. Not an abnormality. And like most human experiences, it serves a function in the human condition. There is a built-in way to "heal" and "recover" from the experience of psychosis. Just as wounds naturally heal when given the right conditions, psychosis can naturally settle given the right conditions.

Second, I wish to provide some perspectives and pointers on the journey back. This isn't meant to be a template or recipe to be followed, but more reflections from someone who "went there" and "came back." I am going to share what helped me along the way and may help others on their unique journey home.

My journey is my own, just as each person's journey is their own. Please, listen to your inner wisdom and guidance. Do not blindly believe or listen to anything I say, I am not an expert. I am not the definitive voice on healing from psychosis. I am just someone who has been there and learned a few things along the way.

In order to share some of what I've learned, I am going to borrow some language and understanding from the Windhorse Approach to dealing with extreme states. Windhorse is a mental health model that emerged in the 80s when a psychologist was asked by his Buddhist teacher to develop a mental health approach that fused Western psychology with the insight and practices from Tibetan Buddhism. This merging is expressed in the community of Windhorse, where I worked for a number of years as a clinician.

I am a trained psychotherapist. Technically, I have a masters in counseling psychology. I am not writing this book as some expert on psychology, counseling, or the Western understanding of psychosis. To be honest, I think the Western medical model's understanding of psychosis does way more harm than good, which we will get into.

I am primarily writing this book as someone who has made the journey, someone who lost their mind and had to find some way back into living again because I wasn't willing to commit suicide.

Beyond being a "survivor" as we are sometimes called, I am a contemplative. My contemplative training has been by far the most beneficial resource in navigating my journey back from madness.

What do I mean when I say, I am a contemplative? In a basic way, I am someone who has meditated a decent amount, primarily in the Zen tradition. I have spent many days in silent meditation and tried to understand the deeper "truths" pointed to by contemplative traditions, particularly Buddhism.

In a way, it is hard for me to describe what it means to be a contemplative. We could go to the basics, the four noble truths of Buddhism. There is suffering. There is a way out of suffering. Follow the eightfold path and you will find a way out.

I like to translate this a little differently: "Life is hard, learn to work with it." So for the sake of recovering from madness, I believe the contemplative approach is best defined as "learning to work with your mind" or, more accurately, "learning to be with your experience in a generative and meaningful way for you and others."

I have waited a while to write this book. The night I lost my mind, when I ingested psychedelics at a party, not honoring set and setting, feels far away from where I am now. I am writing this book because if I don't write it now, the memory of that time in my life might fade too far to bring back.

At this juncture, I am no longer fighting against the modern medical models' understanding of madness. I used to struggle, worrying that my way of navigating what I went through was flawed, some form of denial. I was worried for a long time that I was not willing to admit to my mental health disorder. Now I don't really care. My template, my understanding, has brought me here. It seems to work well enough.

I have been functioning and living for over a decade now, without another break. It doesn't mean that I don't struggle or I don't have significant periods of struggle. To be human is to struggle. I think at its core, saying I have recovered from madness means I am able to integrate my struggle into my life and grow from my experiences, where psychosis can be seen as an inability to integrate one's experiences in a generative way.

If you've had a psychotic break or know someone dear to you who has, this book is meant to be an aid in healing and recovering from those experiences. I am not an expert on psychosis. I am not here to start a new system or model of therapy. I just want to provide some support on the journey that will be unique to you, your loved one, or your clients.

This book is meant for informational purposes only. While I am a trained mental health counselor, this book is not meant as a substitute for medical or mental health treatment by a trained professional. Please consult and seek treatment from a medical or mental health professional if you are struggling in a way that needs support. Any information in the book is educational and meant to be supportive, it does not constitute professional mental health advice.

No Return

I am walking down the street. I can feel my life is falling apart. I am twenty-two and just graduated from college. The plan I had for myself, the PhD program I intended to start in the fall and the accompanying financial aid money I needed are not happening. I failed a requisite class to start.

I feel trapped. Not sure how to move forward. Unable to give up the vision for my life that I have been working toward. I am not sure what to do.

I am instantly taken back by a distinct aroma in the air. My body begins to shudder with a type of existential fear. It is the smell of psilocybin mushrooms.

My last experience with the mushroom was a "bad trip." It was overwhelming, ego dissolving, and I deeply regret the way I behaved toward someone I loved. At the same time. I learned a tremendous amount.

I am curious about the phantom smell of my past but, as soon as the scent passes, my thoughts of that time pass too.

Two days later, a friend's partner offers us chocolate mushroom truffles. I am taken aback by the synchronicity of it all. I ask if she has any LSD as I am afraid of the mushroom and want to bring a "friend" along with me. She reassures me she does.

I consume a moderate amount of psilocybin and LSD. The experience starts like any number of psychedelic experiences I've had in the past. I am brought into a different world while feeling comfortable in the psychedelic space. I am enjoying the sense of freedom I have, after multiple weeks of turmoil.

We go to a house party, it is a playful joyous affair. Then something happens to me. I have an encounter that leaves me deeply disturbed. It is part real-world encounter and part psychedelic.

I leave the party in a panic. Terrified by my experience. I find my way home and start to feel some safety while reconnecting with friends.

By the next morning, I have not "come down" or "come back" from the psychedelic journey. I am still in the altered "other world" experience. I will not "come back" for a number of months. I'm now living in a heightened psychedelic-like landscape. My "normal life" is left behind in a flash of a moment.

I have hesitation in sharing my experiences of madness. In trying to convey to you the experience of what it was like. A number of people have tried to capture the unique flavor of madness, some more successful than others.

I do not wish to do this. As I said, I am more interested in the "return" from madness than the descent into it. With that said, I cannot communicate to you the profound task it is to "come back" without also communicating the loss that occurs in the descent into madness.

I want to be clear. I do not think all madness is the same. I have encountered a number of "flavors." Clinically speaking, these might be referred to as paranoid, grandiose, catatonic, more manic than psychotic, etc. But that is clinical jargon. In my experience, each person's madness has a distinct feel to it.

In the Windhorse Approach, they speak of living in a client's dream. Each person's madness is unique to them, even though there might be generalized categories clinicians use to group them. While I do not believe there is "one" madness, I do believe there is a type of pattern and recognizable experiences that happen when someone goes through what I and many others have experienced.

There is a simplified way of understanding what I went through. I took a psychedelic and experienced a drug-induced psychosis. If the experience only lasted a few days, this would be the case. Since my experience lasted for months, it is more likely that I have an underlying psychotic disorder brought forth by the psychedelics.

These simplified versions of my experience would have two different approaches. If I had experienced a short-term psychosis following psychedelic use, it would be advised that I not take them again. Hopefully I would not be medicated, as medication is proven to increase the likelihood of a future psychotic break. [1]

Since my experience lasted more than a few days, I would be encouraged to be placed on an antipsychotic medication for the rest of my life to manage my illness. Psychotherapy would often be discouraged and a more maintenance-based therapy encouraged instead, one that would ensure I continued to take my medication, with the medication helping me "adjust" to the "real world."

Neither of these outcomes happened to me, obviously.

There is a more complicated response to what did occur. One that doesn't have a definitive answer. There were a number of potential factors contributing to the psychedelics being the "breaking point," pushing me over the edge into madness.

I already described the heightened anxiety and dread I was experiencing associated with not being accepted into the PhD program. This impacted me on multiple levels. First, I wouldn't be able to financially sustain myself any longer without financial aid. Financial worry is real.

Second, I was deeply attached to a "vision" I had for my life. My vision felt like a "calling" and the fact that it wasn't working out, yet it was so close, deeply disturbed my sense of how life worked, a type of existential crisis if you will. I was not sure how to move forward with my life without this vision in place.

---

1 Warner, R. (2004). Recovery from schizophrenia: Psychiatry and political economy. Brunner-Routledge.

I had not yet learned the importance of letting visions go, of not being attached to the outcome of one's life. These lessons would come later. But at the time of my psychotic break, I was still holding tightly to a vision of what I thought my life should look like. My attachment kept me locked into a life that was starting to fall apart, without giving me the freedom to explore other options.

Add to this my history of childhood trauma, with my father leaving me as a child, which had a lasting impact on the foundations of my sense of self. Throw in being overly dedicated to meditation and spiritual practice for the few years previous to my break.

This expresses a certain imbalance in my personality, a type of desperation to get there spiritually. As my current Zen teacher says, "to become spiritually mature." Not in a kind way, or as contemplative researcher Willoughby Britton calls it, "being a spiritual zealot."

At the same time, many spiritual practices are psycho-spiritual technologies that "open" us. Combine these opening practices with the opening agent of a psychedelic and you increase the potential for a psychotic break. I am definitely not the only spiritual seeker or serious meditator who has had a psychotic break. Many recognized spiritual teachers today had their own breaks, although they do not often speak of their experiences openly.

A lot of times when someone who gravitates to a spiritual orientation toward life has a psychotic break, there can be a type of retroactive interpretation of their previous spiritual calling as an expression of their latent psychosis. From this perspective, the spiritual calling was actually an expression of their psychosis all along. The person's spiritual pursuits are retroactively interpreted as an expression of illness.

This just isn't true. It is not as simple as the Western medical model wants it to be. It is a known fact: spiritual, meditative practices can induce psychosis in individuals with no history of trauma or family history of psychosis. [2]

2 *Frontiers in Psychology*, 28 July 2020. Sec. Cultural Psychology. Volume 11 - 2020 | https://doi.org/10.3389/fpsyg.2020.01905. "Progress or Pathology? Differential Diagnosis

It seems, on the spiritual path, there is a potential to lose your mind. Especially if you push yourself.

Include all the other unknown potential underlying currents stacking against me, and in favor of a psychotic break, and there are enough ingredients pushing me out of the orbit of grounded engagement with life into the out-of-control positive feedback loop that is madness.

There is a tendency in the current culture of madness, by this I mean the Western medical model's approach to treating "mental illness," to seek an answer to madness. If you find the answer, most likely a brain or genetic defect, you will be more likely to cure it. This approach sees all mental health symptoms and struggles as expressions of biological illness rooted in the brain's chemical processes.

From this view, the only way to treat these "illnesses" is to find the root cause in the brain's neural pathways or genetics and develop a pharmacological treatment. Unfortunately, after billions of dollars spent, the Western medical model is no closer to identifying the root biological causes of madness. And it continues to neglect caring for those experiencing madness in favor of finding a cure.

From this perspective, madness is an illness that needs to be eradicated. From one level, this totally makes sense. Especially if you are coming from a medical perspective. Who wouldn't want to cure cancer?

However, from my view, mental health crises are not illnesses in the traditional sense. They are indicators of imbalance within a person, a sign of needed healing. In a way, our mental health symptoms are our psyches' attempts to help us heal and live a meaningful life.

I know this can be a radical perspective, that our mental health symptoms are actually trying to help us heal and invaluable to living a full and meaningful life. As someone who has experienced a radically life-altering, devastating mental health crisis, I see what I went through as part of my healing journey. I actually

---

and Intervention Criteria for Meditation-Related Challenges: Perspectives From Buddhist Meditation Teachers and Practitioners"

see my psychosis as a helpful attempt to get me to reset on a fundamental level. Both to my life and the way I related to myself internally. A forest fire if you will. A fire supporting new growth.

This is my story. Whether it is accurate, I do not know. But it has been helpful in continuing to move forward and rebuilding my life post-break.

Sometimes it can be helpful to personify ways of thinking through mythological characters. Right now, our culture is attempting to take an "Apollonian" perspective on healing madness when what it really needs is a "Dionysian" perspective.

Apollo is the Greek god of order, reason, and calm. He drives the chariot that pulls the sun around the earth. He is associated with medicine. So, it would be appropriate to take an Apollonian perspective on healing madness. Figure out the cause and find the cure.

Dionysus on the other hand is the god of wine, ecstasy, blurred boundaries, and of course madness. In his "biography," he actually experienced madness and was helped by a wise figure to come back from his own descent.

If we take a Dionysian approach, having an answer is less important. When you really look at madness, it is often a breakdown of sense- and meaning-making. In a way, as we try to apply order to madness, to make sense of it, we are denying the heart of madness. It is a breakdown in generative sense-making.

If you cannot rationally make sense of madness, how do you approach healing it? Apollo likes to rationally understand, to diagnose the problem. Dionysus on the other hand creates wine. He mixes ingredients together in a certain way, allowing for the emergence of something new. From grape juice, wine emerges. He traveled the world sharing his recipe for creating wine.

For me, when approaching healing from madness, it is more important to first know it is possible to bring forth sanity from madness. They are not in opposition to each other.

Second, the ingredients you bring together are often what allow sanity to emerge from madness. Ingredients like warmth, understanding, engagement in everyday tasks of living, a lack of pressure around "getting better," supporting past activities of health and wellness, etc.

When these ingredients come together, there is a far more likely chance of healing from madness, whatever might have caused it in the first place. From this perspective, the cause does not matter. What is important is the awareness of the potential for healing, and knowing how to bring in the right ingredients to support the healing process.

That is what this book is about, laying out some of the ingredients that are supportive on the healing journey from madness. Some of my hesitation in sharing is rooted in this perspective. The specifics of my madness, both how it happened and my experiences while mad, are less important than the ingredients I had to call on to help in my healing journey.

I am not going to share much of the idiosyncratic expression of my madness. But I would like to share something of the horrific overwhelm that I experienced. The quality of disorientation, of not knowing how to find my way back. Of being lost in a new world that didn't make sense. And of course, the beauty, the wondrous otherworldly experiences I had while mad.

There is a tendency to either pathologize madness or romanticize it. To see everything that happened during madness as an expression of illness. Or to see the mad person's experience as something divine.

I want to honor both of these impulses. I want to be incredibly clear. I was crazy. In the worst sense, completely delusional about who I thought I was and unable to function in even a basic way in everyday life. I had profound experiences that are still meaningful to me. "Real" experiences shaping who I am and how I see the world to this day.

For me, one of the most radical and surprising aspects of being mad was the fundamental alteration of both my perception and experience of "energy" within my body. A lot of time folks see madness from the outside. They hear delusional stories, see abnormal behavior, and can easily dismiss what the person is saying or doing as "not real" or "crazy." What they don't see is the way madness fundamentally alters one's experience.

I remember feeling flooded with a surging energy moving through my body. It was overwhelming, to say the least. I had to do something with the energy, I was not able to contain it. The first few days after ingesting the psychedelics, I found myself desperately creating art. It was the only way I knew how to move the energy I felt.

I remember building a collage-like creation on a friend's wall, without permission, just needing to make it. At the time, I had a moment of seeing myself from the outside, thinking "this is what crazy people look like," frantically writing on walls.

For me, it took the expression of images and art, which was totally weird because I really never made much art before. From the inside, living the experience of "needing" to create, the creation was the only way I knew to move my experience forward, to manage the intensity and overwhelm I was experiencing on an ongoing moment-to-moment basis. A very real and tangible overwhelm experienced in my body and my senses. It was not in my head or thinking, but in the fundamental way I sensorily perceived my body and the world around me.

I was living in a new reality. And it did not conform to my previous experience of reality pre-break. For me, the changes were viscerally real.

Anyone who has experienced madness can speak to the changes of energy in the body, the intensity, the surging feeling, the overwhelm. What is clinically called "pressured speech," a primary symptom of schizophrenia, is literally felt as pressure from the inside, the pressure of the very real energy in the body that is not able to be contained. The need to express the intensity in words, the pressure disorganizing speech, making it hard to maintain the coherence that is required to communicate in the everyday consensus world.

The heightened experience of energy in my body was not just "in my head." A number of times through my months of continuous madness, strangers would walk up to me on the street and say "I felt you from blocks away," sometimes offering me food or rides to places.

You have to understand how incredibly disorienting this was for me. On one hand, I knew I was crazy. I had lost touch with my ability to navigate through life in a cohesive and reliable way. This is the real devastation — the loss of life, relationships, community, engagement with activities, and life goals — often all forgotten within one's extreme states.

I could not even remember to drink water, let alone continue to train to rock climb or start developing my career post-college. On the other hand, people were walking up to me saying, "I felt you from blocks away." I did not know what to make of it. The part of my rational brain trying to make sense of my experience could not hold the belief this was "all in my head" while, at the same time, having real-world moments of people pointing out something was different about me.

No one stopped me on the street before my experience of madness. But the changes in my energetic body were not the only differences I was experiencing. I felt I could "sense" more of what was around me, almost feeling into everyone who walked by. I was not some psychic, knowing facts about people's lives, but could feel the weight of each person's history. It was incredibly overwhelming. People have karma.

I would have these cascades of feelings, senses, and insights constantly moving through me at an accelerated pace, making it impossible to make coherent meaning out of them. I was always trying to hang on, hanging on to some story to make sense of the endless flooding of experiences I was drowning in. Moment to moment, altered-state experiences continuously washing over me. Living in this space of heightened experience day to day, week to week, month to month.

Having taken psychedelics in the past, I was somewhat familiar with the altered-state experiences I was having. On another level, nothing prepared me for living there full-time. This was not some pre-planned four-hour experience I knew would end. I was expected to maintain my life from this newfound heightened experience and state of overwhelm I was in.

On a practical level, I quit my job within days and moved out of the place I was staying. I knew there was no way to keep on living the way I did before my break and, at the same time, had no idea how to live in the new reality I found myself in. I didn't know how to function. How to maintain a "normal" life.

Luckily, I had friends and support helping along the way. I would have these bases I could go to for a few days at a time, rest, and get food before venturing out into the world again. Friends who understood I was struggling and needing support.

The hardest thing for me to sit with is the delusional quality of the experience I was having, the stories I started to tell myself about these new experiences I was having. The stories were grandiose, to say the least. I felt like there must be something special happening to me for me to experience this flood of energy and heightened senses. Some destiny, some purpose to it all.

This is what is hardest for me to hold, the stories I told myself to get me through this experience of heightened overwhelm and confusion. I would often imagine a version of events where I just stayed with these heightened experiences without having to create a story of importance around what I was going through.

I see two ways of interpreting my impulse toward grandiose delusion. First, my life had just fallen apart. Before this, people saw me as someone who had promise, someone who was going to do something interesting with their life. Now here I was, homeless, without money, without anything to call my own. Unable to figure out how to get my life back on track. In that desperation and shame, a story of importance emerged to keep me going, to help me not just fall completely apart. I needed some sense of purpose to get through what was internally happening to me.

On another level, I was having a genuine experience of energy, of heightened perception, and things I had never felt before. I was perceiving reality in a new way. Not necessarily a "right" way or a "good" way but it was very real to me. From these genuine experiences, I created meaning. And as these were intense experiences, I created an intense story.

I want to get at how confusing all of this was for me. How I could not "make sense" of what was happening. But first, I want to share the radical shift I experienced from living a mostly functional daily existence to my life falling away in a matter of days.

Rhythm and Routine

I am running a small division of a non-profit. I am teaching yoga in the local park four days a week. I am finishing up classes to start a PhD program.

I am also connecting with friends, meeting new people, exploring the new land I am living on, meditating daily, and starting to build a life for myself.

Following my break, everything collapses. I am homeless. Without work. Without money. Unable to know what I will be experiencing moment-to-moment.

I can no longer tend to the basics of my life. Food comes at strange intervals. I am no longer drinking water. My hands dry and crack due to the dehydration.

I am barely hanging on to functional living, trying to manage the new flood of experiences I am having. Lost to the altered-state experiences I am living. Deluded. At times, fearful and overwhelmed. In other moments, I am arrogant and determined. Often, I'm living both at once.

I want to convey to you the radical shift that often happens following a psychotic break. How one day I went from living a rather coherent and organized life — going to school, working, teaching yoga, and engaging in the activities of health and vitality I maintained daily for years.

Then, in one evening, I am brought into a new reality I do not understand. Bombarded with a flurry of experiences that shatter my perception of everyday life. From one moment to the next, my life became a kaleidoscope of ever-shifting experiences. I became desperate to get a hold of what was happening to me. To understand. To stop it somehow.

My only focus became navigating the new reality I was in. I gave up everything I knew. Almost everyone I knew. Just trying to make sense of and navigate the craziness I was swimming in day to day. While mad, I remember countless times, looking in the mirror, taking in my reflection, and wondering, "How did I get here?"

Prior to my psychotic break, I was doing alright with my life. I wasn't special or anything. My first two years of college were pretty difficult. I was able to make some changes and reconnect to my spirituality. After a long hiatus from religion as a teenager, I was able to once again find some vitality and meaning in life.

In college, I even won an award for my engagement in the psychology department. My friends and people who knew me often thought I would write a book, lecture, or something like that. I was pretty into Zen Buddhism and Western psychology, interested in the intersection of the two.

This isn't to say I didn't struggle. I didn't have core wounds, childhood trauma, poor coping mechanisms — all that good stuff. But I thought I had a decent handle on it, that I was on a healing journey that was going rather smoothly. I thought my life was moving forward, toward an interesting and fulfilling existence.

In the first few years of engaging with Zen and starting to take my spiritual and psychological health seriously, I experienced significant improvements in my mental state, my ability to connect with others and my sense of meaning and connection to life. The night I ingested the psychedelics and lost my mind, I was not prepared for the radical departure my life would take.

On one level, you can interpret it as becoming homeless, which is terrifying enough for most people. The real terror goes far deeper. One morning, I woke up as Brandon, who was struggling and acutely aware that my current life plan was not working. Even after taking the psychedelics, I was still Brandon. I was just Brandon on psychedelics.

But the morning I woke up still in a "psychedelic state," I was no longer Brandon as I knew myself. The story of Brandon was dependent on some consistency, some grounding, and an ability to maintain functional aspects of my daily life.

Once I was stranded in a state of wide-open perception, flooded with experience and sensation beyond my imagination, I had to become someone else to survive. By this, I don't mean I became someone other than me, but a different me emerged to help me navigate what I was going through. A crazy me.

Before the moment my life fell apart, I wouldn't have believed it would be so easy to erase a life, for it to just fall away. But here I was, living my life, on a life trajectory. I was in communities, working, functioning, and BAM, all gone. Only my heightened experiences and those trying to help me stay afloat through my flood of madness were left.

During the first week of my madness, I saw just how flimsy and fragile life is. How easily it can fall away and we can become something else, be someone else. Knowing this is terrifying. Many people do not want to acknowledge how flimsy the ice we are standing on is, how easy it would be to fall into the currents of madness living beneath all of us.

I also saw more clearly what made me who I was. It wasn't so much the stories I told about myself (or others told) or the life experiences I had. It was more the daily activities of my life.

There were rhythms and routines of my way of living. The time I woke up in the morning. My morning routines. My work schedule. The ways I filled my free time. The people I connected with day to day. My activities of health. The ways I blew off steam. My vices. My creative expressions. My embodied play. The ways I reliably filled my days.

I think we all do this. We all re built by routines and habits we perpetuate day to day. It is in these habits that I believe we truly know who we are. The way we feel, think, and experience the world is as much dependent upon our routines and activities as anything else.

When I stepped into madness, all of my routines, activities, and relational connections fell away. I was swimming in novelty, every day, every moment a type of new adventure. Without the stable foundations of rhythm and routine, I continued to lose myself further and further into madness.

I lived this way for four months. Open to the onslaught of altered state experiences I was having, coupled with the realities of living on the streets. The harassment from police, the need to protect myself, and the ongoing engagement with the public and other homeless individuals. I did not have a break during my months of madness, there was no down time. No time to rest. Just a continuous dream, equal parts nightmare and other-world adventure.

Thank You Jesus for Being Here

I am on a Greyhound bus, going north from Southern California. I have been lost to the "other world" for what feels like eternity but is probably six weeks.

Around the Bay Area, a middle-aged man with gray hair gets on the bus and sits next to me. He is wearing prison clothes. He is jacked in a prison way.

He is sweating, clearly nervous, on edge. When I really look at him, see into him, he is luminous. He is glowing like an angel. I think, "He is a good soul."

I talk with him even though his outward appearance scares me. He tells me stories of his life in prison and his fear of entering the outside world again.

Through our talking, I see his suffering and try to soothe him. To help him settle. He tells me he is going to do something to go back, it's been too long since he's lived "out here."

While he shares, I softly hum, trying to hum his nervous system into relaxation. He relaxes as we talk. He starts to settle a bit from his heightened state. He is less on edge. More grounded.

My bus stop arrives. I wish him luck and start to leave. As I am leaving, a middle-aged woman seemingly coming back from work stops me.

She invites me to her home for a meal. She is offering to take care of me. I am scared of others. Afraid of being "trapped" by someone. I politely decline.

As I am walking away from her, she bows to me and says, "Thank you Jesus for being here." I leave and spend the night on the streets.

I do not share this story to build the romantic side of madness. I share to articulate the deep confusion I was experiencing. Here I was having grandiose delusions of importance, self-narratives of being special, messianic. I am assuming something grand is going to happen to me and rescue me from the horrific place I am in. That my spiritual importance will be recognized and I will be taken care of. I thought I was not really "crazy," but I have broken through in some spiritual way. Some important spiritual way.

I am also deeply aware I have let myself go. I no longer have a life. I am no longer functioning as I once did. My life looks like a wreckage compared to what it was before. I am no longer in contact with my friends, no longer engaged in the community, no longer working or moving toward life goals. Wandering the streets, desperate, without food, without money, just trying to survive.

I do not know how to hold both of these together. Am I just crazy? Should I have let my friend check me into a psych ward, gone on medication, and accepted a broken story of madness? Or am I having some spiritual breakthrough I will be recognized for?

Obviously, the answer is neither of these. And this experience captures the deep confusion running through me during this time. This woman recognizes me as "Jesus" and I am homeless. Not homeless in that cool Jesus way, making fish miraculously out of nowhere. More of an "in the dumpster diving for food" kind of homeless.

There was no simple answer as to how I was going to move forward, how I was supposed to make sense of what was happening to me, how I was supposed to put my life back together from the state I was in. To be honest, in many ways, I still do not "know" what happened to me. What was real and what was "crazy."

These are merely categories. Attempts at rationally understanding the experience I was having. When it seems I was having a more blurred, Dionysian-like experience of both being true. I was having genuine spiritual experiences while totally fucking crazy.

I walk a strange line of not often sharing what I went through with others. Even here I am sharing a select few stories, some that might seem "out there" or unbelievable. These really are the tame stories, the ones I feel comfortable telling. There are other stories, other memories that baffle my understanding to this day, challenge my ability to ever make sense of what happened to me, of being able to understand what is "real."

There was a time in my recovery journey when I would openly tell people I had a psychotic break or I went crazy. It was a way for me to work with the shame, not letting it fester as I was rebuilding a life for myself.

Later, as I started working with folks as a therapist, I would tell my mentors and supervisors. It would be more of a type of disclosure, something I needed to tell, like they needed to know my dark history to approve of my ability to work helping others. Kind of like a confession.

Often, they wouldn't care. I remember I waited to tell my first clinical supervisor about what I went through. After I shared with her, she proceeded to tell me about her manic experience in college where she was hospitalized and missed a semester of class. She was relieved to also be able to share with someone. When applying at Windhorse, I disclosed my period of madness in the interview.

These days, I keep it mostly to myself, telling others when it feels appropriate. I no longer feel I have to disclose it when I work, like I am required to share my brokenness, that it is real. It has taken me many years, a decade to no longer be defined by a story of brokenness.

When I have shared, people have attempted to give their own interpretations of what I went through. I've had graduate school mentors tell me I went through a spiritual emergency. Past college professors have diagnosed me to my family, giving me a mental health condition to capture what I was going through. In my view, highly unethical.

My wife would romanticize madness and think of what I went through as some divine expression not accepted by culture. For me, I do not know what happened. What I do know, I lost the ability to function.

I really think this is the most important thing to take away. You can describe the symptoms of madness, often hearing voices and seeing visual hallucinations. You can look at the changes in personality, the delusions generated in states of madness. Yet at its core, for me, madness is the break of the ability to maintain the life you knew before the madness. It is no longer being able to "hold it together."

In Zen, we have a saying, "Before enlightenment, chop wood carry water. After enlightenment, chop wood carry water." Even if what I went through had genuine elements, I was not able to "chop wood and carry water." It would take years for my ability to function to be restored. Before I could work, keep a schedule, or maintain a rhythm of living that was financially, socially, meaningfully, and spiritually functional.

That is what this book is about. Being able to return to functional living. I do not necessarily mean a cookie-cutter correct version of functional living, but a functional living that works. That allows someone to maintain health, maintain financial needs, have meaningful connections to others, and hopefully feel part of a larger community.

I do not think recovery means being "normal" again or even free of "symptoms." I do not see anomalous experiences as inherently wrong or reflections of an "illness." Anomalous experience is a normal part of everyday life, just denied and pathologized by dominant Western thinking.

In my recovery journey, I never became symptom-free. I never stopped having "out there" experiences beyond the acceptable range of those allowed for in our current consensus reality. It was more the frequency of experiences that shifted. I was no longer flooded by my altered-state experiences after my recovery. They became a part of what I was going through, not the whole of my experience. I was able to work with and integrate the many altered state experiences I would have after I "recovered."

It took some time to accept my alternative way of perceiving and experiencing life. To learn how to both function in the basic boring way and allow for the diversity of experiences I have from time to time. To do this, I had to let go of ideas of "normal" and "acceptable" ways of participating in reality. I had to allow for a more fluid definition of "real."

My new litmus test, the way I gauged my recovery, was rooted in my ability to function. Did I show up to work on time? Could I shoot the shit with co-workers and have everyday conversations? Did I cook my meals? Show up to my commitments? Could I engage in a daily spiritual practice again?

These benchmarks became my new definitions of "normal." Not the experiences I was having as I moved through my day, but my ability to maintain the foundations of my day.

East-West

I am on my way to the North Bay from Southern California. The train has stopped in Stockton. I am confused, not sure why the connecting bus is not till the next day.

I ask a conductor about the wait. He is wearing a traditional conductor's outfit. He has a way about him, like he is from another era.

He slowly tells me, "Trains move easily from north to south but things do not flow as easily from east to west." His statement has a cryptic quality. I am scarred in a deep way. Like he wasn't from the "ordinary world" but was speaking to me from the "world behind the world."

I throw away my ticket and wallet in a fit of fear. I do not want to be "found" by the "world behind the world." I feel like something is hunting or haunting me. I do not know its intentions and it does not feel safe or "on my side."

I have divided the "world behind the world" into some sort of cosmic backdrop of good and evil at war with each other. On one level, I am identified with the "good." On another level, I want nothing to do with the "war" I find myself trapped in. I want out.

I keep trying to figure out how to create a "stalemate" to end the "war." I do not want my actions to perpetuate the "evil" attacking me. I want my life back.

Not knowing what to do, I walk the streets of Stockton. It is late at night. I am wandering, following some current I do not understand.

While walking, I am bombarded by a techno-dystopic feeling taking me over. I feel in "communion" with the city, taking it into my body.

I look down and there are boils all over my body. I continue to walk, swimming in the dark haunted feeling of the city.

By morning, I am freed from the city's grip. The boils are gone. I borrow someone's phone. I call an ex-girlfriend who lives in the area. She is disturbed by the state I am in. Rightfully so.

I do not know what to do. I decide to walk to the North Bay. I have no food or water. During my walk, I am taken over by the spray-painted symbols on the pavement.

My mind is pulled a thousand miles a moment, pulled in a flurry of meaning I cannot keep up with. I am not making sense of the symbols, but they are informing my experience in a way I do not understand.

A cop pulls up next to me. He asks me what I am doing. I say I am walking to the North Bay. He informs me that you cannot walk on the side of the highway. He proceeds to drive me south from the westerly direction I am going.

He leaves me at a travel center gas station in the middle of nowhere. I am not sure what to do. I see an SUV with an animal paw sticker on the back, the sticker has spiritual significance to me. The driver is pumping gas. I ask for a ride. He drives me to the nearest town, leaving me at another gas station.

I do not know where I am. I have no shoes. I left them while walking, although I do not know why.

It is winter. I am wearing every item of clothing I possess. I walk into a local bar to stay warm. I sit at a table alone. I try to be invisible and not draw attention.

Someone walks by and silently places a pint of beer on the table for me. I drink it. At some point, I feel it is time to leave.

I walk to the nearby Safeway to look in the dumpsters for food. I find a box of Raisin Bran and chocolate almond milk. Next to the cereal is a whole rotisserie chicken.

Raisin Bran with chocolate almond milk is one of my favorite meals. I feel like I am safe, protected on this strange journey by forces I do not understand. I enjoy my meal. I find a place to sleep in the shopping center that is my new home.

I am awoken by a cop. He tells me I cannot sleep where I am. I ask what I am supposed to do. He tells me he doesn't know, but I cannot lie down at night. I clarify, asking if I can sit there at night. He informs me I am allowed to sit.

I stay awake. Holding a vigil. Meditating. Trying to fight off the need to sleep. When daylight comes, I find a safe place in the shopping center to sleep.

Rested, I am sitting on a planter box. A homeless man walks up to me. He is older. He starts a conversation with me. He has a good way about him. We talk. Sharing stories.

He informs me he has an opportunity to get off the street. He needs to go to a rehabilitation facility to detox from alcohol. He is afraid to go because he does not "get along with Black people." He is worried he will get in a fight.

I encourage him to go. I feel the commitment energy building in his chest. I tell him he can let go of the hate. He looks at me, kissing a necklace of his protective saint. He thanks me and walks to the detox center.

I am struck by the oddity of my life. I do not understand how it became what it is. I do not know how to find my way back to my old life. I have a fantasy of going to my old Zen Center and being taken in.

Days go by. Same routine. Sleep during the day. Dumpster dive at night. Hold vigil to fight off sleep through the darkness.

I ask to borrow the phone at Peet's coffee. I am not able to reach anyone who will help me. The manager walks outside and gives me twenty dollars. I imagine she's hoping I will leave her shopping center.

I take the BART (Bay Area Rapid Transit) to Berkeley. There is a pizza shop with a beautiful outdoor patio full of patrons. I go and sit at a table. I order a margarita pizza. I eat it, marveling at the strange turns in my journey.

Moments before, I was abandoned in an unknown city eating from dumpsters. The next, I'm casually dining amidst a large number of people, leaving a tip for the server, still with no shoes.

I sell a cannabis pipe on Haight and Ashbury. I buy a bus ticket to the North Bay. I have a formal interview with my old Zen teacher. He is incredibly kind to me, even trading necklaces. It is a beautiful moment I will always remember.

An old friend from college gives me a pair of shoes. Another friend gives me money to get back to Southern California. I still do not know how to find my way home.

This is just one piece, one segment of time in my madness. Just a few days, hopefully capturing in a microcosm of what my experience was like during the months of madness I experienced.

I lived trapped in a world where I felt persecuted by a spiritual force attacking me. At first, I tried to fight it. Thinking I could fight back somehow. Quickly, I wanted out of the "fight." I was consumed with trying to figure out how to "get out" of the "war" I had found myself in.

Eventually, through whatever actions and choices I made, I found my way out. Even though I was no longer at "war," I was still stranded in the strange psychedelic-like landscape I found myself in. At least I was no longer experiencing myself as being "attacked," just lost without a map home.

I lived in this heightened reality for months. Months where every day felt like an eternity of experience. I accumulated more experiences than it feels I will be able to digest in this lifetime.

It is so hard to convey the intensity of mind I experienced while locked in an ongoing extreme state. When in my extreme states, my mind moved at speeds beyond my ability to understand. Like when walking down the freeway.

I remember seeing the signs on the ground and my mind firing and making meaning of them, as if they were somehow a part of the unfolding journey I was on. The speed at which my mind computed and made meaning of the symbols happened at light speed. I could not keep up with the movements of my mind. I was at mercy to them more than they were serving me.

Some say when we enter into extreme states, we taste some of the "secondary process" or "underlying process" of our mind's ability to process and interpret the world around us. Like we tap into the processing power of the mind, a place we should not have access too. We get overwhelmed and confused by the speed and intensity of the mind's capacity to sort and organize the world around us.

It's sort of like opening the backend of an operating system and seeing all the 1s and 0s creating the stable image we normally relate to on our screen. As we are not meant to see the 1s and 0s, we make meaning of them, not realizing they aren't meant for our eyes. They are not meant to be made sense of.

My speed of mind was not the only way my experience was unrecognizable while in my madness. I mentioned the boils appearing on my body as I walked through the streets of Stockton. I understand this one might be hard to believe yet, for me, it was real.

We often like to think of madness as being "in the mind" but it fundamentally impacts the whole person, even their bodies. Just as anxious folks can get hives, strange things happen to bodies while in the throes of extreme states.

People seem to take comfort in regulating the experience of madness to the mind, as if by locating the "problem," their experiences can be dismissed. Most people who experience madness will experience genuine changes in their physiology. Whether through enhanced visual perception or an increased capacity to smell, madness can fundamentally alter one's perceptual capacities, not just what we "imagine."

With my mind firing at these speeds, my body constantly changing, I kept trying to find a way to "get my life back," wanting to find something that would "work." I had countless fantasies, ideas, and schemes to get my life back. Schemes rooted in a mind out of control. Like I am hunting for the right trick that will create a life that works, instantly. This out-of-control method did not get me back on track. At some point, I began to see that nothing I tried was working. I will "give up" trying to put my life back together again.

The List

I have been homeless for months, wandering up and down the West Coast. I am back in Northern California. I am wandering near my old university. It is winter. I am cold and hungry. I go to the 24-hour computer lab to stay warm.

Earlier in the year, I was still a student at the university, using the computer lab to finish my final projects. Living with friends. Feeling my life in front of me.

Now I am homeless. Without money. Without resources. I am giving up hope I will ever be able to "find my way out" of the place I am trapped.

The next day, while walking through a neighborhood, I run into an old college friend. He buys me a bus ticket. Instead of going south, as I had countless times, I go north.

I take the bus to my father's house in the pacific northwest. He takes me in. I give up on putting my life back together.

I land at my father's place broken from my journey. I have forgotten how to be a normal person. I remember the first evening, sitting down with him for dinner, eating a meal at his dining room table. I was staring at the plate in front of me, looking at his table we were sitting at, overwhelmed by the prospect of pretending to be normal again. It was unfathomable to me, with everything I went through, I was sitting down at his table eating a meal like nothing happened. Talk about crazy.

Slowly, my extreme states began to settle. Each day, I started to "come down" from the heightened state I was in. Eating meals began to feel less absurd and almost normal again. I still did not know what to do with myself. How to spend my time. How I was going to find my way back into functional living.

I have this impulse to write a list of things I need to do to get back on track. I have a map finally. Not one of my crazy plans generated in an extreme state. This plan reflects the beginning of grounding taking place. This plan is more rooted in what I know to be helpful to myself. Helpful to me feeling healthy and connected.

I look up a therapist because I know I need to somehow process what I've been through. I find a local Zen Center. Before my break, Zen was an incredibly important foundation in my life, an anchor. I also found a local hot yoga studio with a good first-time student discount. At this point, I have totally lost touch with caring for my body and know I need to find a way to connect again with vigorous activity.

I find a local rock climbing gym to connect to a community and engage in a play-based movement I enjoy. I start to look for a part-time job, nothing serious or ambitious, something in food. It's a skill I know I have, where I can show up and work without having to think or try too hard. Just being able to get back into the routine of showing up to work on time and staying through a shift, things that were impossible in my heightened state.

The list I have is a solid starting place, but I am not able to activate it. I am not able to move toward these goals. They feel like too much. At the place I am in my recovery journey, I am not able to just dive into these activities, even though they are most likely the things I need to get my life moving again. I don't believe I can create a rhythm of routine that will help me find my way back into functional living.

I find myself stuck. Not knowing how to live anymore. It is incredibly difficult to stay with myself from moment to moment. My shame starts to grow. The disbelief about what I have been through grows. I start to retreat into myself. I start to pull away from my father, spending most of my time in his basement isolated.

He gave me an old computer and I find myself watching episode after episode of television. It becomes my only reprieve from the growing shame I am feeling. The growing recognition of what has happened to my life.

It becomes clear I need to go south again to get my driver's license. It has been a few months since I was last in California. I stay with a friend who supported me the most during my ordeal. We had a type of kinship. He looked after me in ways, ways I am eternally grateful for now.

A couple years before we met, my friend was out with his friends, at a bonfire. On the way home, some flowers stood out to him. In his stoned state, he felt compelled to eat them. They were belladonna flowers containing Datura.

Datura is an incredibly strong psychotropic. It is not psychedelic. It is more akin to a delusion-creating plant compound. After ingesting the flowers, he began to live in a world where his friends were apostles, and he was an apostle too.

After trying to care for him, his friends checked him into a psychiatric hospital. A few days into his stay, he realized he had to pretend to be "normal" to get out. Since his time in the hospital, he has lived in two worlds: his everyday consensus world and his "other world."

When we would be together, it was like being with a long-lost brother who understood a shared experience few could understand. He was there for me, supporting me in the basic fundamentals of living.

Without him, I would not be here today. He kept me alive when I was unable to live in both worlds, the everyday consensus reality that we share with each other and the personal world that is uniquely our own.

This distinction is incredibly important to how I view the world. There is consensus reality — an agreed-upon reality we share. Consensus reality is "agreed" upon reality, currently often defined through a Western idea of science, materialism, and secularism. I do not believe there is one consensus reality but multiple consensus realities overlapping each other. Many attribute this strange time we are living in to a breakdown in a shared consensus reality, with folks siloing off into their own shared consensus realities no longer overlapping with others.

And there is the personal world. We all have a personal world. The world of our dreams. The world of our fantasies. I speak of my delusions, the grandiose stories I told about myself in my madness. But we all do this in some way. Not everyone's story is grandiose, but we all tell a story about our lives to ourselves, and then attempt to have others around us validate that story.

Currently, I am telling the story of being someone who has something to offer due to what I went through. As I write this book, I can't help but have fantasies about what it will be like when I finish. I know they are just fantasies, stories I tell myself. And they happen, while I am daydreaming.

This personal reality is what I also refer to as the "other world." When I was with my buddy who ate the belladonna, we were able to be in our own "other world" while together, which to me was the most beautiful thing.

The thing my friend was able to do that I was not able to do at the time, was being able to live in both worlds. While we would go on strange adventures together and share openly with each other about our "other world" adventures, he was able to maintain going to school, working, paying his bills, and having connections with other friends. He was able to "chop wood carry water."

When I went down to stay with him, I had hopes of rebuilding my life. He was open to me staying with him until I got on my feet and could pay rent. I started to look for some part-time work, a pizza shop or something. I had no car, no cell phone.

I realized quickly that I wasn't going to be able to just "start over." I was too impacted by what I had been through, too haunted to just pretend like everything was normal again. Just like I was unable to begin to activate the list of activities I had created. I wasn't ready yet to just step back into normal.

Even though my consciousness was beginning to settle, no longer locked into a heightened state of sensitivity, I was still incredibly raw. Too raw to just go on living like nothing happened. I wouldn't know it at the time, but I was going to need years to let what had happened settle and wash through me. Years until I would really feel ready to start living again.

I also missed the heightened state I experienced while in madness. I missed feeling like my energetic field extended for city blocks. I missed feeling in touch with a deeper cosmic reality. As I had come down, I also let go of many of the extra-sensory and otherworldly experiences I was regularly having. I was starting to become "normal" again.

So I went north again, to my dad's. He set me up with a room in his basement. I locked into the computer I had down there. Pretty quickly, I found myself back in the routine of watching TV during every waking hour I had. When I was not watching TV, I was crushed by the overwhelming shame of what my life had become. Days turned to weeks, weeks turned to months.

I lived in this new routine for over a year. Just watching TV. Avoiding having to be with the punishing self-hate dominating my thinking space. The TV being the only reprieve from the thoughts in my head telling me to kill myself.

I did not shower. I slept during the day to avoid contact with my father, going to the local grocery store at midnight when I needed food. Any moment I was not occupied by television, I was assaulted with the overwhelming thought to take my life.

I would hear myself saying what a piece of shit I was for letting this happen. I was just some fucked-up crazy kid who was never going to be able to "come back" into living again. The fear of this voice kept me locked to the television. I watched A LOT of television, some really good shows.

It was during the "golden age" of television when it was still easy to illegally download shows and movies. To this day, I have an encyclopedic knowledge of actors, directors, television shows, and movies from this period in my life.

Previous to this experience, I had been depressed throughout my life. I first experienced depression as a younger child, having suicidal thoughts while in elementary school. Sleeping through the day, just trying to "check out" from the pain I was experiencing.

Throughout middle and high school, I would come in and out of depressive periods. It was in high school that I discovered cannabis and other substances. I was able to mask my pain through substance use.

In college, I experienced a *crushing* depression. It was devastating. It was the first time in my life that each moment felt unbearable. My family was so concerned, they came up to see me. I eventually came out of that depression. It actually fueled a lot of growth and movement for me. I started to make choices more in alignment with the life I wanted to live and it helped me to reconnect to a spiritual path, after years of agnosticism following my loss of connection to the dogmatic fundamentalist Christianity I grew up in.

I am trying to say, I thought I knew depression. I thought I had experienced soul-crushing depression before this. But the depression I experienced while self-imprisoned in my father's basement was worse than anything I could ever imagine. Each moment felt like an eternity of punishing self-hate.

I completely lost track of time. To this day, I do not know how long I was down there. How many months and years I spent watching television, too overwhelmed by the punishing shame to start building my life back again and, at the same time, unable to kill myself. Unable to find a way out of the hell I was living.

In reflection, there was one bright spot during this time. My father never pressured me to "get my act together." Every few months, while passing him in the hall, he might say, "Are you ever going to work?" I would ignore him and walk back into the basement. By not having the pressure from my father, I was able to wait until something in me was ready to start living again.

If I had tried to get things going before that moment, given a push to get my act together and it didn't work, I know there would have been no way for me to try again. I really only had one shot to make an attempt at building a life.

Early on in my time in my father's basement, my mother came to visit me. It was the first time I had a conversation with someone in what felt like forever. I remember going to eat at a restaurant, being in public. I tried to "be normal" as best I could, but I know I failed. My mom now describes seeing me and how I was "broken" but still me.

The thing that haunts so many parents when their kiddo descends into madness is they can no longer recognize the kid they knew. It is heartbreaking for parents to not see their child in their child. I have heard numerous parents describe to me seeing when their kid "came back" again, and the great relief they felt.

After the visit, I did not keep in touch with my mom. I lost touch with every friend I knew. I gave up everything I knew as me. I gave up my hopes and dreams for my life. I gave up any hope of having a life. I was nowhere close to "me."

Even though my extreme states had resided, I was not ready to start the basic activities of living. Of caring for myself. Tending to my health. Maintaining rhythms and routines of health and vitality. I was not able to maintain the functional activities that allow us to be people. Instead, letting all the functional ways of knowing myself fade away as I tried to manage the punishing self-hate defining my experience.

I pushed everyone I knew away due to the incredible shame I was holding. To this day, I do not know how I survived my time in the basement. It is a living hell I wish to never return to.

It must have been a year later when I realized I wasn't going to kill myself, that I wouldn't listen to my voice of shame punishing me. At this juncture, knowing I wouldn't take action and yet still wasn't able to step back into functional living, I felt truly defeated. Trapped in the limited routine of TV and sleep I had generated for myself.

I saw no way out. No way of starting to live again. And most of the people in my life had lost touch with me. No one was there encouraging me to put my life back together. I felt no one there rooting for me to start living again. As if the world silently watched me disappear further into the hole I had created.

It is one reason I want this book to live. To maybe prevent some of the extremes of suffering I experienced in my recovery journey. I have helped others who were provided with more supportive ingredients than I had. My father did not know how to help, nor did he have the resources. My mother also did not know what to do. She tried. She reached out to psychiatrists and sought support, but no one was able to help her in helping me.

I sometimes make meaning out of what I went through. That I might have endured the suffering that I did so others who have lost their way might have an easier way back. Cause it was fucking hard. So hard. And it did not have to be.

There are easier ways to take breaks after a period of madness, breaks to reset and take time before coming back into functional living. It does not need to be in a state of isolation and shame. It can be in a supportive and loving environment. Where folks are given space, given support, and allowed to take their steps back into living when they are ready.

Unfathomable

I have been in the basement for over a year. I have lost time. I live in another dreamlike reality. Not the kaleidoscoping extreme states of madness. I live the same day over and over. Avoiding the punishing voice in my head that tells me to kill myself. It is my own voice. Not an auditory hallucination.

My hair has grown to my shoulders. This is my only measurement of time. I wear the same sweatpants day after day. I do not leave the basement. I live in a hellish prison I have created. It is a worthy punishment for having lost my mind and given up my life.

I have no will to live. No belief I can have a life again. I cannot imagine returning from the place I am. From the places I have been. How could I pretend to be "normal" again? Just go on like nothing happened to me.

I have resigned myself to my existence. I now know I will not listen to the thoughts repeatedly telling me to kill myself.

My mother sends me a box. It is small. It haunts me. I am afraid to open it. I leave it on a shelf. Afraid even to look at it. I do not know what is inside. I imagine something horrible.

I do not know what changes. I find the will to open the package. I am willing to face my fear. Inside is an e-reader. My mother probably sent it for Christmas. Or maybe my birthday. I have forgotten how long the box has sat there haunting me.

When I see the e-reader, I break. The numbed deadness that had taken me over recedes for a moment. I feel the kindness expressed in the gift. I had forgotten kindness existed. I have only known self-hate for so long. Tears come to my eyes. I have not cried in a very long time. Too afraid to feel.

Something in me feels ready to live again. I do not understand how. A seed of hope emerges. I am afraid of it. Slowly yet quickly, I move into living again.

I take my dad's offer to enter the family trade of cleaning windows. I purchase a used bike with the help of my parents. I regularly attend yoga. I am moving my body again. Exercising. In the world. Even though my mind is afraid, my body reminds me. It knows how to live.

I start to meditate again. I can only sit for a few minutes. My mind horrifies me. I commit again to daily spiritual practice. I am in savasana. I hear a voice. It says, "It can be so much more than you imagine."

I cry with hope for the first time. Hope that I might have a life. A voice that is not my own reminds it is possible to live. While my own voice tells me to kill myself.

Within two months, I am renting a room in the city. I have roommates my age. I am working part-time. I continue to do yoga. I have found a Zen Center. My new routine is now working, going to the Zen Center most mornings.

I make a close friend. He will become my brother. I am going to bars. Going to concerts. Going to the river. Dancing. I am dancing. I am reading again. I am at house parties. I am weaving my bike through the city streets late at night when everyone has gone down. Loving life again. Cooking for friends. Friends. I am living. Life was waiting for me. I just had to say yes again.

I am terrified. It cannot be this easy to come back. I am afraid every moment that it will fall apart again. I will fall apart. This life I love will be taken from me again. This particular fear will last for years.

At this point, I am no longer afraid I can't have a life. I am afraid my life will be taken from me by my broken brain.

I still do not know what opened in me and allowed me to be ready to live again. I did not "do something." I did not crack the code. I did not figure something out. Nothing changed in my external reality.

Yet somehow, a soft willingness to participate in life again emerged. A willingness to try to live despite not knowing if it would work out. Not knowing if my trying would pull me out of the hellish prison of the basement. If it was possible to come back from where I had been. From the altered states of unbelievability to the half-human prison of the in-between I was trapped in for so long.

The only thing I can identify in my life that changed is the e-reader my mother sent. The moment I opened the package, a flood opened inside. Not an overwhelming, taken-over type of flood. But a soft flooding of all the feelings of goodness, kindness, and love I had known in my life.

The basement had become a prison-like cocoon. I was in a constant relationship with my internal voice of self-hate. A near-constant battle of trying to not be dominated by the overriding self-hate that had taken me over.

To survive, I had to cut off from all feeling inside. I had deadened myself. I did this through television and not allowing "gaps" where I could be in touch with myself. Through the act of opening the e-reader, I once again opened to the possibility of having an internal experience beyond self-hate.

With self-hate becoming my constant companion, I had lost awareness of a world where love, kindness, and care existed. In essence, I had cut myself off from life to survive. Life is love for me.

With my punishing voice in my head telling me I could not live again, I started to begin the transition out of my father's basement. Once again engaging in the everyday tasks of living.

As I started to reclaim my life, the hateful voice was not replaced by a loving, supportive voice. Instead, the distortion the hate was telling me was seen through. The hate telling me I could not have a life was wrong, as life was forming again. The feeling I had ruined any chance of having a meaningful existence in the world was being called into question through the very act of living again.

Through this "living again" process, the hate's power decreased. It didn't go away. But it lost its supreme power over me. The voice could no longer tell me it was not possible. It was clearly wrong. You can have a devastating mental health crisis, lose your ability to maintain the basics of being human and come back again.

After leaving the basement, I would continue to doubt the reality of my existence. But in a new way. I assumed I was actually crazy, in the way of the Western medical model, biologically broken and destined to have repeated psychotic breaks throughout my adult life. Even though I was living again, I was destined to fail. A fool's errand. The life I was building would inevitably perish with my next break.

This has not proven to be true. I have not had another catastrophic mental health crisis. I have not lost my basic functioning since leaving my dad's basement. I have known periods of depression. Periods of instability. Periods of pain. Anxiety. Overwhelm. Doubt. Sorrow. Grief. Through all these experiences of being human, my life has maintained continuity. I have not lost touch with the essential thread of my existence like I did all those years before.

I have had to heal many fears, many doubts, address past wounds, let go of destructive beliefs, learn to be kinder to myself, to support myself, to stop pushing myself so relentlessly to be better. But my life has continued. It has not fallen apart. There has been a steady through line.

Soon after I moved out of my father's house, when I left the basement, I tried online dating. I met someone who intrigued me. Who I would fall in love with and we would share a life together. She had a way about her. She wasn't playing the "game" like others. She lived her own way. She created beautiful art that spoke to the depth of her soul.

We are still together. Married. We have a child. I've owned property. Paid taxes. Received a graduate degree. Worked for years at a number of different jobs. I hope it is okay to say I have helped a good number of people as a psychotherapist. Helped them heal from their painful histories, learn to be kinder to themselves, find greater vitality within, and develop a deeper connection to their lives.

All of this was unfathomable to me while I was in the depths of my depressive self-hate in my father's basement. I could not imagine there was a way out of the hell I found myself in. I did not know you could go so far, lose so much of what it means to be human and come back again. I know I say it a lot but I did not brush my teeth for *two years*. I had let go of the most basic task we learn as children.

Not brushing my teeth is a symbol representing all of the other habits of humanness I had abandoned. The basic caring of myself as a human being, let alone the more aspirational qualities such as the desire to grow, to connect, or to offer something of value to the community.

I came out of the basement with a few cavities. Other than that, I was physically okay. Within a couple of months, I was able to find physical health again, meaningful relationships, work, and community. Some of the hallmarks of living.

In a way, I stepped back into the life I had lost years before. I would still have my personal traumas. I would still have my idiosyncratic struggle. I would still have the same goals, the same desires for my life. I was back on the growth trajectory of my life, my aspiration and struggle living together.

After stepping back into the rhythm and routine of living, I was asked again to work on things I needed to work on to grow into a mature human being. I am still working on it. Being a mature human.

But I had a new struggle post-madness to contend with. On top of the normal struggles I carried, I now carried the ongoing doubt I was cheating in some way. The doubt that it was not possible to have a life after a catastrophic psychotic break.

As a teenager, I was pretty into psychology. I was always drawn to it. How the mind worked. What it meant to be human. I read texts on the history of psychology in high school for fun. I eventually received an undergraduate degree in the subject.

In all my reading and studying, I did not know you could recover from a psychotic break. That you could go to the places I went and come back and have a "normal" life. There were no role models. There were no templates. No representation. No theories doing justice to the true possibility of recovery.

Think about the media you have seen. Think about the representations of extreme state disorders on television, of what you see when someone is diagnosed with schizophrenia or bipolar disorder.

Typically, a high school student will either begin to display odd behavior or manic symptoms. They will experience chaos, a deterioration in their functioning. They will lose social standing. They will be diagnosed. They will have a moment of coming to terms with their illness, then they will be medicated. The medication will help "stabilize" their symptoms. They will still be themselves but less "interesting" in a way. A little deadened. They will have to manage the illness for the rest of their lives.

This is the representational arc of more severe mental health diagnoses in the west. It is a medically and pharmacologically driven approach to understanding and treating severe mental health crises. If you are given a diagnosis of schizophrenia, you can never heal from it. Even if you have no symptoms for years, you will always be in remission, much like cancer. This is not the case for depression or anxiety. Those diagnoses you can recover from. But not schizophrenia, it is a permanent invisible scar.

This is what I knew, what was represented to me in the media and within psychology. Due to not having a template to model my life after, a representation of possibility and hope, I was always fighting the story of brokenness inside. Trying to prove to myself it was possible to have a life post-psychosis.

Often through my recovery process, I was afraid I was lying to myself, deluding myself again. I was no longer grandiose in my fantasies of self-importance. I was now trying to have a life. To live a "normal" life.

Based on the internalization of the Western medical model's conception of madness, I was left defending my right to have a life for myself. Defending my right to exist, to work, to play, to have connection to the wider mystery. Honoring my basic humanness felt like I was defying the conventional understanding of mental health.

I was supposed to be medicated. I needed a proper diagnosis. My internal experience was no longer to be trusted. These were the stories the medical model left me contending with.

This was the invisible struggle I carried. Much of my personal struggle post-madness was triggered when something would happen in my life that would cause me to doubt my ability to have a "normal" life, or if I felt my "sanity" was questioned. I would spin out often, caught in a fearful loop with no way out. I was asking myself, "*Can I do this? Can I go on living fully?*" I was terrified the answer was no.

I made a choice at some point to not be defined by the cultural stories of madness. To find my own way into health. Into living fully. Into having a full-hearted life. I can't say when that moment occurred. The final rift, where I said no to the narrative of brokenness I was fighting.

One would think after years of stability I might trust in my capacity to have continuity. Or even after years of helping others navigate their own recovery journeys. But none of these "accomplishments" made me feel safe. I realized at some point that I could never prove my sanity, I could never prove my way out of brokenness. Because it was not true. It never was.

The story of brokenness generated by the Western medical model is just a story. It does not need to be proved wrong. So instead of fighting it like I had for so many years, I had to take the radical leap of seeing through it. Much like I saw through the voice of self-hate telling me I couldn't have a life.

I had to stop fighting the story that I could not have a life and live. I had to abandon conventional psychology and choose to stand apart from our dominant cultural narratives around madness. In this act, I freed myself to be me. To no longer measure myself against some internalized story of sanity and, instead, allow myself to navigate my experience and the world in the way that resonated in my heart. A way that many might think is different or even a bit crazy.

Along the way, I would eventually find representation. I would find a role model who would show me it is possible to truly recover. Show me you can have a rich, meaningful, full-hearted life after a period of madness. He would give testament and become my anchor letting me know it was possible. Without him, I could not be here writing to you.

When I committed to finding my own way, I did not know I would be internally fighting a story of madness, a story of brokenness, for almost a decade. I thought with enough accomplishment, enough time, enough healing, I would find comfort in my solidity as a human being.

Even after taking the "leap" into living life on my terms, I had to untangle myself from the entrenched web of the Western medical model. I had to find my own confidence in my ability to navigate my life independently of our cultural stories of mental illness.

But the shadow of brokenness, mental illness, and brain-based disorders would haunt me well into my recovery. Even to this day, a decade after "recovering," I am still living with the fear of being in a world that defines "crazy" in a way that does not make room for me.

I no longer fear my sanity, but I assume if others hear my story, if they understand what I went through, any credibility I have as a human will be taken from me. For having recovered. For experiencing life differently than others. Because of this, I don't have a right to have an opinion or perspective.

This is the tyranny of consensus reality. If your opinions challenge consensus reality, you are a threat who needs to be silenced, either through character attack, dismissal, or harsher means. Our history is one of violence to those who experience reality differently.

Finding Rhythm and Routine Again

I had been living the same day over and over. Avoiding reality. Avoiding the state of my life. Sitting in my father's basement. Then, almost overnight, the will to live returns. It is not loud. It is soft and gentle. A gentle internal encouragement to "start again."

It is hard at first, but I honor the gentle encouragement. I start working with my father. I start riding my bike to yoga a few days a week. I start to shop for my own food, remembering the recipes I used to enjoy cooking.

Some days, I slip back into the routine of losing myself to television. More days than not, I start to live again. Even when everything in my body says to enter my hole, I push myself onto my bike. Push myself into the yoga class.

I am remembering to honor my commitments to health. My commitments to my life. Little by little, it takes less pushing and I find myself back into routine. Back into living in the world again.

During my months of madness and the following isolation in my father's basement, I was always amazed at how quickly a life could fall away. How quickly my life fell away.

Before my break, I experienced myself as a rather continuous thing. There was a Brandon and, for the most part, I lived Brandon day in and day out. The idea of Brandon was always a bit abstract. Was it my identity? Was it my beliefs? Was it my past experiences?

It was only after my life fell away that I understood. I am my rhythm and routines. I am the activities making up my day. I know myself through the activities which define my life. In madness, there was a complete dropping of routine to manage the onslaught of intensity I was experiencing.

While in my father's basement, I found a routine, a routine of deep avoidance. I knew myself through watching television and avoiding all contact with the world around me. My routine reinforced my self-hate. I imagine at some point they became one, my routine being the outward manifestation of the inner hate I lived.

Once I found the gentle energy to start again, one might say, as Windhorse descended into my life, giving me the gentle push to return back into living, I had to reclaim the activities of health I once knew. I had to remember what it is to commit to a daily routine, to commit to activities of health and wellness.

At first, it felt like I was pulling myself through quicksand, trying to get myself to take those steps into living again. Soon though, my routines began to gain momentum. As I found myself going to yoga every other day, I started to trust in my ability to grab my backpack, get on my bike, and ride myself there. I didn't have to push myself into doing it. It became my routine again. Same with work. I would wake up, gather my gear, and join my dad for a day of window cleaning.

From the place of "not living," the place of stuckness I found myself in my father's basement, I thought it would be impossible to start again. I thought it would be a major undertaking to really live again and, in a way, it was.

But it was the commitment that was the hardest, the willingness to start again. Once I committed to a few activities of health, I was shocked to see my body remembered how to be me. I didn't have to "bring myself back" or remember again how to live and interact. No, the activities of health I once devoted time and energy to before my break stored a living memory of who I was.

It was through connecting again to my rhythms and routines I remembered who I was. Where I remembered the pace of my mind, the way I thought, the determination in my body, my ability to physically push myself even when tired. I remembered I was someone who knew how to live in the world. I remembered the kindness I felt to others. My desire to be of service.

For so long, I only knew my own suffering, the hell I lived in. I forgot to look out and see the world, to see the sea of suffering so many of us swim in. By entering into the world again, I was able to remember my heart, who cared about the suffering of the world. The heart that wanted to be of benefit.

In my shame and struggle, I was not able to generate compassion for myself. But in the world, I could see the suffering and wanted to find a way to alleviate some small sliver of the ongoing pain so many of us live day in and day out.

These forgotten aspects of myself were not abstract ideas I had to generate. They were living realities stored in the memory of the activities I once engaged in. By reconnecting to the actions I once knew, I was able again to connect to myself, to know myself in the world.

For me, this is the most fundamental aspect of recovery, reconnecting to the activities of health and wellness that store a living memory of who we are. When we can connect to these things, we connect to a somatically embodied aspect of our personality. A part of our personality not defined by the history of madness, nor by the destruction and loss that occurs during a psychotic break.

My ability to play basketball does not care if I had a psychotic break. My ability to play basketball only cares about moving my body in a way that is conducive to playing. When I am on the court, I can drop all the stories I accumulated through my break. The stories of brokenness, of shame for losing my life, of lost time and opportunity. None of those matter. The only thing that does is moving in the rhythm and timing of the ball.

I had to remember there was more to me than my break. There was more to my story than madness and isolation. I had to see these were just recent experiences, recent additions to a long life. Through reclaiming activities of vitality, I could remember that my vitality lived beyond any story of limitation I had created about myself.

This is how I restored my ability to function. I connected to activities that reminded me of this inherent ability. These activities helped me recall the functioning self who was living inside of me the whole time. The self who was lost to the madness and buried in the isolation. It just took a little work, a little effort to commit to a few activities of health for me to start to recall who I was.

Once I was able to reclaim simple activities of riding my bike, going to yoga, and cooking food, I was able to gain the confidence to start working again. To find a room in a house with roommates. To live again on my own in the world.

The first six weeks to two months where I only focused on reclaiming these activities felt like a type of physical therapy. They were the foundational months that allowed me to build on top of something, on top of my history of health and sanity.

I was able to remember the me who fell away to cope with the madness and isolation. A me who was waiting to be reclaimed when the timing was right.

Zen

I am lying awake. Unable to sleep.

Tears are streaming down my face. There is overwhelming relief flooding my body. I did not know how afraid I was. Scared I could not live a spiritual life after what happened to me.

I am able to practice Zen again, to walk a contemplative path.

I have been meditating for days. On a week-long meditation retreat, a sesshin. I have not lost my mind. I have been sleepy. I have been in fantasy. I have been in agonizing pain. I have not moved.

I have stayed with my experience. Returning time and time again. I have reconnected to silence. To the gentle embrace of this moment.

My commitment grows. To work with my mind, to stay in this moment. Over time, I will learn to stay in this moment with a loving embrace.

I have a path again.

I grew up religiously, raised in a fundamentalist Christian household. I accepted Jesus into my heart and wanted to do right by God as a child. I would attend those big mega-churches with rock bands and PowerPoints.

Over time, as I learned more about science and comparative religion, I began to doubt the dogmatic foundations of Christianity. Obviously, I am not the only one this has happened to.

I remember being fairly stoned one day. I'm not sure why I wasn't at high school. I was watching a documentary about the Greek pantheon; Zeus, Hera, Ares, and the like. I had this thought, "If their religion is now a myth we look down upon as primitive, what does that mean about my religion?"

I believe this was the thought that started the unraveling of my faith. When I lost my faith, I lost the spark, my connection to the greater-than-me world. I wound up feeling alone and dry inside for many years. Not quite knowing what was wrong while knowing something was missing.

I would not be able to see how much losing my faith cost me until I was in college, when it returned. Not as a dogmatic faith, but a more spiritual openness to life again. To the sense that there is something more.

I distinctly remember the day I reconnected to the "more." I felt a charge in the air again. A charge I had forgotten. In the charge was possibility. A sense that this moment, this life, mattered in a way I couldn't understand from my limited perspective.

Shortly after the spark of living returned, I found my way to Zen practice. I started meditating on a gut feeling. This was before mindfulness was all the rage. I was in my early 20s.

Within a few months of starting to meditate in college, I attended my first week-long silent meditation retreat. It was during the start of summer break between my sophomore and junior year. It was not a Zen retreat. It was in the Insight tradition that is popular in the west.

During the retreat, I had a strong sense of coming home. It was the most profound experience I'd had up until that point in my life. It was not loud or overwhelming, like the psychedelics I had taken. It was softer but louder in a way. The access to silence, to spaciousness, was profound. It showed me that with effort, focus, and intent, healing and growth are possible. And in short periods of time.

I began to understand the power of working with my mind. Of learning to recognize when I am caught up in thinking and fantasy, and release. It showed me how to stay with difficult emotions and not run from them. Returning to them over and over until they open and reveal their hidden gifts.

Shortly after my first meditation retreat, I started meditating twice a day with commitment. I eventually found a Zen Center near my college. I fell in love. With the practice of Zen, the community, and the land the Zen Center was on. I was hooked.

I would spend my school holidays on retreat, staying at the Center during the summer. Often I would spend weekends there too, practicing with the monks who lived there full-time. A few of them became friends of mine.

I assumed after college I would become a monk at the Zen Center and pursue my spiritual path there. Something inside called me in a different direction. Into living in the world and trying to embrace a spiritual life. I gave up on becoming a monk.

I imagine if I stayed at the Center, I might not have lost my mind in the same way. Some of the learning, the lessons I needed on my journey, might have unfolded more slowly. In the gentler, more supportive environment of the spiritual community the Center offered.

Instead, I chose to live in a lively party town. I did not have the support I needed to anchor the experiences I was having. I was not able to "come back" smoothly. I have met others who have had breaks through psychedelics, who had the support of a spiritual community and were able to integrate the experience more fluidly, without having to give up so much.

I guess I learned the hard way.

In Zen, we have a practice called formal interviews. It is a long-standing tradition, centuries old, where you enter a small room and sit with your teacher. Sitting eye to eye, knees almost touching, you ask a question or share your experience. And your teacher responds to you.

Sometimes there is dialogue, sometimes there isn't. The teacher usually has a bell and when they feel the encounter is through, they ring the bell and you leave.

Over the years, I have had hundreds of interviews with my former teacher. The first time I interviewed with him, I let him know what I had been through. The Cliffs Notes version. I had a severe psychotic break due to a psychedelic experience. I had not engaged in active functional living for almost two years and I was just starting to put my life back together again.

I was expecting a cautious response. A warning to be careful when meditating with a fragile mind. Possibly even a suggestion that a meditative spiritual path might not be right for me.

In a lot of circles, if you have a psychotic break, you are discouraged from meditating. It is thought you are too fragile or too open to meditate and it will do more harm than good. I think there is some wisdom in this view, but not a universal wisdom.

This approach does not take into account the process of recovery and how, at certain stages, it might be best to not meditate. But at other stages, it becomes incredibly important to learn to work with your mind. It does not mean you have to meditate, but it is important to learn to be with your mind. To learn techniques of being with agitated mind states, to learn how to disidentify from thought and anchor attention in the present moment.

Instead of a warning to put meditation down, my teacher was indifferent. He didn't seem to care that I had a psychotic break. It felt almost like he shrugged. In his lack of response, I heard, "That doesn't even matter."

It was the most liberating experience I had up until that point. I had put so much focus and energy on having had a psychotic break. It had become such a definer of who I was on the inside, even though I rarely talked about it with others. It was what I was fighting with the most on the inside. *Am I crazy? Can I go on living after everything I've been through? Can you come back from what I've experienced?*

These were the questions eating at me at this point in my life. And here was someone who did not care, nor saw it as a problem. My break was irrelevant.

My teacher was not ignorant. He had a PhD in clinical psychology and was a trained psychoanalyst. He was familiar with psychosis and its impact on someone's life. He knew I would be on a journey of recovery for some time. He supported me for seven years on my journey, and he never made a deal about it. This was one of his great gifts to me.

In Zen, we talk about "mind-to-mind transmission." This is the idea that the teacher transmits something of what it means to be a Buddha to their student. My teacher showed me to hold my experiences lightly, to not put so much weight into my past. He let me know it was possible to not be defined by what I've gone through but to put more weight and possibility into who I was in this moment.

For that first year, I put a lot of focus on rebuilding my life. Learning how to honor a work schedule again. Managing money for the first time in years. Finding friendship and connection. Dating and finding a partner. Reconnecting to my body. To health. To food. To joy. To connection. To possibility. Caring about my appearance. Learning to live in a new city.

There was a tremendous amount of focus on rebuilding the foundations of my life. The core components that would allow me to create a functioning and meaningful life going forward.

In that process, there was so much fear of it all "falling apart" suddenly. Fear I would have another break. Or I would get called out by some authority for being full of shit for thinking I could just start over after everything I went through.

One of the first things I did when I started working again was buy a meditation cushion. At the time, it was a lot of money for me. But it was important to reconnect to my biggest passion, one of the things that mattered most to me, living a contemplative life. The cushion is still with me, I sat on it before writing tonight. It is torn, stained, and my friend.

Even though I was meditating daily again, 20 minutes a day is not the same as going on a meditation retreat. retreats are profoundly challenging endeavors. They are typically a week long. You wake before six and meditate until ten at night. Everyone I have met has told me their first meditation retreat was both the most difficult and most profound experience they have had.

When I signed up for a retreat that first year into my recovery journey, I thought I was just going back to one of the things that made me who I was. Something I loved. Like rock climbing. Just reconnecting to an activity of health that was once important to me.

It wasn't until I was in the middle of the retreat, sitting day in and day out, that I became aware of the deeper fears I wasn't acknowledging in my act of rebuilding the foundations of my life. I had swallowed a lot of the assumptions around madness, assumptions I didn't consciously know I held. One of those beliefs being that after a psychotic break, you no longer have a sound enough mind to engage in intensive spiritual or transformational practice.

Many meditation centers and other transformational retreats will screen for people who have had psychotic breaks. You have to fill out a form informing them of your mental health.

In a way, this screening can be helpful, ensuring that folks are stable and supported enough to engage in more challenging transformational work. A lot of times, transformational work is destabilizing. It breaks down the ego, pushes defenses, and forces us to look closely at ourselves.

For someone with a shaky foundation, a loose grip on consensus reality, intense spiritual practice can intensify the instability. Hence the hesitation in letting folks like me do these practices.

It wasn't until I was lying on the floor crying, listening to the snoring in the room, that I could really see how much I doubted my ability to have a rich inner life. To live a transformative journey. I was starting to trust that I could maintain an exterior life, an outward life With a job, friends, rent, and other responsibilities of being a person.

I didn't realize how afraid I was of being cut off from the richness of my inner world. It was during the retreat, when I was able to reconnect to parts of myself I had been cut off from for the last two years, that I saw I could have a spiritual life also. I could live in consensus reality and my personal "spiritual" reality together. My life could have depth and be "shallow." I could have a full life.

It was on this retreat I would first meet Paul. I have mentioned him throughout, my representation. My story doesn't exist without this man. Without him, I would never know it was possible to live a full and meaningful life after a psychotic break.

Paul

I do not remember the first time I heard Paul's story. Whether it was in a group setting, or if he shared it directly with me.

By the time I met him, he was in his late seventies. Old by most standards. Yet he was alive. He had a glean in his eye. A way of connecting with others. A loving way.

We fell into a routine of getting coffee after our morning Zen meditation. He often shared his life story with me over our hot drinks, and later over hikes. I was thirsty for his story. I needed it desperately.

Paul had been a spiritual seeker most of his life. We had that in common. He was originally drawn to Christianity and maintained a connection to the tradition throughout his life. He once attempted to become a monk in the Benedictine tradition. They kicked him out for being too much of a "contemplative."

In the 70s, after leaving the monastery and a marriage ending, Paul ended up in San Francisco. I do not know all the details but I know he had an opening, where he felt in touch with God, bathed in His light.

Following the opening, Paul felt pursued by "dark forces" and ended up homeless. A "wino." Drinking a bottle of Carlos Rose each day.

He lived this way for seven years. Until he accepted help from a Catholic priest, allowing himself to be on "disability" and was able to put his life together again with financial assistance.

Paul's and my story are not the same. We did not go through the same experiences, nor suffer in the same way.

> *Yet here he was, sitting with me, old and alive. I mean really alive. Paul had a rich life and a rich spiritual life. We would go on dozens of meditation retreats together. He would become one of my closest friends.*
>
> *Paul was my anchor. The root which allowed me to believe I could live a full life. He was a living example of finding his way home and living fully again. After his break, he had rich experiences. Starting to practice Zen, caring for his dying mother, and semi-adopting a young man.*
>
> *Paul was my mentor, my spiritual teacher, and my friend. Without him, I am not.*

When I met Paul, he was just a grumpy old man on a meditation retreat. The first time he stood out to me, I was in the bathroom avoiding a meditation period. My body hurt. I was tired of meditating. I was hiding.

I came out of the restroom and saw everyone lying down in the zendo, which was weird. But I was so relieved. I didn't need to sit through the agonizing knee pain I often experience during meditation retreats. I was hiding for no reason. I got to lie down and stare at the clouds floating through the skylight.

When I went to lie down, Paul was lying next to me. We were practicing cloud gazing, watching them pass by. There are a lot of metaphors around clouds and sky in Buddhism, the thoughts being the clouds and your awareness, who you really are, being the sky.

Paul fell asleep and was snoring at the top of his lungs. Filling the silent meditation hall. In my mind, he was ruining my lying down meditation period. I was annoyed, to say the least. My angry thoughts toward him filled my mind like the clouds floating through the sky.

It wasn't until later that I learned Paul had a severe encounter with madness. He spent his early 30s homeless and mad in San Francisco. I met him close to 50 years after this, when he was close to 80. In the period in between, Paul had lived a rich and meaningful life.

I didn't know the day he was snoring that he would become one of my closest friends, my role model, and my teacher. He would be the anchor who would let me know it was possible to go the places we have been and come back, living a full, rich, vibrant life.

I cannot do justice to the importance of Paul in my healing journey, my story of recovery. Paul is the beacon who let me know it was possible to come back and have a meaningful life after madness. If you look at pop culture, there are no representations of people recovering from psychosis, of finding functional grounding in everyday life again after a severe mental health crisis.

Paul was not "sane" by some textbook definition. He was uniquely himself. A beautiful anomaly. He told me stories of having another break later in life, being pulled into delusions that disrupted his life in a Zen community he was a part of when he was in his 40s.

Even when I knew him, he would at times say, "I'm feeling manic right now," particularly after meeting his future wife. Yet his anomalous experiences, his fluctuations in mood, did not derail his life. He worked with them. He was able to stay with his experience and maintain his life.

It would be years until I would hear stories of other folks who have made the journey back and reclaimed footing in both worlds of consensus and personal reality. Most notable was John Thomas Perceval, an English aristocrat who underwent a period of madness and was confined to two English asylums between 1830 and 1832. During this period, Perceval spent eight months confined to the Victorian equivalent of a straitjacket.

Even in deplorable conditions, he was able to learn to work with his mind. To see through his hallucinatory process, allowing himself to ground and anchor himself again in consensus-based reality. His story and descriptions of madness were influential to Edward Podvoll and the community who developed the Windhorse Approach to working with extreme states.

Like Paul, Perceval was able to see through his delusions, to let them go and start again. He married, had four children, and became an advocate for the refinement of asylum treatment in Europe.

In describing how he wished he was treated, Perceval shared:

> "It may be asked of me, what course I would have pursued towards me, seeing there was evident danger in leaving me to my liberty? I answer, that my conduct ought to have been tried in every situation compatible with my state; that I ought to have been dressed, if I would not dress myself, that I should be been invited to walk and down my room, if not quietly, in the same confinement as in my bed, that whilst implements what might do me hurt were removed, pens, pencils, books, &c., should have been supplied to me; that I should have been placed in a hackney coach and driven for air and exercise, towards the sea shore and round the outskirts of Dublin. Few can imagine the sense of thirst and eager desire for freshness of air which the recollection of that time yet excites me." [3]

Perceval and Paul exist in a long history of individuals who have "recovered" from madness and gone on to live meaningful and rich lives. This is the unspoken history of madness. The one denied by the Western medical model and the expectation of lifelong use of antipsychotic medication.

For me, these stories, the stories of possibility, of healing, of leading a rich and meaningful life, are the necessary ingredients missing in our current culture of treating madness. Clinicians are trained to believe schizophrenia is a lifelong condition requiring "maintenance." Their clients are more often than not provided daily antipsychotic medication proven to increase symptoms and

3 Podvoll, E. (2003). *Recovering sanity: A Compassionate Approach to Understanding and Treating Psychosis*. Shambhala Publications.

hospitalizations while negatively impacting their ability to integrate into and lead full lives.

These clinicians provide a treatment that denies hope and actively thwarts an individual's ability to heal. They have no understanding of the possibility of healing for folks with psychosis. Their belief systems are then transmitted to the clients and their families. Often clinicians see the removal of hope as an act of kindness, "preparing" clients for their future lives.

It is time clinicians step back and understand that their inability to treat madness is not due to the nature of madness, but due to their own limitations as healing professionals. Limitations they've inherited since the 1800s, when madness was first integrated into medical treatment and seen as a biological illness.

Clinicians are unable to heal madness under the current worldview and practices of the Western medical model. These clinicians assume the "illness" itself must be the cause of the current trajectory of madness. They do not see the models' understanding and treatment of madness as the primary limitation in treating extreme state disorders.

My rant here does not even take into account the calamitous impact of the integration of pharmacological companies with the medical model. Of antipsychotics being marketed as safe and curable when it has been known from their first implementation that they cause what is equivalent to traumatizing and degrading the brain, a lobotomy in pill form.

This is where the real irony lies. With the medical model describing madness as a chemical imbalance in the brain, yet its treatment actually disrupts brain functioning, creating the symptoms and outcomes they attribute to the "illness" itself.

For me to meet a friend "in the wild" who clearly has lived a full and meaningful life was the greatest challenge to the Western medical model. It was the foundation that allowed me to start to question the model's assumptions. Assumptions I had internalized without realizing it. Assumptions of brokenness. Assumptions of future psychotic breaks. Assumptions of a brain meant to decline over time.

Paul was my counterexample to the long-standing narrative of traditional mental health and the medical model. I knew him for years. I saw him through ups and downs. I saw him navigate his life for years with kindness, wisdom, and trust.

Paul showed me it was possible to go my own way. To create my own life. To discover my own meaning from my experiences. To make my own way. Through Paul's role-modeling, I was slowly able to shed the Western model's story of madness and begin to discover my own story. To learn to make my own meaning from my personal journey.

Most importantly, I saw Paul fully engaged with his spiritual life. He would leave our coffees after an hour of meditation and go take the Eucharist at his local Catholic church. I watched him grapple with and make sense of his own spiritual life. Always moving toward greater love and kindness.

During the retreats, we had a community practice of eye gazing, where we'd stare into each other's eyes for half an hour. I loved doing this with Paul, he was my favorite partner. For some reason, on one particular retreat, I was focusing on concentration, being able to maintain my focus on one object for a sustained period of time. While eye gazing with him, I engaged the concentration practices I was using.

It was the only time I had ever seen Paul directly mad at me. He shamed me for "losing my gentle touch," for "getting hard" in my ways of relating to others. For him, to see me concentrating while engaged in eye contact was a denial of our connection, of our ability to be together in shared silence.

In the past, I would attempt to let Paul see me, to relax into my experience and let him witness me as I am. He redirected me back to this practice, to the radical act of bearing one's tenderness for the world to see.

For this, I am ever grateful. He reminded me what was important to me. He was the role model in this radical tenderness. Anyone who talks about Paul now speaks about how loving he was. How kind he was. These are the markers of a man for me. Not his career accomplishments or material possessions, but his heart. This is what Paul left in his death.

Paul's dedication to his heart paved the way for me to let go of "being normal" or "proving my sanity" to others. He showed me it was okay to be me. To honor my unique callings in life. The way I want to show up to this life, with kindness and openness.

For me, this book is a continuation of Paul's story, a passing on of what he offered me. I wish for there to be new stories, new possibilities for those experiencing madness. Where individuals are taught they can learn to work with their unique experiences and discover their place in the world, instead of always having to accept or fight a medical model's story of brokenness and damaged brains. It is time we let go of the old stories and make way for the new stories of possibility to take root.

I dream of a world where clinicians are confronted with their limitations. Where they can stop blaming clients for not getting better or for there being no "cures" and, instead, understand their own limitations in meeting extreme states. Limitations of their training, their worldview, and their perceptual understanding of the world around them.

It is time clinicians understand their own humility. The Western medical model is an extremely limited understanding of the human experience that positions itself as the radical answer to life's suffering. We've been grappling with suffering, madness, and the human experience for millennia. Our new vogue concepts of psychology, the brain, and chemical imbalances are just one attempt to make meaning of human suffering. And a limited one at that.

It's time clinicians take some cue from those who have lived experience to begin to understand the healing conditions that allow for the natural recovery from psychosis, which often does not take place in the allotted hour for a therapy session nor in the prescribed medications to manage one's symptoms.

How Do You Not Be Crazy?

I have reconnected to Zen. I am meditating regularly, working with my Zen teacher. I am a month into living on my own. Out of the basement. In the rhythms and routines of everyday life. Work. Chores. Laundry. Brushing teeth. Grocery Shopping. Cooking meals. Being with others. Moving toward life goals.

I am grabbed by a koan, which is a Zen parable of enlightenment encapsulated in an exchange between teacher and student. I cannot let this one go. I am chewing on it. It is chewing on me.

The master would say to himself, "Master, Master," responding "Yes," to which he would ask, "Are you awake?" He would again respond "Yes" before reprimanding himself, "Don't fool yourself."

The koan works on me, a reminder to be real with myself, to "not fool myself." The koan passes. I no longer sit with it as much.

I am on public transit, heading home. I hear a voice. It is not mine. It says "Brandon!" I am terrified. I am trying to believe I am not crazy and I am hearing voices.

I will hear it throughout the day. "Brandon!" It will haunt me for over a week. I do not know what to do. I pretend like everything is okay. Deep inside, I am horrified. On edge.

I am grocery shopping. I am cooking a meal. I am alone in my new home, cutting carrots for fried rice. Again, I hear the voice, "Brandon!" I am terrified. I do not know what to do. How do you not be crazy?

I pause. I breathe. I turn toward the fear. I feel under the fear. I try to let the fear in, let it wash over me. It is intense. Almost too much.

As I continue chopping the carrots, I doubt if I can have a life. "I am fooling myself," I think. "This will not last."

Just three months ago I was lost. Not human, barely existing. Now I am pretending to live again. Pretending to work. Pretending to have friends. Pretending to be healthy. Who am I kidding?

I break. I am crying. I am heaving. I feel the "voice" is helping me. It is pointing out my fear. I embrace the fear I am unconsciously fighting, unintentionally pushing away. I acknowledge how afraid I am to lose my life again. How much I want to live.

I now actively work with the fear when it comes up, no longer pushing it out of my awareness.

I do not hear a voice shout "Brandon" again.

This was the first turning point. The first time I really had to confront this dividing line I had constructed between sanity and insanity. As my life opened again and began to take shape, it felt as if everything was too easy.

I had gone from the hell of the basement, my continuous state of not living, to once again reentering living, feeling a fully formed life around me in only a matter of months. It was a blink of an eye in recovery time. I felt like I was pretending, almost cheating in some way. I feared that before I knew it, it would all come crashing down. Like a drug addict relapsing. This was the story I was fighting as I moved into stabilizing my life.

For me, the worry was not that I would relapse into substance use but madness. I was afraid I would lose my ability to maintain contact with consensus reality. I would lose my ability to engage in the everyday tasks of living that allow life to perpetuate itself. Working, exercising, cooking, maintaining relationships. The basic acts of living.

I was afraid I would get so caught in my "other world" that I would lose touch with "this world" again. Allowing the rhythms and routines I had built to slip away. Once again drowning in the cacophony of extreme states that swallowed me up before.

Here I am, only a month into recovery, hearing voices. In my madness, hearing voices was not a primary component of my struggle. That doesn't mean it didn't happen from time to time. I was not that kid walking down the street talking to himself, lost to everyone around him. I was the kid who was living in his own reality, no longer in touch with consensus everyday shared reality.

I had no idea what to do about the voice shouting "Brandon!" I was too terrified to talk about it with others. The last thing I wanted was for someone to know I was crazy, the very thing I was fighting. I did not seek "professional" help. I was terrified of a diagnosis. A label that would haunt me forever.

When I was able to turn toward the fear underlying the voice, I was able to connect to the deeper dimension of doubt I was too afraid to hold. As I was rebuilding my life, I was too scared to hold the possibility it would fall apart again.

In a way, this is healthy. I had to do the courageous act of taking a leap of faith. A leap into living. Now that I had taken that step, my life started to take shape and I started to find rhythms and routines again. I was finally able to sit with my deep underlying fear of everything falling away because I was actually crazy.

To this day, I do not understand the nuances and humor of the healing journey. It was an internal voice, an auditory hallucination that allowed me to understand how afraid I was of being crazy. I am not wanting to go metaphysical here. To try to understand the "reality" of hearing voices. That is above my pay grade. Instead, I want to focus on an incredibly important distinction: fear of anomalous experience vs terrifying anomalous experience.

Years after this incident I would read Dr. Paris Williams' book *Revisioning Madness*. He would articulate the difference. First, a common definition of an anomalous experience is:

> *"an uncommon experience or one that, although it may be experienced by a significant number of persons is believed to deviate from ordinary experience or from the usually accepted explanations of reality according to Western mainstream science"*

I've found that, of anomalous experiences, hearing a voice that is not your own is the most stigmatized in Western culture as it is most associated with schizophrenia. There is research-based evidence that up to 15 percent of people will hear a voice that is not their own talk to them. There's also epidemiological evidence that up to 60 percent of people will hear a voice talk to them in their lifetime, with most incidents being incredibly positive experiences, while under 1 percent of individuals are diagnosed with schizophrenia. [4]

When I heard the voice say "Brandon!" I was terrified. Not because the experience in and of itself was terrifying. But because of what I was afraid it represented, me being crazy. Only crazy people hear voices, right?

This just isn't the case. People occasionally hear voices. In spiritual circles, this is a more accepted phenomenon, whether you are a medium or channel. Because I was so afraid of being labeled as crazy and not being able to live a fulfilling life, I interpreted this rather benign experience as indicative of my long-term ability to lead a meaningful life.

Unlike a fear of anomalous experiences, some people experience truly terrifying anomalous experiences. They might hear violent, destructive voices telling them to do horrible things. They can have horrific visions that shake them to the core. They may encounter threatening "presences" in the world. These experiences are horrifying. I've experienced a fair number of them.

When I was in my depressive state, the punishing voice that told me to kill myself was my own voice. It was not a hallucination, just self-hate directed toward me in the form of my own suicidal thinking. Ironically, punishing self-hate is seen as more "sane" than a positive auditory hallucination.

---

4 Jim Van Os. "New Visions for Psychiatry". Madness Radio. March 21st, 2016.

Many people hear voices. They hear their own voice refer to themselves in the second person, with *you*. "You're a loser." "You'll never be successful." Folks with everyday depression often hear these negative internal voices.

There is a commonly accepted term for this, it is "the inner critic." Our culture has begun to move toward a more multiplicity-based understanding of the self, while more pronounced experiences of hearing a voice outside of ourselves are still in the realm of crazy. This needs to change. It is not the voices that we hear that matter but what we do with them. How we respond to them internally, and how we express them in the world.

Many years later, while working at Windhorse, I would make a weekly "Sunday dinner" for the community. Staff and clients join to cook and eat together. One day, a client was my "sous chef." She was excellent. I asked her to make a sauce for a dish. She created a delicious one without any need to check in with me. Her cooking station was clean. She was organized and executed her role awesomely.

The client was also talking to herself throughout. She was able to engage with me, to break contact with her inner dialogue. But she was talking to herself all while she cooked, just as I was thinking thoughts to myself.

Another staff member walked into the space, saw her, and had a visceral reaction. The staff pulled my client aside, asked if everything was okay, and then continued to hover over her the rest of the night. The only focus was on the client's dialogue with her inner voices.

The clinician did not notice how the woman was demonstrating expertise, creativity, and engagement in other ways. This is the demonizing of hearing voices. So many of us live tormented by our own thoughts of self-hate, but we are not "crazy." Just depressed.

I am brought back to car rides with my grandfather. He would pick me up from elementary school often. These rides would be "silent." By silent, I mean we were not talking. He was clearly in an argument in his head. Fighting with someone.

I assume he was replaying a past argument or planning for one in the future, something people do all the time. I felt his anger and would see him going through his disagreement, his lips slightly moving. He was regarded as sane.

Our understanding of anomalous experience as a culture is deeply flawed. We need to make room for people who experience reality differently. We need to acknowledge that anomalous experiences are part of being human, and some folks experience them with more frequency. We need to learn to distinguish between people who are struggling to be engaged and connected to everyday consensus reality and those who have experiences of the "other world" while still being able to engage.

This is the crux. People can learn to work with anomalous experiences. They can learn ways of working with "uncommon experiences that deviate from common experience." What we think of as crazy might be less about having anomalous experiences and more about how we are able to work with the unique experiences we are having.

It's probably clear by now. I do not experience reality according to the ordinary experiences accepted by Western mainstream science. Most of the time, I do. But I frequently have anomalous experiences.

Often, like the auditory hallucination shouting "Brandon!," these experiences are helpful to my life, or at least benign. It would take me many years to learn to accept the ways I experience reality differently. I more often experience what is described as visual hallucinations, which is not really accurate. I do not see things that are not there. It is more, when I look at things, sometimes I see into them and there is more there than just the surface object I am viewing. Like the glowing moving box I referenced earlier.

I was once providing therapy to a client while this was happening. She was telling me a story about her childhood, an experience with her mother. While I was listening to her share, she morphed in front of my eyes.

On top of her face was superimposed another image. An image of a TV character I had seen recently. This was deeply disturbing to me. Why was I seeing this character? I "erased" the image, trying to see just my client again.

The character returned, superimposed over my client's face while I could still perfectly see her.

I did what I do with most anomalous experiences, I accepted it while not trying to make a "special" meaning out of it. Just allowing it to be there. I continued to listen to my client's story.

The woman told me about her mother's Munchausen syndrome by proxy. How her mother would seek attention from doctors by pretending my client was sick and bringing her to the hospital. A disease I had only just learned about because the TV character in question, the one superimposed over my client's face, had the same condition.

By having this hallucinatory experience with my client, I was able to more fully trust what she was sharing, to not doubt her story. I was able to emphasize. The hallucination gave more evidence that what she was sharing was true. If I had not had the hallucination, I may have doubted my patient's story and another person in her life would have denied the challenges she faced as a child.

To have anomalous experiences is human. For some, it is more the norm than not. Madness is not about the anomalous experiences we have, but our ability to function no matter what experience we are having.

There was the possibility that the voice shouting "Brandon!" might have driven me into an isolated state. Maybe the fear would have grown, and the frequency and intensity of the voice might have increased. From a place of fear, I might have locked myself away, cut myself off from the world again.

I would have done this not because the voice I was hearing was threatening, but because hearing any voice is a sign of being "crazy." By trying to fight being "crazy," I might have stumbled into another psychotic break.

I am grateful I had some of the training I did, some of the contemplative training that allowed me to learn to stay with my experiences. To not fight what was happening to me, but to be curious. In my curiosity, I was able to see the underlying fear I was holding. The fear that I was destined to be crazy.

The moment I decided to not care about hearing a voice and instead honor my underlying fear of not having a life, was the first moment I decided to live life on my terms. To let go of normative definitions of sanity and choose to define it on my terms. To determine health on my terms.

Now I do not care what voices I hear or what experiences I have. I do care about my ability to care for my son, to be relaxed in my body, and to notice the world around me. These have become *my* benchmarks of sanity.

If I allowed myself to be defined by the Western medical model's story of madness, I might have checked myself into a psychiatric ward for hearing the voice shouting my name. If that happened, I don't know where my life might have ended up. If research is any indicator, not well.

Pulled to Madness

I am standing behind the main desk. It is late. I am tired and almost finished with my swing shift. Mary walks down the stairs to get her evening medication. She is wearing a long red wool coat. She really is royal in her way.

I place her mandatory evening medication in her hand. She swallows the tablet, showing me her tongue to prove she has taken the pill. It is the atypical antipsychotic she has consumed since it was released in the mid-80s.

Mary looks me in the eyes, saying in the way only she can, "What makes you different than me?" before pausing, then, "Why are you standing behind the desk and I am over here?" She has an accusatory tone.

I look her in the eye and say, "I am better at pretending than you." She raises her head, huffs, and indignantly walks back to her room.

Later, I accidentally give her an extra dose of her evening medication. It impacts her. She loses motor coordination and verbal functioning. She slips and falls. She is not injured.

I help her up, realizing my error. I support her up the stairs. I feel horrible. She is so clearly impacted by my mistake and the cognitive impacts of her medication.

The next day, Mary greets me with great warmth. She does not acknowledge my mistake from the night before. I can tell she is affected by the kindness and concern I show in my guilt. She is softer and more tender with me. It is returned.

Our human connection deepens. We know each other for years. Playing countless games of Gin Rummy. Although, I eventually realize that the game she played was not Gin Rummy, and I do not actually know Gin Rummy's rules.

To this day, I do not know what pulled me back to the world of madness so soon after my own break. I was only out of my father's basement for six months when I started working at a group home for "Severe and Persistent Mental Illness" (SPMI). In recovery time, six months is a blink of an eye.

My job at the food cart was not panning out financially. In a strange twist of fate, my boss hired two people for the same role. The other person would become one of my closest friends in the world. With our role being divided into two, so was our paycheck. I decided it was time to find new work.

I learned quickly that having a bachelor's in psychology didn't open many doors. There weren't many entry-level jobs in the field paying well. The one I repeatedly came across was a Residential Associate. A Residential Associate is a frontline care worker. In the case of where I ended up, it was someone working with folks with SPMI.

SPMI was a term developed in the 80s by the National Institute of Mental Health. [5]The term is vague and generally refers to individuals who need ongoing state care for mental health struggles. They are not in crisis but in a state of permanent need.

Typically, individuals who receive an SPMI designation are not able to maintain daily functioning. Their family is not able or willing to support them. They are considered in need of round-the-clock care. Many folks in group homes for SPMI were part of the state psychiatric hospital system that closed down through deinstitutionalization from the 1950s to the 1980s. [6]

---

5 Zumstein N, Riese F. "Defining Severe and Persistent Mental Illness-A Pragmatic Utility Concept Analysis." *Frontiers in Psychiatry*. 2020 Jul 6;11:648. doi: 10.3389/fpsyt.2020.00648. PMID: 32733295; PMCID: PMC7358610.

6 Scull, A. (2015). *Madness in Civilization*. https://doi.org/10.2307/j.ctvc77hvc

I was surprised by the group home setting when I arrived for my interview. It was a normal-looking suburban house in a working-class neighborhood. From the outside, there were few indicators it was being used as a group home for those experiencing significant mental health challenges.

Really, the only thing separating the home from other houses was the front desk in the entryway. The desk was a blocked-off area where staff would gather and medication was kept locked up. It had a security desk vibe, it was clear clients were not allowed behind the desk. There were two computers and staff would hang out there during their shifts, tending to the comings and goings of the clients. It was a clear division between staff and clients, with clients not allowed behind the desk.

And of course the locks. Everything was locked up. Cigarettes were locked up. Food was locked up. Shampoo and conditioner were locked up. If a client needed almost anything, they had to ask staff to unlock it.

On the day of my interview, there were two staff members at the desk. One was playing with the house cat. The cat was feisty and loved to claw anyone who came near. The other was handing a client a small plastic cup of shampoo. The client was clearly pissed. She wanted more.

I would later learn this client always felt dirty and would compulsively want to wash herself clean, often using a whole bottle of shampoo. Hence the limiting of this item. I often wondered what happened to her in her life that left her feeling dirty, no matter how much she cleaned herself.

I decided to take the job, but still doubted my own discernment. If I were working with someone today who had a similar background to mine, I would definitely challenge whether they should be working so close to psychosis while in an early recovery process.

From one perspective, I was an early twenty-something kid working at a group home for "mental illness." A common thing to do with my degree. On another level, something in me felt called to step back into the fires of madness. Not my own madness, but others. I did not know what I was working out at the time but there was something I was trying to make sense of.

My first therapist who supported me through my integration and recovery process would like to say, "I played with fire." Something in me was called to go back to madness and wanted to understand. Not necessarily understand what happened to me, but understand how we got to this place. To this place where people are expected to perish, to fade away after receiving a diagnosis categorizing them as someone suffering from SPMI.

I've come to learn that I really wanted to understand why I contained an inherent assumption that one could not return from madness. That once someone experienced a psychotic break, they were destined to experience breaks for the rest of their lives.

This belief is not isolated to me. It is the rhetoric of the mental health field. Later in my journey, when working at Windhorse, I would hear families talk about encounters with high-end treatment facilities. Not your typical state-funded group home like the one I first worked at, but treatment facilities for families who could afford to provide their kiddos with adequate care.

One mother described being walked through the grounds of a facility and the director pointing out a man in his 40s, sitting at a table, shaking and talking to himself. The director told the mother, "This is what you need to expect for your son. This is where he is ending up." Which was not the case. Her son received nine months of treatment at Windhorse, returned to college, finished his degree, and is living his life. Upon leaving the team's care, he was off medication.

It would take me years to untangle this embedded assumption of no return, of once gone, lost. After my years working in the field, in institutions like this group home, I would have a real sense of the collective story around madness and the assumptions driving our care. I would understand it from a clinical point of view, through my training in the Western medical model and alternative understandings of madness, like the Windhorse Approach.

I would also understand it from the inside, the part of me who was terrified of the Western model being true. True in the sense that I had to give up having a full and meaningful life and accept a partial life of medication and living with a mind I couldn't trust. Like the director suggested to the mother.

In the case of the group home for SPMI, care was minimal and impersonal. It did not allow for much human connection, growth, or the possibility of ever increasing one's engagement with life. Food, medication, and minimal social support. This was the baseline of care. These are not the core ingredients I see as necessary in supporting folks navigating through a psychotic process.

It is so clear when working at a facility for "severe mental illness" that our culture does not believe people can recover. The treatment provided in no way provides the conditions needed to support a healthy and grounded return from a descent into extreme states.

When I first descended into madness, it was as if two selves lived concurrently inside me. One self could clearly see I had lost it, I was no longer sane. I was able to see I had lost my ability to navigate consensus reality. To move through life in an ordered and reliable fashion. I knew I needed help. I was drowning and did not know how to get my life back on track.

The other self, the one lost to the other world, was living out a different story. It was a similar story of being lost and needing to find my way back. But that self was lost within a spiritual dimension I needed to free myself from. I was not concerned with sanity/insanity, functioning, or mental health. I was engaged in a struggle larger than whatever was happening in my consensus-based reality. Larger than a kid graduating college and losing his mind after taking psychedelics at a house party and needing some sort of mental health treatment.

The part of me who was aware I had lost my mind, the part seeing me drift further and further away from consensus reality wanted absolutely nothing to do with traditional mental health treatment. I was terrified of being "treated" by our Western medical model.

Please hear me out. It was not my madness, not my stories of grandeur, not the spiritual warrior playing out an epic battle. No, it was the part of me who clearly saw my predicament of having taken a psychedelic and lost my mind that wanted nothing to do with the label and treatment of schizophrenia.

I admittedly refused treatment at every turn in my struggle. At the onset of my descent, I refused to be admitted to a psychiatric hospital. When I first started to find grounding in consensus reality again and descend into the depths of my depression, I refused the medication a doctor suggested.

Even after I started moving back into engaged living, leaving my dad's basement and rebuilding my life, I waited over a year to start therapy. Mostly it was because I didn't have the financial resources to afford therapy, but also because I wanted my internal foundation before I allowed myself to be "treated" by our mental health system.

When I was ready for therapy, I was incredibly careful in the therapist I chose. I looked for someone who I hoped would not pathologize my struggle with madness, not reduce it to a brain-based disorder to be treated and "managed."

The therapist I chose supported me for seven years after my break. She helped me through graduate school, getting married, purchasing a home, and becoming a therapist myself. All along the way, I felt she was someone who wanted me to live in the world, to express myself, to find a place for myself. She did not ask me to be less.

Occasionally, she would hint at me writing about my experience. She never once asked about "symptoms" or assessed my sanity. She supported me in processing the impact of having lost my mind, of having a gap in my life story. A two-year gap where I was lost and trapped in my own personal nightmare.

Through her help, I was able to acknowledge what had happened to me without having it be a definition of who I was or who I would become. Much like my Zen teacher who presented an indifference to my period of madness, I never felt my therapist defined me through the lens of psychosis or any other diagnostic label.

I have met many people who are scared of the mental health system. Scared of the labels that get placed on us. Scared of our experiences of being reduced to pathological brain disorders. People who want the opportunity to find a way of expressing their lives without inhabiting a story of brokenness. A story required to be "consumed" by clients in order to receive treatment for madness by many providers. Just like the expectation of consuming medication as a required foundation of treatment for extreme state disorders.

Some individuals even deem themselves survivors of psychiatric care. They see the treatment of their "illness" as more damaging than the illness itself. If you look back at the history of madness, you see centuries of "treatments" and "cures" that ended up being more damaging to the individuals receiving care than letting the "illness" of psychosis play out.

Early on in my madness, while traveling up the coast of California, I was visiting a close college friend. Someone I saw as a brother, as family. I opened up to him. I let him in on the depths of confusion and distortion I was experiencing. He saw how deeply I had changed, how lost I was, and immediately offered to take me to a hospital to receive treatment. I felt his kindness in the offer, I did not feel threatened by him. So I went along.

While we were in the hospital waiting room, the admitting clinician came out. He briefly interviewed me. I sensed a grounded kindness from him. He asked about the voices I was hearing. I told him, "They don't seem that much different than thoughts." He asked about the visual hallucinations. I responded similarly, "I'm fine with those as well."

Simplifying schizophrenia to visual and auditory hallucinations is so incredibly limited to the actual experience of being lost to madness. Had the admitting clinician asked, "Do you know how to find your way back?" or "Do you remember how to sit still?" or even "Do you remember what it is to feel safe?" I might have responded differently.

I knew I was not going to be taken through the locked doors and placed under "treatment," so I walked away. Afterward, my friend dropped me off. I would continue my wanderings for months, lost and not knowing how to find my way back. Desperately wanting respite, a place to feel safe to sort out what had happened to me, and was continuing to happen to me.

The only respite offered to me was behind locked doors, where upon entry I would be forced to consume medication I was not comfortable with. My family would be called. They would be informed of my diagnosis. They would be educated about my future, a limited future with little hope of living a full life.

The clinicians would tell my family that if I was lucky and started on medication, I might have what looked like a normal life. This would place my family on constant lookout for symptoms or signs of my deterioration. I would feel watched and scrutinized, the intensity of their gaze driving me further into isolation.

I would lose my ability to reach out and connect. I would have to hide any struggles I do have to prevent them from worrying. For the rest of my life, my actions would be interpreted through a lens of crazy or not. In the clinical world, we call this expressed emotion. It's a strange phrase for what happens to someone when they become "the patient" within a family, the problem needing to be fixed or the object needing monitoring.

I am able to describe this path because I have seen it happen to many young people. I've had to educate parents on the misinformation provided by most inpatient hospital staff. Staff who only see clients at their worst and release them, not knowing what happens after their two-week stay in the acute care facility.

These clinicians do not track the long-term outcomes of their clients' lives. They do not know what meaning their clients make of their madness and struggle. They do not see the life they create post-madness. These staff plant a seed, a seed of brokenness, of a difficult life, without any awareness of the possibility of recovering. Often, the family then takes on the role of nurturing the seed. The cycle is brutal.

Odds are, these hospital staff have not joined anyone on their recovery journey. They have not seen anyone find their feet again and be able to walk through life after psychosis. They most likely have not seen anyone regain their ability to express themselves within consensus reality. To find meaningful activity. To find human connections and relationships. To have purpose. To feel a calling and possibility. To know the joys of being human.

Clinicians are blinded by the story they inherited through their education and training. The story of madness being a permanent condition, an illness with no way back.

These clinicians and staff often do not know history. They do not know the roots of our modern story of madness. They assume our current story of "schizophrenia" is true without question. They don't even think to question it.

When clinicians provide their pitch to families about the treatment approach based on "maintenance," they assume they are providing kindness. Like the director of the high-end treatment facility, telling the mother what to expect from the course of her child's "illness." They do not know this approach is a byproduct of a lie. It is rooted in the belief that psychosis is a degenerative illness that can be "slowed" through proper interventions, primarily antipsychotic medication.

This just isn't the case. It is a vestige of thinking from the nineteenth century. [7]I will hear from clinicians I trust, deeply learned psychologists who have helped many people with their struggles, regurgitated stories of psychosis being a chemical imbalance, something therapy doesn't help with. Often because they have never tried.

It was while working at the group home that I first started to conceptually understand my deep-seated aversion to "treatment." After seeing this treatment firsthand, I knew I made the right choice in avoiding this traditional form of help.

I really didn't know what to expect when I started working at the home. I typically worked the swing shift from early afternoon till evening. I would arrive and begin prepping dinner for the community. A staff member would make lunch and dinner every day.

At times, I would help clients complete their daily chores. It was the one thing expected of them during the day, besides for following their medication regimen. I would help with the tasks they needed — getting more cigarettes, doing laundry, getting money. Basically, when they needed something, I had a key to help them get into their locked personal items.

---

7 Scull, A. (2015). *Madness in Civilization*. https://doi.org/10.2307/j.ctvc77hvc

Even snacks were kept locked away. On my first day, a tall strong-looking woman asked me for a snack. The other staff member let me know it was okay to give her one and gave me the key ring with the snack key on it.

This client had a detached, distant quality to her with what are sometimes called negative symptoms: limited facial movements, monotone expressions, and limited engagement with others. For me, it seemed like she was really inside herself and did not "come out" to greet others often. Human contact seemed unimportant to her. She minimally engaged with the world around her, but she did love snacks. She loved snacks so much, she was restricted from having her own. Hence the lock and key.

Not knowing the ins and outs of working with this client, I opened the cabinet. She frantically reached in and grabbed boxes of snacks. I tried to stop her and she quickly swung on me. She was close to hitting me in the face.

Here is someone who is cut off from the world, not able to connect or be with others and there is something she clearly loves: snacks. She loves them so much that when she's given a moment, she seizes it and acts in a "crazed" way, grabbing as many snacks as she can. Unwilling to let my "authority" stop her.

What a lost opportunity to explore how to support her relationship with delightful, tasty snacks and encourage her to be more connected to those around her. Maybe she eats her snacks at the community table. Maybe we taste-test different snacks and rate their deliciousness. Maybe we cook the snacks she loves. Instead of finding the snacks as a doorway to connection, they are locked up because of her "health."

The policing of space was my primary job. Keeping the refrigerator locked up. Providing medication and ensuring each person took theirs, with no cheeking allowed.

I remember I would have to ask the snack lady every night if she was wearing socks. She would have to show me and, if she wasn't wearing them, I would have to ask her to go get them before she received her cigarette. More often than not, I wasn't wearing socks myself. I was at a period in my life where I wasn't really into socks. I'm not sure I've ever left the not wearing socks period of my life. But, anyway, these are the types of rules created for people in "managed care."

I would love to see a breakdown of spending in one of these group homes. The amount of medication we provided was tremendous. Everyone had at least 5-8 medications they were given at regular intervals. Up to three times a day. All paid for by the state.

Yet, the home I worked in was in a near-constant state of disrepair. The food was horrible. The living conditions were minimal, to say the least. Think of a few Ikea paintings randomly hung up with Goodwill furniture.

Often, we were so short-staffed I would work 16-hour shifts alone with eight clients, cooking and tending to the house. I was so divided that I had no time to create genuine connections with the clients. This was not even thought of as part of the job. Maintaining the space. Keeping it orderly. This was the role. No one expected you to build relationships, to develop friendships, to support clients' engagement in consensus reality.

At this juncture in my recovery process, I was more concerned with building the foundations of my life. I wasn't yet ready to dive into the history of madness, to understand how we got to this place. A place where people are assumed to deteriorate with no thought of finding their way home.

When at the group home, working, friends, and community engagement were what mattered most to me. Feeling connected to life in a deeper way. Learning how to be human again. Enjoying being twenty-five.

In the years that followed, I would become curious. I wanted to know where my internalized sense of brokenness came from. Why was I fighting so hard to be able to have a life after madness? Why did I think it was impossible to heal? Where did this deep-seated doubt in the possibility of recovery come from?

No one told me you couldn't heal from madness. I wasn't taught this in a class. My sense of fighting a destiny of decline was pre-built into my understanding of what madness is, an assumed part of my belief system.

I wouldn't know it, but working at the group home would be the start of my expertise by training. My learning how to be with others struggling with extreme states. Struggling with minimal care. Struggling with being marginalized by a culture that does not believe you can heal from madness and is unwilling to support those who have lost their way.

For decades, NAMI (the National Alliance on Mental Illness) has pushed to destigmatize mental illness and mental health symptoms.[8] For most people, this is considered a wonderful thing. To normalize mental health struggles, to increase empathy for those struggling with their mental health, and to decrease people's resistance to seeking treatment.

Most people are strongly in favor of destigmatizing mental health symptoms and mental illness. I personally am not. I feel it causes a tremendous amount of harm for the good it does cause. The scales do not balance.

In many ways, de-stigmatization has been incredibly helpful to the proliferation of the Western medical model of mental illness. If you believe the model's stories, you are fine with destigmatizing them. Stories of chemical imbalances, of the necessity of medication for managing mental health, of genetic predispositions to mental illness.

Through the movement to normalize this specific model's understanding of human struggle, many people are receiving treatment who didn't in the past. However, when you look at madness, at psychosis, this may not be the best thing. To receive treatment. The Western model, in my view, does more harm than good in helping first-incident psychosis.

It has been known for almost thirty years that an individual who has a psychotic break is far more likely to recover if born in a third-world country than those born in an industrialized society like the United States. Please take this in. People in third-world countries recover from first-incident psychosis at rates higher than in the industrialized West. [9]

---

8 https://www.nami.org/Blogs/NAMI-Blog/June-2020/The-Evolution-of-the-Mental-Health-Movement https://www.nami.org/Blogs/NAMI-Blog/June-2020/The-Evolution-of-the-Mental-Health-Movement

9 Padma, T. Developing Countries: The Outcomes Paradox. *Nature* 508, S14–S15 (2014). https://doi.org/10.1038/508S14a

The efficacy of treatment in the United States, essentially the helpfulness of our current approach to treating madness, has seemingly not improved in the last hundred years. This stagnation has occurred within the era of both first- and second-generation antipsychotics. As we've praised and spent billions on the proliferation of antipsychotic medication, individuals are experiencing a decrease in quality care, as care is no longer considered human but pharmacological.

I have my personal theories on why this is, but I am not an academic. I am not a researcher. I am not a doctor. I am not a pharmacologist. I am not an epidemiologist. I'm just someone who's tried to understand why I assumed I could not heal from a first-incident psychotic break. Someone who, while in a desperate state of needing treatment, refused it at every opportunity. Someone who had to find my own way back, my own way of honoring my recovery journey from madness.

I am someone who has experienced madness, who has had an acute psychotic episode and recovered. I'm also someone who has helped other people recover from acute psychotic episodes.

We need to acknowledge what we are doing is not working. The current belief is the treatment does not work because psychotic mental health disorders, like schizophrenia, are permanent brain-based disorders that have no cure. And the only real treatment is the lifetime use of antipsychotics. This is not science as we know it.

These assumptions have existed as far back as the 1800s. Before we had MRIs, before the human genome was mapped, scientists were excited by the emerging science of phrenology, the study of bumps on the head to indicate intelligence. The eugenics movement was wide-ranging and had a specific target, sterilizing individuals struggling with lunacy and other extreme state disorders. One country grabbed on strongly to the narratives proliferated by the eugenics movement, Nazi Germany.

The T-21 program was the testing ground for the gas chambers used to enact genocide on the Jewish population. One of the primary subjects used for these tests was the "deranged," another word for madness in the twentieth century. It is speculated that over 98 percent of Germany's deranged population was killed during testing of the T-21 program. Within one generation after this testing was completed, the number of people considered deranged returned to pre-genocide levels.

When schizophrenia is destigmatized, there is an assumption that the underlying understanding and treatment are accurate. You are destigmatizing a story that is sold to people. The story of schizophrenia is just wrong. It is not accurate.

People recover from madness and do not develop schizophrenia. People who have not had treatment, who've had no professional support, are able to recover from madness. People like myself, who've found their way back on their own.

I can almost guarantee that if I had received the Western medical model's treatment for schizophrenia with the built-in assumptions this model holds, I would have not recovered. I would be fighting an "illness" for the rest of my life. Always on guard. Off and on medication. Unable to pursue my life dreams because I need to be careful and "maintain" any functioning I have.

As of writing this story, I feel less fight. Less struggle with my internalized stories of brokenness I've inherited from the medical model. Instead, I feel acceptance for the way I move through the world. I've come to appreciate my differences in perceiving reality. To understand the value of living my personal reality while engaging in consensus reality. I even see some of the value of honoring my personal anomalous experiences, despite what consensus reality deems "accurate," "objective," or "true."

In truth, the medical model is a damaging story. A story that tells people they are broken and have little possibility of leading meaningful lives. Some believe rebelliousness is a potential key characteristics of individuals who have recovered from psychosis. Rebelling against the story of brokenness provided by the model's story of madness.

To understand this story, you have to go back to the 1700s and chart the emergence of the asylums, lunacy, and the purchasing of madness by the medical establishment. Remember, before science, religion cared for the soul. And lunacy, as it was called, was a disease of the soul.

As I said, I am not an academic. I am someone who tried to understand why I assumed there was something wrong with me for recovering from my psychotic break. Like I had cheated the system. For many years, I felt like I did something wrong. It was almost something I was ashamed of. I recovered from a psychotic break and was living a functional and meaningful life.

I did not celebrate my accomplishment, I hid it. I still hide it. Even now, I am uncomfortable writing this book. Uncomfortable in calling out the lunacy of our current treatment of extreme state mental health crises.

Someone like me, someone who is open about their experience of madness, is easily dismissed as crazy. This is my legacy. Fighting other people's stories of madness. People on the outside. People who have not been there. Who have not lived through it. People who assume an understanding of things, an understanding of how madness works. Whose careers are predicated on the belief that those suffering from madness are lifelong patients.

This is not meant to be a history book on madness. Others have written those. I encourage checking out *Mad in America* and *Madness in Civilization* as starting points. I simply want to share some of the meanings I've made.

In the 17th century, a book was published that I believe changed the course of our current understanding of mental health, *The English Malady*. In it, the author claims that Victorian symptoms of melancholy and nervous disorders, what we might now call depression and anxiety, are actually by-products of being civilized. Through shedding primitive ways, one is cursed with these conditions. This book sought to normalize anxiety and depression as expressions of the upper class, of being civilized.

Here is the beginning of destigmatizing mental illness. Categorizing certain mental health symptoms as "elevated," as reflective of a class status of civilized, and bracketing off other mental health struggles, like madness, as reflective of being "primitive" or, in modern language, a brain-based disorder. This same trend is witnessed in present-day diagnosing. Black individuals are far more likely to receive a diagnosis of schizophrenia while White individuals are more likely to receive the often less-damaging label of bipolar.

It was in this era when insane asylums began to pop up all over Europe, especially in England. If you have a civilized mental health illness, a nervous disorder, it was suggested you take relaxing trips to the coast to be treated by the healing waters. If you were experiencing more extreme state symptoms, you could be locked up in an insane asylum against your will. Like Perceval, who was locked against his will for over two years while suffering from extreme states.

It was around this time the claim of madness as a brain-based disorder began to take hold. It wasn't a natural movement toward science but a literal purchasing of lunacy away from the religious institutions who saw it as an illness of the soul. At this time, surgeons were not the elite medical professionals they are today. They were more akin to barbers in the social hierarchy.

These surgeons began propaganda campaigns claiming madness as a brain disorder and, therefore, must be treated by the medical establishment. A lot of money was starting to circulate in the state treatment of lunacy. Like the clients I worked with in the group home, their care was state-funded.

It was of interest for the surgeons in pre-modern England to make the case that madness is a brain-based disorder. By it no longer being a spiritual issue of the soul but biologically rooted, it was in the purview of medicine to care for those experiencing madness.

Lunacy began to become a business. In the 1800s, governments started to pay for the cost of treatment. Being a director of a state-led lunacy hospital was a prestigious title with significant financial compensation.

Please remember what people thought of the brain in the 1800s. It is not our current understanding of mental plasticity, interpersonal neurobiology, or current brain imaging. During the Victorian era, there were rudimentary assumptions about the brain, mostly based on autopsies.

Due to lunacy becoming brain-based, physical treatments became more prominent. The dunking of individuals in freezing water became commonplace. Spinning contraptions were developed which kept patients spinning for hours, leaving them disorientated and "docile." Being locked up by chains, being burned, and bloodletting were all common practices of "medically treating" individuals.

Perceval was locked in chains in his bed for over six months, at times being placed in soaked blankets that would dry and cut off circulation throughout his body, resulting in extreme pain. As things progressed, insulin-induced comas were developed and lobotomies became common practice. The removal of teeth was thought to reduce symptoms. Clinicians even surgically removed vital organs — all types of treatments to "cure" the brain-based disorder.

This would give way to electroshock therapy and the widespread usage of antipsychotic medication we see today. When antipsychotic medications first entered the treatment market of the West, they were known to chemically degrade the brain, creating Parkinson-like symptoms in clients. This was considered a benefit. Antipsychotics were akin to lobotomies, the practice of pushing an ice pick through the eye socket and removing vital connections within the neocortex of the brain.

Because people cannot heal from a brain disorder, the primary treatment is about reducing the cost and human labor it takes to "manage" these individuals. Not in helping them navigate their unique experiences and learn to integrate back into society. It is this dividing line, between symptoms that are reflective of life's challenges and biologically rooted illness, that still exists in the medical model's understanding of mental health.

It is okay to have depression. People can get depression for all types of reasons and not expect to be depressed for the rest of their lives. It is not possible to recover from schizophrenia. If you receive a diagnosis of schizophrenia, you can only ever be in remission. Even though evidence points to almost 30 percent recovery rate for individuals diagnosed with this condition. This statistic is from the industrialized West, often considered one of the worst places to receive treatment for schizophrenia. [10]

I will come back to diagnosis in the next part of this book. For now, I want you to sit with the possibility that de-stigmatization is harmful, normalizing barbaric biological treatments for psychotic breaks that often cause more harm than good. Leaving people with increased symptoms, increased likelihood of

10 Warner, R. (2004). Recovery from schizophrenia: Psychiatry and political economy. Brunner-Routledge.

future psychotic breaks, and significantly reduced abilities to be in touch with themselves and their loved ones.

The current treatment for extreme state disorders like schizophrenia and bipolar disorder is the maintenance approach. I'm not even sure if this is a technical term. To me, someone in the field, it is just what it is known as. It is what was taught in graduate school. It is what parents describe to me when they relay what other providers have told them about their kids' future lives. Like the mother being walked through the grounds by the director of the treatment facility.

The maintenance-based approach is best described by anecdotes. I am in graduate school in a psychological evaluation course, learning about Rorschach tests, the Myers Briggs, and that type of stuff. Somehow, the professor is going on a tangent, talking about a client he once had. A client who, at the age of seventeen, began to display psychotic symptoms.

The professor did not elaborate on the kiddos' symptoms. In his most sincere "caring about the client" voice, he repeated what he told them and their family.

> *"You need to adjust to the life you are going to live. Whatever plans you had for college, for your future, need to be changed. You are going to be placed on a medication for most likely the rest of your life. You should expect to maintain your life."*

After he described his encounter with this kiddo who was starting to display symptoms of madness, the professor informed us that he was doing them a favor. He was preparing this client for his future life. While it might sound harsh, his statement was likely actually helping the kid to have appropriate expectations for his treatment and the outcome.

Hearing this, I was appalled. I just sat there dumbfounded. I did not say anything. I did not want to disclose my own recovery journey. I did not want to argue with the professor. I knew my rage was hot. I would not be able to be civil. I think of this kiddo being sold a lie. A destigmatized story of brokenness. I am scared to think of their future.

Later in the same program, in another class, a professor recommended not doing therapy with someone displaying psychotic symptoms. "I tried it once," they said. "It didn't work." The maintenance-based approach is rooted in the assumption that extreme state disorders are permanent biological illnesses with no cure. The only treatment is to reduce the impact of the symptoms through medication. Because there is no cure, there should be limited expectations of having a rich and meaningful life.

If you look back at the history of these disorders, this makes total sense. Before schizophrenia was called schizophrenia, it was called dementia praecox. The term was made into a diagnostic category by Emil Kraepelin and literally means a chronic deteriorating brain condition, implying incurable madness. Kraepelin was the first to separate classes of psychosis: manic depressive psychosis, modern-day bipolar disorder, and dementia praecox, the precursor to schizophrenia.

Kraepelin terminology requires that a person who receives the diagnosis of dementia praecox does not recover from the illness. It was even reported that he would move people from dementia praecox to manic depressive if they started to show some improvements. This is still evident in the elevation of bi polar over schizophrenia.

When you look at the history of madness and the initial formulation of schizophrenia, built-in is the assumption of decline. The assumption is that the best practice is to slow the inevitable decline through a maintenance-based treatment approach.

What Kraepelin didn't know at the time was what he was describing was not madness. He was most likely describing encephalitis, a biological illness that had not yet been discovered. It would still take twenty years until this occurred, revealing that encephalitis is a brain-based illness that often results in madness and is characterized by a steady deterioration of functioning.

When we normalize treatment through campaigns to destigmatize mental illness, we do not realize we are normalizing a story. In the case of madness-based disorders, the story holds no possibility of healing. Why would we want to proliferate this story? Can't we come up with a better understanding that reflects an inherent truth that when given the right conditions (and sometimes without), people recover from psychosis?

Traveling

I am traveling for the first time since my descent into madness. I've been out of my father's basement for almost two years. I am staying with a college friend, the only friend I am in contact with from before everything unraveled.

I am walking the streets. Passing time. Not sure what to do with myself. My friend will not be home for a few hours. At some point, I lose my way. My phone is dead. I cannot get directions. I am lost.

I am overwhelmed by a pronounced fear in my body. I feel myself on edge, terrified of falling over into it. What it is, I do not know.

I try to soothe myself. To anchor myself in presence. I do not know what has taken hold of me. I am barely holding on in the "inside." While on the "outside," I am just another person walking down the streets. I am shopping. Being a "normal" tourist.

I find my way to a bookstore. I am wandering through the books. I come across a lawyer's personal account of madness. Her journey is different from mine. She struggles to be in consensus reality. Identifying with the diagnosis of schizophrenia. Trying to "hold it together" with great effort. I resonate with her in my moment of barely hanging on.

As I read, I am slightly calmed. No longer on the streets confused. I feel into the lostness I am experiencing while traveling and am reminded of the lostness of madness.

I am without my normal routines, the familiarity I have come to know. My newfound anchors. The structure I have built that allows me to know myself.

I begin to anchor myself into my life. Remind myself of where I am. I am traveling to attend a conference. I am in graduate school studying to be a psychotherapist. I have a partner at home waiting for me. I have a family. There is a cell phone in my pocket. I have a bank account with money in it.

I am able to remind myself I am not lost. I am not abandoned to madness. I am not homeless. I begin to steady myself, find ease in my body again. I tremble as the fear is released.

I am able to find my way to my friend's house without Google guiding me. While we eat dinner, I am reminded of friendship, of connection, of my history beyond madness.

Later, after he has gone to sleep, I am again looking through books. A book stands out on his shelf. "Recovering Sanity." It is written by a contemplative psychiatrist. I am immersed again in reading about madness.

The psychiatrist writes of a model of treating madness. A model rooted in inherent sanity. He describes a community-based approach to working with folks in extreme states, the Windhorse Approach.

I know this model. It is familiar. It reminds me of how I helped myself heal.

Later, I talk with my partner. We discuss moving to where there is a Windhorse Community so I can work there and learn their ways.

I tell her it will be years until I feel ready. My recovery is too fresh to imagine helping others so directly.

Once again, I don't understand why. but when I first made my list of activities that would help me re-anchor myself back into my life, I wrote I would attend graduate school for counseling. Before my break, I had no desire to work with folks in a healing capacity. Now, over ten years in, I can't imagine a different life for myself. To be with others on their healing journey is one of my great joys in life.

When I first wrote "training to become a therapist" on my list, I thought it was absurd. Who was I to think I could help others? I was someone just out of a psychotic break, unknowingly entering a period of severe isolation and depression that would span almost two years.

Yet, something in me must have had confidence in my ability to heal. Some faith I could be where I am, lost and broken, and still become a support for others on their healing journeys. Or I was still delusional when writing my list.

The finding of *Recovering Sanity* was the beginning for me. It was the beginning of me really trying to understand what I went through. Of making sense of my story. Once again, I was not trying to make sense of madness. I think understanding madness is a rather silly endeavor. As silly as trying to find its "cure."

It was more about making sense of the post-madness, the recovery journey. Trying to understand how on one level, my recovery was "easy," and on another level, it was one of the most difficult things I've ever been through. A journey I am still on, recovering from the story of brokenness provided so freely by our therapeutic culture, rooted in a Western medical model's damaging understanding.

After the torment of madness, after the excruciating depression, I was able to find my way back into everyday living with some ease. I was able to find structure, community, meaning, and begin again to tap into the thread of my life. Stepping back into the movement of my life, working on my growth edges, understanding my struggles, and placing myself in situations to heal and move forward.

In a way, it couldn't have been easier. When I am speaking freely and not packaging my language in psychological terms, I tell people, "Life was waiting for me when I was ready to step back into living."

It was me who had put the brakes on my life. I needed a break. After my madness, I knew what I needed to do to put my life back in order, I had a list. But I wasn't ready yet to take it on, to start rebuilding a life again. I needed a solid time away to regroup and reground myself into everyday consensus reality.

The way I was able to do this was by isolating myself and watching TV until I was ready to step back into living. Not the healthiest way to get back on the ground, but it worked for me. When I look back at the time I spent in my father's basement — the isolation, the crushing shame, the timeless depression with no end — I remember it as one of the most painful, difficult periods of my life.

At the same time, It is hard for me to remember now how I felt then. To be so subsumed in shame, so lost to the world that the only thought I had was to kill myself. Hence the necessity of television. TV allowed me to take my attention from my inner landscape of punitive shaming and connect to something else, something outside of my pain.

From one side, it was the worst, most painful place I could be. On another level, it was exactly what I needed. I needed space. I needed a break. I needed time for my extreme states to settle, for the anomalous experiences to fade into the background. To have distance from the delusional narratives I created for myself. The stories I told myself that helped me both make sense of my madness and navigate through the radically different experience I was having while in its extremes.

It was only with time that I was able to let go of what had happened. To no longer be defined by those experiences. To feel "fresh" to reenter living again.

I now think of my time in the basement as a type of hibernation, a break from the demands of "functional living" to settle and regain a sense of connection to myself. A time to let the intensity of the extreme states settle. A time to let the stories I told myself about myself, you know delusions, too fade with those states. A time to recover from what I went through in my experience of madness. The experiences I had and their impact on my body and nervous system.

I have watched several other folks, people who experienced their first break, need months to find their feet again. Time alone. Time watching TV. Time taking it slow, slowly stepping back into life.

I remember later in my journey, when I was supporting others on their return journey at Windhorse, I was working with a young man. He was in his early twenties and had his first break, a devastating break. His life fell apart. He was so raw when I first met him. Almost like a newborn. Just trying to remember the basics of navigating everyday reality.

I spent almost a year with this man. Seeing each other every other day for a few hours. Mostly just hanging out. Reading books. Going to get lunch. Drinking many cups of tea. Watching movies. Being people in the world together.

One day, after a hike, we were driving. We were pulling into the local food co-op to grab some lunch. He turned to me, clearly upset, in a state, and confessed his shame. His shame for having been in the Windhorse program for as long as he had. He admitted his fears, his worry about what I would think of him for needing this much help. At this point, I'd probably spent over two hundred and fifty hours with him. And I was just one person on a team of three others who saw him as much as I did.

My heart broke at that moment. Broke in ways I couldn't share. When I work with folks, I rarely tell them my own story of madness and recovery. Colleagues would question my choice to keep my story to myself. Wondering if it would be of benefit to share with clients. I always liked to think the people I worked with knew, on a certain level, on an unspoken level, the kinship, of having gone places unspeakable and trying to live in the world again.

Sitting with this man in the car, my heart was breaking for all the things I couldn't say to him directly. The honor that it was to watch his recovery journey. To see him coming back into himself. How I wished I had the human support and time he had. How I would have given anything to have companions during the hard months and years of isolation when I wasn't yet ready to be on my own in the world. Having people to be there with me and not push me when I wasn't ready to step into the world of doing, of structure and responsibility.

Instead, I shared an anecdote. I told him I thought taking his time was the best thing for him. I compared what he went through to a traumatic injury. Like a traumatic brain injury. These injuries take years to recover from. Hours of physical therapy. No one expects you to work, to have it together after brain surgery.

It was at that moment that I started to become truly enraged at the system's treatment of what I call catastrophic mental health crises, like psychotic breaks. If someone were to have brain surgery, it would take weeks if not months to recover at home, not including the year of physical therapy to regain their skills, coordination, and capacity.

The standard treatment for a psychotic break is a two-week stay in a hospital's psych ward, where you are provided a stabilizing medication, typically in a dose that is not sustainable for being in the world, working, and functioning. You are then usually discharged. Hopefully, you are set up with a psychotherapist. Often you are not, with medication management being the primary treatment.

This is just not enough. It is not enough to help someone come back. What someone needs on their journey back is people. They need human support. They need people to be there with them while things settle, while they pick up the pieces and begin to make movements toward engaged living again.

Human care is expensive. The treatment facility I worked at, Windhorse, was close to 200K a year, around the cost of brain surgery. It could be done for cheaper but not much. I still to this day do not know why we do not provide the proper financial support to see people through their recovery journey. Why is brain surgery covered by insurance but someone recovering from a psychotic break is not provided close to the same level of care and treatment?

Cultures that do support recovery see a radical improvement in recovery rates. Finland, which pioneered the state-run Open Dialogue approach to treating psychotic breaks, has an over 80 percent recovery rate. [11]

I imagine what it would have been like to have my break in Finland, in western Lapland, where the Open Dialogue approach was developed from what I understand. As soon as my behaviors began to change, as soon as I started to lose my ability to hold it together, a team would be called in. In my case, hopefully within a couple of days of taking the psychedelics that initiated my descent into madness.

The team would be comprised of doctors, social workers, and therapists. They would meet with my family and me. There would only be team-based group meetings. Nothing would be hidden.

The first order of operations would be to develop a language, a way for me to describe my inner struggle, which is so hard to articulate when you are lost to the other world. I would develop a way of letting my family know what it was like, and when I am struggling more than other times. Through developing a shared language, a bridge is built. One where I can communicate with my family, friends, and mental health providers. Through building this bridge, the number one intensifier and prolonger of psychotic symptoms would be addressed: isolation.

Medication would be used minimally, mostly to support the stabilization period during and after the psychotic break. Of the roughly 80 percent of folks who have recovered through the Open Dialogue approach, only 33 percent maintain regular medication use. [12]

---

11 Seikkula, J., Alakare, B. & Aaltonen, J. (2011). The comprehensive open-dialogue approach (II). Long-term stability of acute psychosis outcomes in advanced community care: The Western Lapland Project

12 Seikkula, J., Alakare, B. & Aaltonen, J. (2011). The comprehensive open-dialogue approach (II). Long-term stability of acute psychosis outcomes in advanced community care: The Western Lapland Project

Compare this to my friend who ate the belladonna flower. Who had to "pretend" to be normal to be released from the hospital. His providers were not interested in creating a bridge for him to explain his unique experiences and struggles. Instead, he had to pretend his struggles didn't exist to be let go.

My friend is not a solitary case. The Rosenhan Experiment is a well-known research project from the 1970's. David Rosenhan wanted to devise an experiment to test the validity of mental health diagnostics, of a clinician's ability to determine if someone was sane or insane. He and his graduate students admitted themselves into psychiatric hospitals across the country. Upon being admitted, they would report fear after hearing a non-threatening voice say their name. Sound familiar?

The "sane" researchers were often held in psychiatric wards for up to two months and only allowed to be released once they admitted to the hospital staff's narratives of them having a degenerative mental illness. Often, anything the researchers did was interpreted through a lens of pathology.

Even when they took notes for their research, the facility staff would interpret the behavior as part of their paranoia. However, the clients of the facilities would often identify the researchers as faking their way in, even calling them out for being journalists or researchers.

This is the nature of our mental health system, where clients seeking help in a time of need are required to accept a label of brokenness, of degenerative illness, in order to be released into the world. But to receive treatment, the support they need when they are struggling, they must accept the medical model's story of psychosis.

If they don't, they may be deemed "resistant" or told they have "low insight" into the nature of their "illness." The less insight they have, the easier they are dismissed and discredited by their providers.

In the Open Dialogue approach, there is no diagnostic procedure, you do not receive a diagnosis. Your symptoms are not tracked. There is no pathologizing of the patient and their behavior. It is more oriented toward building a community around the individual to support them through their process. Trying to learn what the client needs on their recovery journey.

This is what is needed. True mental health crises need to be recognized for what they are, a catastrophe. Not just for the individual, not just for the family, but for the whole community.

Often, I get the sense that family and friends do not know how to show up for folks when they are struggling in madness. It's common for loved ones to be pushed away. There is also this sense that people step back, as if they have no way of supporting their loved ones through their crisis. Like they need "special" care. This just isn't the case.

People who are losing themselves to madness need more than anything to be reminded of their humanity. To be brought back into human relating. Often, in the height of a psychotic break, this is incredibly difficult. But psychotic breaks do not typically last long. They are incredibly hard for the body to sustain.

After the intensity of the break begins to wane, when the extreme states begin to subside and the speed of mind begins to slow, there is an incredible window for someone to be supported. To be reminded of their humanness. If that window is lost, the person will often fade into isolation, grabbing hold of their stories of madness that gave them meaning through the throws of their extreme states.

It is during this window that the person needs the contact of humans, especially loved ones who are able to be there with them. Not trying to fix them. Not trying to "help." Just willing to be a person with another person who is in distress.

When we are lost to madness, so often we lose touch with the self we knew before. It is as if in the intensity of madness, our sense of self, our identity, and the ways we know ourselves are augmented through the process. (I will talk more about this later.)

In being connected to the human relationships we have known, we can remind ourselves of the self we were before madness took hold. We can be reminded of how we were through the rhythm and cadence of the relationship.

We can reconnect to our consensus-based self, the self who navigates the world of relationships, outward responsibility, and community.

The trip to see my friend was the first time I was able to step back and understand what I went through as a trauma. Typically, trauma is defined as either experiencing or witnessing a life-threatening event. This is a pretty outdated interpretation. In the wider sense, it is now used to describe anything that has negatively impacted us, "that was traumatic."

I am not an expert on trauma. I've read the books. I do trauma work with folks. But others are better suited to define the term. On a basic level, I see trauma as a reorganizing of the self to protect from another life-shattering experience occurring. Our body sends out warning signs, through flashbacks, feelings, and dissociative states, trying to protect ourselves from another negatively-charged, life-defining moment.

It was while I was walking down the streets, lost and without a phone to orient me, that I saw the traumatic impact of my psychotic break. I was able to reinterpret much of my experience post-break, post-leaving my father's basement, as processing the trauma I went through. The complete falling apart of my internal and external realities.

It is as close to death as one can come, in one way. The death of a stable experience of life. The death of a coherent sense of self. To lose your sense of self, your orienting principle for navigating life while the structures fall apart. It is one of the most disorientingly horrifying experiences.

Often what we love most about travel is the sense of stepping out of our set routines. Of possibility. Of the magical happening. So many people can relate to the unexpected turns that happen while traveling. The surprise encounters. The spontaneous events that define our journeys.

This in a way is madness. It is a continuous stream of unexpected moments. Moments that are often overwhelming and mind-defying, challenging our previous understandings of the world around us. It is in this intensity of experience that madness emerges. Making sense of the intensity of the experience is madness, not the experience itself.

For me, in the moment of travel, of actually being lost, I was brought back to the lostness I felt in madness. The unanchored quality of floating through a reality that did not make sense. Where I did not know the rules, the ways of engaging, or how to even modulate the experience. Madness was a flood of experience that did not stop.

When walking down the streets while traveling, my body could not distinguish between the lostness of madness and the lost quality of traveling. It began to freak out. No part of me wished to lose myself again to the degree that I did before. My body was screaming for me to do something, to prevent the descent into madness.

In this case, I was okay. I was just traveling. I had to remind my body I was okay. I had to let myself know I was safe. This is often the work of trauma. To know you are no longer trapped in the world that created the trauma. No longer with your abusive family. No longer in a violent relationship.

Yet when we tell people you cannot recover from madness, when we provide a maintenance-based story of no recovery, one is not able to truly process the trauma due to the inability to find security or safety. Through the narratives provided by the medical model, there is no safety. Your mind can no longer be trusted, your experience can no longer be trusted. You are asked to outsource any ability to work with your mind, to tend to your inner experience through medication. The medication is what will keep you safe.

This is what I fought for. I fought for the inner right to have a full life. Due to the inherent narratives of brokenness, I did not know it was possible to recover. This doubt, this hesitation, caused a basic anxiety in my body. A sense of unease, like any moment the other foot was about to drop and I would see that I was truly "crazy." That any of the healing and growth that I experienced, the rebuilding of my life, was a lie I was telling myself.

From this mindset, it took me years to be able to trust that I was safe, that I was okay. From that embodied sense of safety and okayness, I could begin the work of processing the trauma of the psychotic break. Processing the impact of my life falling apart in a matter of days. Processing the impact of the years of isolation, of not seeing or relating to another human. Grieving the previous life

I thought I was going to live and honoring my new life, as someone who has gone to the other side and back.

When I was finally able to see I was okay, I was safe and it was okay to go on living, the tears started. So many hours of crying. Releasing the impact of what I had been through. In order to process, to move through trauma, you have to let go. Letting go of the holding in your body that says, "Don't relax. Something bad will happen if you let your guard down. Don't let your vigilant watch down."

Through trying to vigilantly "watch for crazy" inside myself, I didn't give myself the space to allow the healing process to unfold. Healing from trauma is a natural, organic process once you allow the letting go to take hold and the movement of emotion and stored energy to be released.

Remember Mary, the woman who thought she was royalty and who I'd play Gin Rummy with? One time, the walls in her bedroom were painted and the new color was close to that of the state hospital in which she was first hospitalized. That hospital was notorious for horrific treatment, one of the reasons it was shut down. When she saw the paint color, she decompensated. It's a silly technical term that refers to an intensification in symptoms.

In a way, while I was walking the streets lost, I was decompensating. I was losing my grounding in consensus reality. I was being pulled back to a time when I was lost in madness, forgetting the life I had built for myself. I started to feel overwhelmed, confused, and didn't know how to act in a "coherent way."

It took the healing of friendship to really help bring me back. The connection I shared with my good friend. We talked. We shared stories. We remembered good times. I was reminded of my basic sanity. Of my ability to connect and share experiences with others.

For me, madness is an inherently traumatic experience, one where someone's "sense of self" gives way and they are hurdled into the kaleidoscoping, ever-changing intensity of extreme states. It is horrifying. Anyone who has gone there typically has no desire to go back into the lostness. Into confusion. Into madness.

Then to come out of the madness and be provided a narrative of brokenness, where you are told your mind is not a safe place to inhabit. A place to be distrusted. A place that will give out and you will be thrust back into the extremes of madness due to "biology."

With this narrative, a barrier is placed. A barrier to healing from the experience. Without the ability to cultivate a "safe space" within our minds, to have some trust in our basic sanity, it is incredibly difficult to process the trauma of madness. Leaving someone's body in a state of alert, vigilance, and often on overdrive. The very conditions that can tip the scales toward another break.

If this was it, it would be enough work for anyone. But it is not. Many people who have been through the mental health system, people who identify with an extreme state diagnosis like schizophrenia, bipolar, or schizoaffective disorder, see themselves as survivors. Not survivors of madness but survivors of our mental health system.

They see their time being "treated" as a form of trauma, as an invalidation of their humanness. They see it as a form of degradation. Where their symptoms are looked down upon and not seen as a part of the human experience.

Often, people struggle to "untangle" themselves from this system. Taking months if not years to taper from medication and detox from its impact. Years to learn their differences are not symptoms. Their differences are what make them who they are. It is less about healing from "symptoms' and about finding a way to function in the world. To have friendship, community, meaning, and a connection to something more.

I feel lucky. Lucky that I was never "treated" for my "mental illness." In one way, I had to struggle. To struggle alone. Denying the help I needed because I was not willing to accept a narrative of "brokenness" to receive treatment. On another level, I was freed. Free to find my own way. Free to make the possibility for my unique recovery journey. A recovery that I defined on my terms.

At first, my recovery was rooted in being functional. Doing the basics of humanness that we need to maintain for our lives to move forward with meaning and possibility. During this period, I would sometimes struggle with any experiences I had that were out of the range of "normal," anomalous experiences. Like the experience of hearing my name called by another voice, much like the graduate students who entered the psychiatric wards of the 70s. The experiences would terrify me because in my definition of "functional," I assumed one had to be "relatively normal." Hearing voices was out of the question.

It was okay to accept non-ordinary experiences. Have mystical experiences on meditation retreats. Transcendental states of experiencing beyond the narrowness of my small self. Being lost into something greater than the me that holds me. That was okay. Hearing voices? Definitely not okay because it could potentially interfere with my "functionality."

But over time, I dropped more and more assumptions of what was required of me to be functional. I made room for the possibility that my inner experience was mine and got to express itself in the ways it did and did not necessarily impact my ability to functionally navigate through the world.

I imagine what it would have been like to receive a more traditional treatment. Where they might periodically check in on my altered state experiences, using these experiences as a rubric to determine my recovery. With a decrease in "symptoms" being an increase in health.

This story of normal waking consciousness being the "best" consciousness, the healthy consciousness, is a form of top-down ownership of what it means to be "normal." In our culture, we have significantly cut off access to non-ordinary states of knowing. We have let go of our communal practices that allow us to enter ecstatic states together. We have given up shared stories of transcendence. With this loss, the waking normal consciousness has not only been privileged above other ways of knowing, but seen to be the only consciousness that is "real."

In other cultures, waking normal consciousness is not elevated above other ways of experiencing one's self and the world. I remember hearing about an American who was trained in Columbian healing practices, particularly the use of Ayahuasca. His teacher once mentioned he saw a panther. The American student asked if it was in person, on a psychedelic journey, or in a dream. The teacher looked at him like he was stupid. He refused to answer the question because it was so preposterous. Why would you distinguish between states of consciousness? The dream, psychedelic experience, and real life are all the same reality to this person's teacher.

Later, while on my graduate school campus, I was buying books for the upcoming semester. A book on the shelf called to me; it was *Mindsight* by Daniel Siegel. In the book, Siegel makes interesting claims on the interpersonal quality of the brain or mind. He sees our brain as a relational organ that supports our connection to others. In a way, when we connect to others, we are "sharing" in one unified mind. He calls his academic study interpersonal neurobiology.

Siegel has a basic definition of mental health and, in turn, mental health pathology. The balance of structure and novelty. The brain is built on having structure and coherence while at the same time, it is essential that the brain has novel pathways. Structure and chaos working together.

If you apply this understanding to mental health, you can track the understanding of most mental health "illnesses." They either involve too much structure or too much chaos, with madness being on the extreme end of a lack of structure and an influx of novelty. My therapist's mentor would say, "Sometimes you need to take people apart," and, "Sometimes you need to put them back together again."

When trying to understand madness, this is one of the most basic and honest ways of relating to it. A lack of structure to integrate the influx of novelty one is experiencing. with the person in madness living on the too-novelty side of the continuum of health. So often, the healing ingredients are rooted in structure. In regular rhythm and routines. And to be honest, in boring, mundane everyday tasks.

This basic approach of structure and chaos works for me. It captures so much of the human experience and the struggle of being a human, maintaining this basic balance. In a way, this model captures what is great about travel. A break from the structure, an influx of novelty, and new experiences to refresh someone as they back into the structure of their lives. It also speaks to why my experience of travel was terrifying. It reminded me of a time when I didn't have enough structure.

I think this model captures the heart of madness. The structure of someone who has experienced madness is not able to hold the novelty of their experience. There is not enough structure to contain the influx of novelty. This academic model describes a similarity to census-based reality and our personal realities or other worlds. This balance of our imaginal, fantastical self with the tangible self that exists within a rhythm and routine in relationships, communities, and places.

The structure of someone who is mad is often in need of support. Support to become a more organized and coherent structure.

An Interlude

Before moving on to the next section: **Expertise by Training**, there will be a brief detour into a potentially different way of thinking about mental health diagnosis, mental illness and psychological pathology. A *functional understanding* over a medicalized understanding.

Catastrophic Mental Health Crisis

I am on a bus. Headed to a Windhorse BBQ. I am reading a biography of William James, the first American psychologist. He is recounting his experience of the 1912 San Francisco earthquake.

James describes the streets filled with humans coming together to face the quake's catastrophe. He describes being "elated" by the scene in front of him. People at their finest, coming together to support each other.

At this moment, I break. I am crying, profusely, for a bus ride.

Psychosis is a catastrophe.

It is not a crisis of an individual.

It is a crisis of a family. Of a community. Of our culture. The individual lost without a way home.

We have gotten it wrong. We isolate. We separate. We blame. We do not gather.

We do not see psychosis as our problem. It is someone else's.

The job of hospitals. Of experts. Of medications.

Rarely is it ever our job.

This word catastrophe came alive for me after reading James' account of the 1912 earthquake. It changed something in me. It was a turn away from the individual toward the recognition of an individual always existing in a context.

An individual in a family, a community, a city, a culture. We think of ourselves as a self but this self is not a separate isolated individual. We are an individual interwoven with our communities, rhythms, and activities. All of which happen in a context, in a place.

This turn away from the isolated individual pivots the understanding of crisis within the mental health world. Not all mental health crises are catastrophes. Within mental health, I see the catastrophe being a more fundamental breakdown of functioning. When the basic functionings that make up a self are lost.

This distinction need not be separated by diagnosis. It is a functional diagnosis without a clear definition in the DSM (*Diagnostic and Statistical Manual of Mental Disorders*). When an individual is no longer able to "hold it together" or has a "break," they are breaking from a functional makeup, the functioning that makes up the self.

When we lose our functioning, we lose ourselves. It is at this very moment of loss that we need our loved ones most. We need community and a feeling of being part of something tangible and real. When someone is in an extreme state or recovering from one, it can be a type of work to connect to people in a more consensus-based reality-like way.

I know for myself, in my extremes, I would have to slow myself. To steady myself to the pacing of "everyday conversation" versus the hyperspeeds my mind was firing at. This act of connecting with others, when the connection feels relatively safe, is a great anecdote to the speed and alienation of extreme states. It helps bring one home.

Community anchors us. It reminds us who we are beyond our experiences of the extremes. It connects us to our histories, our families, our effort and mastery.

Mental health is an individual problem. It is my health, not yours. But a catastrophe, a catastrophe is *our* problem.

The important thing to remember about diagnoses is they have almost no correlation to symptoms. Symptoms determine the category of mental health diagnosis. It does not guarantee one's admittance into a diagnosis.

Functionality is the true gate to diagnosis. All mental health diagnoses are predicated on functionality. If you are functioning, you do not have a mental health illness. If functionality is lost or threatened, then one has entered the realm of mental health diagnosis.

As a clinician, I am always looking for signs of functional impairment. Not because I think it is important to think about, but because I need to justify to insurance companies why my client warrants medical intervention for their mental health. Their symptom expression does not warrant treatment, only the impact those symptoms have on their ability to participate in and navigate their lives.

If there is no loss in functioning, services are not justified to receive financial payment. Most folks who enter treatment are experiencing a threat to their functioning or maybe a loss of some aspects of their functioning. They are struggling to go to work. Struggling to maintain relationships. This degradation of functioning is what drives most folks into therapy. And yet, they have not lost functioning.

In college, due to my depression, I would often be unable to hold up my class schedule through the duration of the semester. I could hang for a couple of months but, by the end, I would invariably end up disappearing from class. I had functional impairment warranting support.

I typically maintained a B average. So, I was still able to play lacrosse for my school. Live in the dorms. Participate in the communities I was a part of. If my depression descended to the degree that I could no longer muster the will to get by in school, I might have been kicked out. Probably returning home ashamed. Compounding my depression. After some time withdrawing, disconnecting from activities of health and vitality. I imagine with my health degrading, it would be clear a catastrophe had emerged. The functional self had broken. A new order of crisis needed to be attended to.

To lose functioning is something else. I am talking about the dropping of the rhythm and routine that allows someone to know they are human. For myself, while in my post-break depression, I gave up most markers of humanness I had known throughout my life. I engaged in the minimalist of caring for my hygiene or appearance. I didn't talk to another human other than minimal contact with my father. I couldn't keep a regular sleep schedule or interact with the world really in any way.

I lost the functioning allowing me to know myself as Brandon and as a "valid" person. Prior to my break in functioning, I had no idea how far an individual could slip from functional living. How quickly someone could lose the fabric of their life.

I had experienced serious depression before. Depression that impacted my grades. My connection to friends. My engagement in meaningful activities. The total loss of human functioning is another order of struggle. It is a catastrophic crisis.

I anchor the word catastrophe within mental health crisis to remind us that we need to come together. We need to support our loved ones when struggling, not just wait for them to get better or get right. We are part of the mechanism that allows someone to "come back" from more devastating losses of functioning.

Human relationship is one of our primary anchors to functional living. We are human for other humans. We exist in relationship. In community. We know ourselves through our connection to others.

Friends, family, colleagues, and others are the greatest anchor in tethering someone back into consensus reality. Back into the rhythms and routines allowing someone to know themselves.

When we remember who we are, it is so much easier to engage in the activities of health, vitality, and connection we've practiced throughout our lives. The sports we play, the hobbies we engage in. The meaningful activities that remind us where our heart comes alive. Volunteering, engaging in communities of shared meaning.

Catastrophic mental health crises are not relegated to any one mental health illness in the DSM. Any of the illnesses outlined by the DSM can drift into a catastrophic mental health crisis. A depression so bad you can't get out of bed. Anxiety so crushing you can't leave your house. OCD so dominating you can't move through your day.

It is felt in our bodies. The dropping of the routines we've known throughout our lives. It is the feeling of seeing through a lie. A lie that we need to be a "certain way." We see that we can let go of all the things that made us who we are and still be here. A person without function.

By borrowing a word from the collective, not the individual, catastrophe is a reminder. Individuals suffer alone so we, as a whole, do not have to face the realities of the impact of our way of living, of our culture. If we acknowledge mental health as a shared problem, as *our* problem, we would have to change our collective ways of being to support the healing of the individual. The individual suffering would become an opportunity for collective change.

A catastrophic mental health crisis is a fundamental breakdown in the functioning of an individual due to their struggle. It is a great loss. For everyone. We are all needed.

Currently, we place the burden of a mental health crisis on families. On social systems never designed to support recovery. If someone is struggling, beyond their ability to function or to keep it "together," the burden of care gets distributed to the family or loved ones, who are often lost without any knowing of where appropriate care is. Many families don't know where to turn when a loved one encounters extreme states.

It seems that when someone enters the realm of a catastrophic mental health crisis, the community around them pulls away. So many people I've encountered who know someone who had a psychotic break describe the distance that is created, the isolation. The person "fading away." The person did not fade away in the true context of the word. More often than not, people fade away from individuals struggling with extreme states. Sometimes quickly, sometimes slowly.

Based on the rate that it happens to individuals struggling, it seems almost natural the way individuals are isolated from previous communities. Isolating them to the degree that they either permanently “fade away” or recover enough to appear to “fit in” again.

This is why we need a counterbalance, a recognition of the community’s function in supporting the healing of the individual. We have to remember we are a we with power. The power to support those we love.

Section Two:

Expertise by Training

I WAS FORTUNATE to receive a majority of my training in working with extreme states within the Windhorse Approach. This is an approach that positions human relationship as the greatest healing agent we have.

In Windhorse communities, an individual who is struggling is brought into a team and provided with their functional living needs. A type of family or community is formed to support the client's recovery.

The person struggling to function due to extreme states is surrounded by folks whose main function is to connect and support the recognition of shared humanity. The team attempts to support the emergence of a more grounded functional engagement in the world. Through this aim of connecting to a shared humanity, individuals lost in madness begin to remember their more grounded humanness. This is not a teaching thing.

Through the team supporting engagement in activities connected to the client's history of sanity, the client is brought back into themselves. To their functional, consensus self. To allow the restoration of a more full and engaged life. Increased connection to loved ones, friends, and community. Often restoring work, school, or other functional aspects of surviving in our financial culture.

This building out of one's roots is what often allows a more balanced integration of heaven and earth. One's consensus self, working in alignment with one's personal self.

Where's My Training?

People who suffer physical ills may want to depict their struggles, but they don't write primarily to critique their treatment or challenge the expertise of their doctors.

A surprising number of mental patients, however, write for just these reasons. Their treatment hasn't worked or it's made them worse. Or their doctors have ignored crucial information about their lives that they think should be considered. Or they've figured out a better method of treatment and want others to know about it. Or they've gained a crucial insight into madness and want people to benefit from what they've learned.

In other fields of medicine, patient narratives don't directly challenge doctor's theories. Someone who writes about having diabetes, for example, doesn't think he is contributing to endocrinology. But there's no blood test for schizophrenia, no brain scan that can detect manic depression. No mental illness can be diagnosed on the basis of an objective measure. This makes psychiatry far more ideological than other fields of medicine. There's no agreed-upon metric to use in evaluating its claims so psychiatrists have to rely on the power of rhetoric to stake out their domain. [13]

Agnes Jacket

Gail A. Hornstein

---

13 Hornstein, G. A. (2009). Agnes's Jacket: A psychologist's search for the Meanings of Madness. https://openlibrary.org/books/OL18732947M/Agnes's_jacket. Pg 163-164.

It wasn't until I read Gail Hornstein's book, *Agnes's Jacket: A Psychologist's Search for Meaning in Madness*, that I first heard the distinction between expertise by training and expertise by experience. On some level, I knew my experience of madness gave me a window into a human experience that psychologists, psychiatrists, anthropologists, and others trying to understand madness did not share.

Often, more clinical and academic attempts to describe and conceptualize madness feel like an attempt to understand something that academics' faculties of reason limit them from understanding. Not in a negative way. If you haven't been there, you haven't been there.

Like I mentioned previously, madness is not about understanding but more about the breakdown of a consistent vessel that is able to understand. It is the transformation of understanding and meaning-making that is the primary hallmark of madness.

One day, someone can have a perceptual, meaning-making apparatus moving through the world. In another moment, after the accelerator of the psychotic break, another perceptual, meaning-making apparatus is perceiving and making sense of the world.

From the outside, this is madness. Before you made sense and were like this. Now you don't make sense and are like this. The psychotic break is often the gap between the two selves: the pre-break self and the post-break self.

All this is to say, experts are trying to understand something that is often elusive to them. There are some who have tried and get closer to capturing how I relate to the experience of madness. But most miss the boat. Instead of really stepping into the phenomenology of madness, experts try to understand the "how."

How did this happen? From the humors of ancient Greece, to possession in the Middle Ages, to early childhood experiences in the height of Freudian times, to modern chemical imbalances in the brain. All these expert opinions have done little to actually change the nature of treatment. To support the necessary ingredients allowing an individual trapped in a cacophony of extreme states to settle and return to a more grounded, consensual, relatable self.

I had hoped when I entered graduate school to train as a therapist that I would have been given some education in working with madness. Some doorway into the healing modalities and understandings that support recovery. One professor did assign a book about madness, which we never discussed. Instead, I was provided stale, outdated assumptions from people who did not know how to support madness. Professors who were brought up with a maintenance-based approach to treating madness.

I heard professors say, "I tried to treat someone with schizophrenia. It didn't work. I don't recommend it." To me, this was a knife in my side — to hear, "I tried it once, didn't work, wouldn't recommend it," while I sat in the class having already recovered from a psychotic break. In a way, I heard this professor saying, "You don't have a right to exist here." "People like you cannot be healed." More importantly, "Don't talk about your experience here."

Later, I heard professors describing how to let someone down who's showing signs of madness. Let down a client from having a full life. Prepare them for the limited, medication-filled life ahead of them. Essentially, indoctrinate young clients into the medical model's understanding and its treatment approach. For me, these are the moments that stand out in my formal expertise by training.

Of course, most early therapists end up working at community mental health clinics, where they are almost guaranteed to have individuals on their caseload suffering with some degree of madness. I know for myself, as a mental health intern, I had numerous folks struggling with some degree of psychosis on a regular basis.

According to those practicing, the people who taught me at least, therapy was not seen as being helpful. Yet, here we were as therapists expected to help folks suffering from madness by providing therapy.

Later, as I became trained in Gestalt Therapy, there would continue to be little acknowledgment of the treatment of madness. As if therapy did not address this domain of human suffering.

Even when I told a beloved trainer in Gestalt, a mentor and someone who I look up to with great love, that I was working with people experiencing "schizophrenia," he was shocked, stating, "I thought that was just a chemical imbalance thing." This is one of the most heart-centered humane therapists I have ever met, saying, "I thought that was their brain," which is another way of saying, "I can't help with that."

These examples are not isolated. They exist within a continuum of history. This is the nature of the asylum system developed in Europe and perpetuated in the United States. Individuals who experience madness need to be locked up because there is no hope for them.

There was a woman working in an asylum in the 1930's, at an upscale treatment facility in New York, who thought otherwise. She broke with Freudian tradition and started to provide psychotherapy to individuals experiencing madness at Chestnut Lodge. And she was successful. Successful enough that one of her patients went on to write *I Never Promised You a Rose Garden*, a seminal biography of one woman's recovery from madness.

Frieda Fromm-Riechman was ridiculed by contemporaries for her belief in the possibility of recovery from madness. Her protege, Harold Searles, was also ridiculed during his time. Searles would go on to train Edward Podvoll while Edward was a trainee as a psychoanalyst at Chestnut Lodge.

Edward would eventually head west to help his Buddhist teacher, Trungpa Rinpoche, start the first Buddhist college in the states, Naropa University. While Edward tried to leave behind his days working with those suffering from madness, life had other plans for him. A woman, who knew of his work, hounded him. Begging him to help her sister who was being held at a psychiatric hospital, displaying signs of madness.

While developing the psychology program at Naropa, Edward reluctantly agreed to help this young woman. He would visit her regularly. Essentially, just spending time with her. Soon he recruited his students to spend time with her too. They began to develop what would later be called Basic Attendance, a therapeutic approach exploring how to be with individuals suffering from extreme states.

As time progressed, they decided to take this young woman out of the psych ward and provided her an apartment with a roommate while continuing to spend periods with her every day practicing as a team what evolved to become Basic Attendance. A new treatment approach was being developed, what would later be called the Windhorse Approach.

It was this approach I first read about while staying at my friend's house in the previous chapter on traveling. He had been a student at Naropa University and was required to read *Recovering Sanity*, Edward's book describing his understanding of madness and, more importantly, the Windhorse Approach to treating extreme states and the recovery process.

Windhorse is unique in the treatment of psychotic disorders. It believes human relationships are one of the primary curative agents in supporting individuals in recovery. Not any human relationship, but relationships rooted in mutual dignity, shared understanding, and co-healing. A relationship of equals, not of superiority.

It was at Windhorse where I received my true expertise by training. Ironically, my training was not about becoming a better therapist or clinician but more about letting go of my therapeutic training to learn to be a person with another person who is struggling. This is the hallmark of the Windhorse Approach.

Windhorse is rooted in a contemplative orientation. In the introduction, I described a contemplative approach as "working with our minds." At Windhorse, the training was less about learning to "help" people suffering in extreme states and more about the clinician learning to stay grounded and centered while in a relationship with someone who is experiencing extreme states. We view our capacity to stay in touch with our wholeness and a grounded mind as the most curative element to offer someone suffering in madness.

Instead of learning some protocol to treat madness or even learning a theory of madness, I learned what I already knew from my recovery journey. Grounded, wholesome activities help to create a grounded, wholesome mind. By supporting grounded engagement in everyday life, someone will almost naturally begin to return to a more settled, in-touch version of themselves. From this space, they will be better able to navigate consensus reality, especially human relationships.

None of this is about removing or healing symptoms. It is about one's ability to connect to others and the world around in a meaningful way. This is healing from madness. A return to participating in relationship, community, and generative meaning.

The Windhorse Approach consists of a number of ingredients to support the recovery journey. Over the years, it has evolved into an elaborate treatment modality. At its heart, the treatment is rooted in developing a therapeutic community around someone suffering from madness.

I no longer work for Windhorse. This is not a Windhorse book. It is not approved by the Windhorse community. I am simply sharing the elements of the Windhorse Approach I found curative in my own healing journey. The ingredients I think others might take with them to support their healing journey too.

The only reason I worked at Windhorse was because the healing journey they described resonated with my journey. I truly believe that through Edward sitting down and joining a woman in madness, co-discovering with her what was helpful, he was able to tap into a deeper core of the recovery process. In a way, letting the process of being with this woman on her recovery journey teach him about the recovery process.

To me, this is the magic of the Windhorse Approach. It is not trying to put a conceptual understanding of what madness is. Instead, it developed a treatment protocol based on supporting a recovery process already underway.

Windhorse acknowledges what has been known for ages: individuals recover from madness. If they recover, what supports the journey that is already underway? What gets in the way? How do we facilitate the natural process of recovery?

Human to Human

I am walking on a forest trail, in a city park near the Windhorse offices. I have been working there for a few weeks. Our first official client has arrived. We are on our first Basic Attendance shift together. He is raw, fresh off a descent into madness.

As we walk, I can tell how hard it is for him. To be in his skin. To be a person. Having to be someone new.

Just being in the world felt hard for him. Being on our walk together. I feel his confusion. His rawness. It is as if he struggles to remember who he is. Struggles to remember how to be a person with another person.

As we are walking, I too am confused. I do not know how to be with him. My graduate school training did not prepare me for this.

I do not know what my role is. Who am I in this person's life, this person taking their first steps on the recovery journey? I am not his therapist. I am not trying to fix him. What am I doing?

As we walk, I take in the trees. I allow myself to be there, walking with him. I turn to him, and I feel into my role. My role to be a person. Just a person in his life who cares.

I feel how useless all my training, my years of school and internships training to be someone's "therapist" or "helper," is at this moment. My training is a distance between me and him. I will try to just be a human walking with another human.

It will take years for me to learn to shed my need to help, to figure out how to best be there for someone. I will always hold on to some self-protection of being the one "helping." Over time, I will learn to show up as myself more and more. Show up with my struggles, my shortcomings, and my idiosyncrasies.

I will take on more responsibilities in the organization. Continue to try to understand how to be a human in my growing roles.

A colleague will watch me one day with clients, see me laugh in the exaggerated way I do. Later, he will approach me saying, "I figured out why you are so helpful to clients, you are just being yourself with them."

It is the greatest compliment I will receive while struggling to be just this person.

Windhorse is a distinctive institution, a unique place to work. Even the name stands out. Most mental health institutions have fairly generic names. Windhorse is named after a mythological figure in Tibetan Buddhism, Lungta.

Most people know Lungta as the Tibetan prayer flags that are prominent. From my understanding, within the Windhorse community, Lungta is seen as the "wind" that brings forth uplifted, positive energy. It is the wind that allows us to move from negative, trapped mind states to positive, spacious mind states.

As I reflect on my recovery process, I see Lungta as the force or energy that allowed me to feel ready to step back into living again, the breeze entering my body letting me know it was time to start. The breath of life reminding me I could live again when everything inside said it wasn't possible to start over. It was a faint breath, a light breeze, a gentle hum encouraging me to step back into the journey of becoming.

The Windhorse Approach is a community-based model for supporting individuals struggling with extreme states. Technically, it is a semi-residential mental health facility. The approach is rooted in creating a team to support individuals struggling with madness and other extreme state mental health crises. Like the one I suffered from.

Individuals at Windhorse are brought to a community home, where a caretaker helps with cooking and maintaining the shared living space. Uplifting the environment is one of the key ingredients to supporting a return to basic, intrinsic sanity. By helping create a clean and inviting space, a client is able to relax and experience ease in their environment.

So often, folks like myself who struggle in extreme states will create environments that mirror their inner reality. Some spaces will be chaotic and overwhelming. Some will be barren, like there is no life happening. Some will even be overly organized or too controlled.

By creating an environment of relaxed uplift, the client can step out of their inner chaos for a moment and taste ease and relaxation in the space. This is the hope and intent for new clients within the community home. Providing a safe, uplifting environment while they discover what it means to be at Windhorse.

When a patient lands in their new living space, they meet their team. This team consists of four to seven individuals. Almost everyone is a trained therapist. A team leader is assigned. This leader has the largest role on the team, tending to the client, tending to each team member, and tending to the client's family. They are the binding agent that holds the team together.

The team leader's co-pilot on the journey is a psychotherapist, in Windhorse language, an intensive psychotherapist. The psychotherapist meets with the client two to four times a week, depending on the client's needs. They practice a traditional style of psychotherapy rooted in psychoanalytic thinking.

Other members of the team are team counselors who practice Basic Attendance, which is the heart of the Windhorse approach. From the outside, Basic Attendance consists of meeting with a client for three hours at a time. The intention is to connect and explore being in-relationship together, often with the hope of finding a shared activity to participate in.

The shared activity, called a shared discipline, is typically rooted in the person's history and reflects their history of sanity. An activity that connects them to a grounded, clear version of themselves. We all have activities that help us settle into ourselves. Listening to music, playing sports, being in nature, going to cafes. These activities allow us to feel human.

When I first started at Windhorse, I worked on several teams at a time. I would spend up to nine hours a day in Basic Attendance. I spent a lot of time joining people in their experiences of extreme states and recovery.

In Windhorse, we would talk about learning to be respectful of others' dreams. That we were entering someone's dream space and ways to be non-intrusive within their dream, respectful to the space they found themselves in.

The final member of the team consisted of a housemate. We would find a client an apartment and pay someone to be their roommate. This isn't someone to keep an eye on the patient or oversee them. The housemate's job was to live their life. They were expected to participate with the client in the maintenance of the house and food. Other than that, they were asked to have a life, to work, and to maintain friendships – to model healthy engagement with life.

One of the foundational beliefs within Windhorse is relationships heal. Not hierarchical, helper-helped relationships, just relationships. We would work to cultivate relationships that were not rooted in the patient getting better but in finding shared connections, interests, and common ground.

Of course, the client is there to heal, to find a way back into a more functional integrated life. But that is not our job to figure out. We provide the necessary ingredients that support healing and integration. From there, we support the emergent process of recovery or, in Windhorse language, the emergence of sanity. Dionysus brings the ingredients and conditions together to turn grapes into wine.

Basic Attendance is a way of being with others in distress. It is also a way of being with ourselves while we are in distress. To learn to attend to ourselves with kindness, in a gentle way. To not put too much pressure on ourselves. To support our chaotic mind states with grounded natural wisdom. Taking it slow. Sticking to the basics. Knowing when to push a little and when to let go of pressure.

Basic Attendance is the art of meeting the moment with graciousness, kindness, and dignity. Respecting the intensity of extreme states of mind while acknowledging the possibility of radical sanity emerging at any moment.

In my recovery, I would have to allow for the intensity of mind to be present, to not see it as a barrier in my recovery process. My training as a contemplative helped with this. Prior to my break, I had attended many meditation retreats. Sitting long hours of the day watching my mind do its thing. I knew a mind could move from chaos to settled in a brief moment.

This allowed me to meet some of my more intense moments on my recovery journey with faith. Faith that my "crazy" mind was not my only mind, just one expression. Just as clear-headedness was an expression. Just as a gentle loving connection was an expression. Just as tired was an expression. The mind has so many faces.

At the first Zen Center I practiced at, there was a life-size statue of Avalokitesvara, the embodiment of compassion in the Zen tradition. She stood there with a crown of 7 different faces, each representing a different state of mind. Avalokitesvara was able to maintain compassion for any of our states of mind – loving, compassionate states of mind and angry, wrathful, chaotic states of mind.

This is the practice of Basic Attendance, allowing for the many facets of our mind to express themselves without it being an indication of brokenness or craziness. One moment crazy, the next sane. This is human.

Anyone who sits down long enough and watches the movements of the mind will see we are all crazy on some level. This mind is something we think we control, but we do not. People who are sane are not in more control of their minds. It is more that the degree of movement of their minds is within an acceptable range, while the range of movement of someone in madness is unacceptable. It is extreme.

Basic Attendance is learning to stay with our extreme states of mind while learning to bring the elements of groundedness and wholesomeness to our experiential moment. What are the activities and relationships that support sanity to emerge? What helps us settle? What aggravates the mind? What makes our extremes more extreme?

These are the questions to be curious about. How do we create the conditions that allow more sanity to emerge? That allow for more groundedness.

More connection. More generative meaning. To attend to our minds is to allow them to be where they are while creating the conditions for a settled, easeful mind to emerge.

Basic Attendance

I am immersing myself in the Windhorse Approach. Leaning into and discovering Basic Attendance. The practice and art of being with another. I am learning and still have a ways to go.

I am with a newer client. We have found a rhythm to our Basic Attendance shifts. I arrive at his place. We shoot the shit. Connect. He grabs a smoke. We walk to our local Mexican restaurant.

He gets the same burrito every time. I get a different one every time.

We cross the street and get donuts, arguing about which one is better. The glazed donut I love or the cinnamon donut he loves. He repeatedly tells me his donut reminds him of the perfect donut he would get on family trips to Hawaii. I tell him I do not share his nostalgic memories to share his opinion.

After eating, we walk to the hippie bookshop down the street. He searches for another Miyazaki film to watch. We go back to his place and start the film.

I am only ever able to watch half of the movie. Since we spend the first half of our time together on our meal routine, there's generally not enough time left.

This day, I am incredibly tired. It's hard to stay awake and the movie doesn't help. I lose my ability to keep my eyes open. Bobbing my head up and down each time I momentarily drift to sleep. Not following the plot.

I am having an internal battle. Should I just let myself sleep? It would be the most natural thing to do. Or should I fight sleep?

Fulfill my role with the client. Be a good team counselor. Maintain my wakefulness while working.

At some point, the battle becomes pointless. I have fallen asleep.

I awake restored. The client turns to me and says, "I told you his movies were relaxing."

I now understand why these films are an anchor for my client. He is seeking relaxation. Peace from the storm of the mind.

I deepen my respect for our routine. Leaning into relaxation and shared connection. I stop questioning if watching a movie during our time together is a "good use of time," if it is "helping him get better."

Over time, things evolve. The client gets an apartment. Reconnects with friends. Starts to go to school. Moves in with friends.

Toward the end of our time together, he picks up a skateboard again. His parents are elated. He used to love the sport. Now we grab burritos at a new spot, spending the remainder of our time at the skatepark.

While skating, I take in the surreal nature of my life. Where I have come from and where I am now. I am grateful for everything that has brought me here.

Basic Attendance is an elusive concept for many people. It's really more of a practice. A relational practice of being with another in a supportive way while not trying to fix them. Not fixing can be hard for many therapists. It's kind of our job. Or at least what most clients expect from us. And what we're trained to do.

The practice is rooted in human relationships. When you are practicing Basic Attendance with a client, you meet for a three-hour period of time. This time frame has evolved over the years and reflects a good amount of time to have a full experience together. What you do during your three hours is an evolving and emerging process. It takes different shapes depending on the client's unique needs and history.

I've gone to movies, had cups of coffee, gone to bookstores, sat on a couch and not talked, and sat on curbs while clients were too distressed to connect. I've gone on countless walks, to pumpkin patches, skateparks, churches, and museums.

So often, like I did, folks in extreme states will isolate themselves from the world. One of my functions when practicing Basic Attendance was to support them to be in the world. To stay connected to the community they were in.

Toward the end of my time at Windhorse, I would occasionally teach this practice to clinicians. I would often start with a journaling exercise. I'd ask them to remember a time when someone was there for them while they were struggling. I'd ask them to think back to a time when this felt supportive and a time when it felt harmful.

People often easily remember when folks have been there for them in ways that are less than helpful. It is harder for them to remember times that felt supportive while in their struggle.

We have all experienced being supported by another in a time of need. Where our dignity as a person is honored, and our struggle is honored. Sometimes the support is gentle. Sometimes it is tough. Sometimes it is playful.

One coworker described a time when he was about to step on stage to perform in a musical concert. He was expressing his fear and doubt to a mentor, who told him to knock it off. As my coworker said, his mentor "verbally slapped me in the face." This shook him out of his self-consciousness and helped him feel ready to step onto the stage.

I remember telling a training group for therapists about a recent nightmare I had. It involved themes around shame and self-disgust. At one point, a coworker (and friend) started laughing. Here I was being deadly serious while sharing in a training setting, and my friend just starts uncontrollably laughing. At first, I was offended. But soon, I saw the humor of the dream, my shame, and my fear of judgment. So silly in a way. His laugh was healing.

What people do not understand is the way you are treated when someone has decided you are mad. Whether it is through your behavior, your speech, or the stories they have heard from others, you can feel when they "turn off" to you. I describe it as the denial of subjectivity. When someone can discredit your subjectivity due to you being "crazy," your thoughts, feelings, and experiences are not to be respected, not to be understood. They can always be dismissed as an expression of your madness.

I would do this often while working with clients. I remember while at the group home, Mary coming down the stairs to tell me her mother was picking her up and she would need money. I dismissed what she said. Her mother had never picked her up in the time she was there. I assumed it was another delusion. Of course, her mother did come to pick her up. I scrambled to get her money from the safe.

This is so common. My example is benign. Others are not. John Read, a researcher of madness, tells a story from when he was being trained as a psychiatrist. He was on a psych ward. A young woman was catatonic, she hardly spoke or moved. The staff had dismissed her, leaving her to her own private reality.

John, being a new clinician, decides to spend time with her in the evenings. Sitting in her room. Over time, she starts to talk, saying one word a night. The first night she said, "My." The next night she said, "Father." The following night she said nothing, and the next night she said, "Me." [14]

John deduced she had been raped by her father and it was unspeakable for her to say. He will be ignored. Her symptoms of schizophrenia were from a brain disorder, not a result of childhood trauma. John would go on to spend his career researching the ways subjectivity is denied to those who are deemed mad.

---

14 Read, J., Mosher, L. R., & Bentall, R. P. (2004). Models of madness. In Routledge eBooks. https://doi.org/10.4324/9780203420393

Basic Attendance is about restoring this rift, the rift between mad and sane. From people who "know" the real world and can judge others' worlds as not being real, in the process denying their right to be a human with autonomous, unique meaningful experience. This is why so many people in extreme states can retreat away. When their worlds are denied, their whole person is denied in a way. It is better to be alone than to be denied by the world around you.

I am not saying that everyone who is mad is in touch with a "real" world. The idea of "real" has little value for me. I am much more rooted in a pragmatic approach of what is "functional" or helpful to the task of living a meaningful life. A lot of beliefs and experiences of individuals who are mad do not help them inhabit their lives in a way where they can connect with others and share in the human experience of being in community.

When on a Basic Attendance shift, you are intentionally honoring the person's humanness, essentially allowing for a basic human connection to form rooted in friendship and mutual understanding. The hope is the client will be allowed to be a person again. They will not have to defend their reality, defend their beliefs. They just get to be themselves.

Most people have goals to better themselves. Going to school. Making friends. Working. Learning an instrument. We all want to move our lives forward in a meaningful way. I believe the desire to grow, to move into our desired life, is one of the functional tools helping us let go of the aspects of madness that do not support functional, engaged living. By having goals and moving toward them, we can work through some of the less-than-supportive aspects of our personal struggles.

Our desire for living, for expanding our life, allows us to face the limitations of our madness. Encouraging us to learn to work with our minds. To heal the wounds that need healing and to counter the narratives of a culture that denies returning from madness.

I do not tell a client what they can't do or think. I help them move toward what they desire and support them in becoming the version of themself that can live up to their goals and dreams for their life.

Basic Attendance is rooted in ten principles. These are guides to support an individual to stay in relationship with another person. A relationship that is inherently healing without trying to heal. A need to heal or fix is considered taboo in the Windhorse Approach. When someone is creating a top-down idea of what someone's healing should look like, this is referred to as an asylum mentality.

Asylum Awareness

Hospitals were dangerous places - one might never leave or might come out worse than when one went in. Today a relative upsurge in patient advocacy has provided more than enough documentation that psychiatric hospitalization is still dangerous.

We seem inescapably drawn to re-create conditions of treatment that are bound to make it difficult, if not impossible, to recover from psychosis.

On examining our own systems of treatment, we might ask: How has it come to be that, in spite of our best intentions, we are haunted by the possibility of reproducing the environment of a lunatic asylum? Why haven't we learned how to a run a hospital better than that? It is because creating an asylum stems from a particular state of mind, an ***asylum mentality****, which can resurface anytime and anywhere and recapitulate the history of the asylum. Contact with insanity tends to provoke it: a reflexive way of responding to instance people that can, in a moment, generate all the notoriously punishing techniques of treatment used in supposedly bygone era. Even in the most benevolent of institutions, asylum mentality erupts as a series of self-deceptions and primitive beliefs or superstitions about what madness is and how it should be treated.*

Edwar M. Podvall, M.D.

Recovering Sanity

Asylum mentality is a concept that emerged as the Windhorse model of treatment was being developed. For me, it is one of the core principles of the Windhorse approach. Asylum mentality is a recognition of the propensity in humans and especially in mental health treatment programs to use methods of control, aggression and a fundamental disregard for the dignity of the patients being treated in the name of "helping". Ed Podvol, the founder of the Windhorse method, speaks of the possibility of even the best intentioned treatment facilities drifting into these methods of control and denial of dignity.

In the Windhorse community, we saw it as our job to recognize this propensity within ourselves. Asylum awareness was considered a practice, the practice of recognizing our tendency as clinicians to control and attempt to dictate the lives of our clients to minimize our own discomfort and lack of agency in "healing" their madness. Often, there is a belief, if only they do what I think they should do then the client will get better. This is the thinking often leading to gross mistreatment and harming of clients.

I would like to share a story of my own Asylum mentality. It is a subtle story, not gross mistreatment of a client, although I have done that at times - disregarded a client's autonomy, humanity and dignity through my attempts to "treat them". These disregards are the heart of asylum mentality.

> *I have been working for a client for over a year. We have a close connection. He is rather lost to his other world, immersed in his attempts to change it to fit his view of how things should be.*
>
> *The client is able to step out of his other world and meet me at times. We have wonderful conversations about the world, music, and even our relationship.*
>
> *At other times, he really struggles. Many times, I sit silently on a curb with him while he is unable to connect or speak, clearly struggling internally. My aim is to just be with him, providing him with human connection when he is not able to connect.*
>
> *These shifts are a great honor. To attempt to be supportive while also not being intrusive, lending my humanness to the*

situation so he is not alone. Not forcing him to manage or even engage with my humanness in a way that overwhelms him.

I get promoted within the organization. I am no longer only providing Basic Attendance to clients, but I'm also starting to become a team leader.

The shift into my new role is difficult for me. I feel the pressure of "managing" the team and being in charge of the direction of treatment for the client. I feel the weight of the responsibility and utilize control to manage my anxiety.

One evening, I am out getting food with my wife and friends. The restaurant is near the client's home. After eating, I walk the half block to the corner to see if the client is outside smoking as is his evening routine. He is.

As I walk up to him, he smiles in a bright way. He is in a good mood. With a calm excitement, he starts to tell me about a one-hit wonder song. He often likes to share music trivia. I am relieved to see he is in good spirits, like I am somehow now in charge of his mood because I am his team leader.

After a couple minutes of shooting the shit, I say to him in a more serious way, "How you doing?" He looks at me sharply, he is incredibly sensitive and astute. He shakes his head and says, "Don't do that to me."

I immediately recognize what he is saying. I had become "team leader" with him. I had taken on a mantle of responsibility and it was now interfering with our human connection. I had assumed a role of control and responsibility for him beyond what was needed.

At that moment, he was clearly safe, in good spirits, and we were having a relaxed conversation. But I activated my power, activated my authority, to see if "he was okay" because it was now my job to track his mood and symptoms.

I will never forget this moment, the palpable shift I made away from being a human with another human to being a human in charge of another human being. It became my practice to honor the human connection first and foremost. The same practice I had before, but now holding a role of "responsibility" in the client's life.

At times, I would have to be a "team leader" with him. But he helped me see that it was just a role I played in his life and our relationship was more than a role. Our connection was real and needed to be honored, even when I needed to be the authority in his life to keep him safe or enforce community rules.

Asylum mentality is not a set of behaviors, although I could list out behaviors associated with it. It is a state of mind, a way of relating that places you above someone and needing to control them. Where your skill and accolades as a professional have earned you the right to treat somebody, even if the treatment is against their will. Edward Podvoll, the founder of the Windhorse method, speaks of the possibility of even the best-intentioned treatment facilities drifting into these methods of control and denial of dignity.

In the Windhorse community, we saw it as our job to recognize this propensity within ourselves. Asylum awareness was considered a practice, the practice of recognizing our tendency as clinicians to control and attempt to dictate the lives of our clients to minimize our own discomfort and lack of agency in the name of "healing" their madness.

Often, there is a belief that if only they do what I think they should do, then the client will get better. This is the thinking that often leads to gross mistreatment and harming of clients.

As I mentioned in my own asylum mentality story, I have done this at times. It was a subtle story, not a gross mistreatment of a client. But I still disregarded their autonomy, humanity, and dignity through my attempts to "treat" them. This disregard is the heart of the asylum mentality.

Within the Windhorse community, they teach you to recognize when you are coming from an asylum mentality. We even would call each other out at times for our asylum behavior. No one liked to be accused.

For me, my struggles went deeper than how I treated clients. While I worked at Windhorse, I felt a level of respect and recognition from other clinicians for the dignity and humanity I had for patients. Not that I was perfect, but I was trying to work with my own asylum mentality. Because I had to. The asylum lived inside of me.

Through my own process of recovery, which often looked like me trying to appear sane or healthy, I had created an inner police-like figure. This part of me would assess which of my behaviors were sane or not. It was on a constant lookout for any ways I could portray myself as "crazy" or even different to the world.

The thing I wanted most was to be "sane" because, if I was sane, I could have a full life and not have opportunities denied to me because of my "mental health." If someone made a comment alluding to my mental state or even asking if I was doing alright, I would feel the need to present this balanced healthy individual to protect from any perception of my lack of sanity.

It generated significant anxiety on a day-to-day basis. I would live in the world of "mental health," spending my days with the guardians of sanity. I often felt like a spy or con artist, pulling one over on the mental health establishment by just existing in their space.

I directly tie my doubt and fear around not being able to have a full life post-break to the inner asylum living in me. The ways that our cultural understanding and treatment of "crazy" people became internalized into my inner stories of sanity, mental health, and being "crazy."

The belief I couldn't recover from madness is a byproduct of the asylum, of the locking away of individuals with no expectation of healing or recovery. These mindsets we carry as a culture, our assumptions around madness we've maintained since the enlightenment, now live inside of each of us. Especially those of us who have been to the other side of sanity and back.

The other day, while talking to a family member about this book, I asked if they thought individuals could recover from schizophrenia or psychotic breaks. They thought about it and said, "No, I guess I don't think people can." He was talking to me, knowing my history and journey.

This family member doesn't see me as damaged or lacking mental functioning or capacity. Yet, he didn't believe you could recover from a psychotic break. This is how deep these assumptions go. How convinced people are of a narrative of madness, of no return, of the broken brain. People who have no psychological training, no understanding of the history of mental health, firmly believe these stories of permanent brokenness.

This is the perpetuation of the asylum. The power of the asylum to infiltrate our thinking and shape the treatment and outcomes of madness in our culture. Just like other forms of oppression, we need to look at our deeply held assumptions around madness. Freeing the culture of these outdated beliefs so we can help individuals live in cultures where their recovery and healing are recognized. It is more acceptable to discuss your recovery from severe drug addiction than to discuss recovery from a psychotic break. This needs to change.

Just the other day, I was at a conference for individuals building businesses that support mental health. A young man walked on stage and described having had a psychotic break and not being able to receive culturally appropriate care as a Native American. I was shocked. Someone outing themselves as having gone there, to madness, in front of others. For me, it was a radical act of bravery to break the cycle of denial, denying that recovery from madness is as natural and normal as any other healing allowed within this new world of normalizing and destigmatizing mental health.

This is what we need. Voices to speak up and share the reality of recovery. Not some maintenance-based recovery, where we take our medication and good patients accept our pathologically-based "diagnosis." No, we need people who've lived rich meaningful lives. Lives of connection, creativity, and possibility. People who've worked with their minds, discovering how to find groundedness and ease within their "symptoms."

The Cocktail

> *The entire "cocktail" (or even any combination of ingredients), has a traumatizing effect on one's total physiology and chemistry... The function of every internal system is altered. Chemicals, energies, impulses, and reflexes normally held in a delicate balance are disrupted. The early investigators of psychosis often said that it was an illness of "disharmony."*
>
> *Edward M. Podvoll, MD.*
> *Recovering Sanity*

In the Windhorse Approach to treating extreme states, madness is not considered a brain-based phenomenon created by chemical imbalances or inherited genetics. The approach does not deny the importance of the brain, of neurotransmitters and the harmony of the bodily system. What it sees differently than the Western medical model is the cocktail.

The cocktail is the ingredients each person brings together to create the "transformative" moment of the psychotic break. In the mixing of these ingredients, the brain does alter. Our cocktail changes our chemistry, impacting our ways of thinking and connecting to oneself, others, and the world.

Anyone can create their own cocktail that breaks them through into madness. Put another way, we all have the potential to lose our minds, no matter how sane we've appeared at different iterations of our lives. What makes the cocktail different is that it does not relegate insanity to a select group of people who are predisposed to madness. We are all predisposed to madness. If you have a mind, you can lose it.

One theory of madness often dismissed by the medical model is that it starts when we lose sleep. Anyone who is deprived of sleep will begin to display signs of sleep deprivation psychosis. They will hallucinate, their sense of self will change, and they will lose contact with their everyday reality.

This is why lack of sleep is used as torture. Ultramarathon runners will often talk about the changes that happen when they hit a certain hour into their run, approximating it to twenty-four hours without sleep. The body changes, the mind changes, and you start to lose it.

David Blaine, the magician and a performer of endurance challenges, describes his own experience of starting to lose his mind after spending over sixty-three hours awake. In an interview with Tim Ferriss, Blaine said, "...when your brain starts to go, when you start to lose control of your mind, there's nothing as horrific imaginable."

In the case of the ultramarathon runners, they have a particular cocktail they've created to bring about madness. For them, their goal is not madness, but to finish the marathon. They know in the process of completing their race, they will potentially lose their minds. The cocktail is based on the ingredients of a predicament, an intention, exertion, a substance, and mindlessness.

Ultramarathoners run a race longer than any human should. By running for longer than a day, they've created a predicament known to generate symptoms of madness. There is some motivation, some inner drive, propelling them toward this unheard-of thing of running for over 24 hours. This is their intention.

The exertion is obvious. They are running for hours on end, pushing themselves further than they have ever been pushed. Exertion is considered a necessary ingredient in breaking us through into madness. Our body is designed to not go mad. So, you have to push through its attempts to hold back madness – in this case, sleep.

Substance is often thought of as drugs, which generally induce states of madness, like in my case. With runners, it is most likely the neurotransmitters being released while moving for such intense durations, also known as the "runner's high." The runner's high allows these athletes to push themselves beyond their limits, to truly push their physical limitations, into madness.

Then the ingredient of mindlessness. This word captures the necessity of "checking out" or even over-focusing on one aspect of experience. Mindlessness allows people to check out from the signals, from their bodies and lives, telling them to slow down. By being mindless, we do not interrupt the madness taking hold. We keep applying the exertion, intention, and substances to break through into it.

If we listened to our body telling us to stop running, we would stop and not complete the race. Many runners cultivate mindless states to maintain their endurance. A friend told me about his dad's trick of paying attention to his thumbs while running, a practice of mindlessness.

For ultramarathoners, madness is not the goal. But Edward Podvoll believed individuals often intentionally re-entered into states of madness by applying their own cocktail to break through. The individual's cocktail becomes their preferred pathway into extreme states. The original title of his book *Recovering Sanity* was *The Seduction of Madness.*

While I do not agree with Edward's interpretation of people suffering from repeated experiences of madness as "choosing it," I do see the wisdom in acknowledging our unique cocktails that broke through into madness. By understanding these cocktails, we can become more aware of our areas of sensitivities, the places where we are prone to lose touch with consensus reality and drift too far into our own personal reality.

The language I am using has a flavor of shaming to it. I did not "create" my cocktail. It is only now, after everything I went through, that I can identify some of its ingredients. I think it is important to look at the unique ingredients of each person's break to determine their cocktail's ingredients.

I see my cocktail as being pretty normal if you will. I was in the midst of a major life transition, a common place for people to have breaks. My transition was not going well. I had invested in attending a PhD program and it was clear it was not working out. I over-committed to this plan for my life and did not leave room for a backup. My predicament involved being committed to a plan that was falling apart before my eyes.

Due to feeling a "spiritual calling" toward my plan, I thought it was protected in some way. If I just kept moving toward the goal, it would turn out well for me. It has taken years to shed much of my naivety around the integration of spiritual experiences and how my life expresses itself day to day.

I now see I was attached to my plan. I was keeping it alive well beyond its expiration date. I was not able to adjust with the changing currents of my life, to adapt to the circumstances presented to me. Instead, I got locked in, over-committed, and unwilling to let go of "my vision" for my life.

Couple this with the substance of a psychedelic and I pushed myself through to the other side of madness. But for me, it wasn't just the psychedelics. It was also the years of intensive meditation practice I was engaged in before the night I lost my mind. For years, I was on a systemic endeavor of learning to open up, to increase my awareness and connection to the world around me. Adding the "natural" opening of committed meditation practice with a psychedelic let me blow open in a way I wasn't prepared to deal with.

Within my committed meditation practice, I also had an overly zealous attitude toward spiritual practice. I brought my young, twenty-something male energy into the endeavor of spiritual practice and growth.

Researcher Willoughby Britton, who studies the negative effects of meditation in her research project "*the variety of contemplative experiences,*" describes folks like me, often dudes, who take their spiritual practice too far and end up losing touch with reality for a period of time. She even created a group home to support monastics who have had a psychotic break and need care to come back to their consensus selves.

Britton does not see psychotic breaks as an expression of a brain-based disorder. Through her research, she has found that anyone who embarks in serious spiritual practice has the possibility of losing touch with reality. It is a known aspect of the spiritual path not often acknowledged within the mindfulness world.

Chögyam Trungpa Rinpoche, an important influence on the Windhorse Approach and Edward Podvoll's Buddhist teacher, describes a point in his journey where, while in his twenties and living in Oxford, he said to his wife, "I'm at the fork in the road where you either become enlightened or you lose your mind." Trungpa's traditional Buddhist education prepared him for the possibility of losing his mind on the spiritual journey.

My life falling apart, psychedelics, engaging in the opening practices of meditation, and being a bit obsessive about my "spiritual journey" were all compounding factors leading to my break. It was the cocktail of ingredients pushing me over the edge.

Once on the other side, Edward would talk about the ways he witnessed his clients engage in different "practices" to maintain the mania or the psychosis. For me, once I broke through into madness, I definitely did things to try to stay balanced. Which is a weird concept, staying balanced while in madness. By staying balanced, I also maintained the state I was in, madness.

One of the primary ways I managed the heightened energy coursing through my body was with breathwork. I had previously been trained in yogic forms of breathwork. While in my madness, I followed some inner intuition and engaged in breath practices that often left me in a state of total sensory overload. I was only the buzzing energy and nothing of "me" was left. From my view within madness, I did this to balance the energy flowing through my body. Only later would I realize I needed to let the energy settle and leave my body, not try to maintain or balance it.

Many people forgo sleep when in madness, perpetuating the state they are in, just like the marathon runners. Folks use their own concoction of substances to maintain their state of mind. I know for myself, I would rarely sleep and was pretty open to taking the drugs around me.

However, the biggest factor impacting my extreme states was being homeless. By being in a perpetual state of uncertainty, I was creating an external environment that was mimicking and perpetuating my inner state of chaos and uncertainty.

The core idea is all of us have a cocktail or ingredients we bring together which generates the possibility of breaking through to madness. So, if you've had a break, it is important to look back at the time before. What was happening in your life? What choices did you make? Were any of the conditions or choices you made unknowingly ingredients in your cocktail?

I know for myself, that whenever I am in a transition now, I am careful. I work to stay grounded, to not get overwhelmed or caught up in my transition.

Just like traveling, transitions remind me of the transition I was in during my break, building a life after graduating from university. It was in this transitory time that I lost touch with the ground of my life. Now, whenever I am in a period of transition – changing work, moving houses, having a kid – my body enters a heightened fear. A memory of what happened when I didn't navigate a transition smoothly.

There was a period of over a decade where I did not touch psychedelics, to prevent a future break from happening. At some point in my journey, I felt "safe" enough to start to explore working with psychedelic medicines again. Really learning to honor "set and setting," not just play lip service to it.

I am also careful when I am "called" to something in my life. I try to watch for the inflation that comes with a calling. To notice the ways I try to force my callings to happen. Over the years, I hope I have gotten better at seeing callings as more intuitions, less about me making them happen and more about me working with the currents of my life.

One of the most important elements of the cocktail is the acknowledgment that we all have the propensity to go mad. It is not a brain-based disorder. It is not hereditary. It is human. Some humans may have more of a propensity to lose their minds based on history and temperament, but it's not an illness. It is a process that has key ingredients in it. Apply these ingredients to someone who is sane and there is a good chance they will lose their minds.

Not everyone has the same cocktail. That is why it is important to be curious about the conditions that bring forth madness for you. To look at the events and, at least in the beginning of your recovery journey, watch out for recreating your cocktail. Be careful with your mind. Give it time to settle and heal before introducing elements of your cocktail that came together to push you over the edge.

Typically, no one cocktail ingredient is the "culprit" of madness, and we have to be aware of the impact of certain choices and environments that propel the intensity of extreme states. In my view, it is not right to blame or demonize certain aspects of common cocktails. While cannabis is often a factor in a person's break, it is not the determining factor. It is only part of the cocktail.

In other circumstances, ingredients in our cocktail might be explored or we might reconnect to them. For many folks, new love can be a primary catalyst for a break. This doesn't mean folks should shy away from love or romantic connection if it is part of their cocktail. It only means you have to be aware of the impact of your unique ingredients on your mind and functioning.

Power

Whatever else mania is, it is also living dangerously. One sports with powers, energies, intensified mind, amplified senses, and altogether unleashed egotistic impulses, one becomes vulnerable to seen and unseen influences of all kinds. What begins as a glimpse of vastness, unity, interdependence, transcendence, "god consciousness," or whatever else one calls it, may end only in the confusion of self-aggrandizement.

At the onset of any such psychotic experience, dramatic changes are occurring in the body, in the perceptual systems and in the activities of the mind. One feels a growing sense of physical vitality, mental agility and personal freedom in relationships. One might even experience some form of "absolute truth" and sometimes it feels like the beginning of a "new life." These feelings may last for only a short period of time - much to one's dismay - but they are nevertheless remembered and longed for. One's curiosity about the nature of the experience is a powerful force. And the desire to repossess the power of that experience becomes a seed for future episodes of psychosis.

Edward M. Podvoll, MD.
Recovering Sanity

The notion of power is a subtle theme throughout Edward's exploration of madness, his attempt to understand the non-understandable. While I worked at Windhorse, we never spoke of power. It was only referenced once by a founding member in a training session. Yet, each time I read *Recovering Sanity*, I pick up this theme.

Edward does not dismiss the psychotic experience as "made up" or "in your head." He goes out of his way to acknowledge the fundamental impact psychosis has on the total self. "One sports with powers, energies, intensified mind, amplified senses," he says. "At the onset of any psychotic experience, dramatic changes are occurring in the body, in the perceptual systems and in the activities of the mind."

Edward fully acknowledges the holistic impact psychosis has on our total selves. All aspects of experience are altered, intensified, or made extreme. Hence the common phrase, extreme state. But he goes a step further. There is one line that has always stood out to me, it is almost a throw-away line, "one becomes vulnerable to seen and unseen influences of all kinds."

This line makes room for moving beyond a limited, isolated self-experience to the possibility of our experience being impacted by everything around us, everything "seen and unseen." The Windhorse Approach is rooted in Tibetan Buddhism which, in my view, is an integration of indigenous Tibetan shamanic practices, Bon and Indian Buddhism. There is a great deal of acknowledgment of a pantheon of deities and spirits supporting Buddhism in Tibet.

Sometimes in a modern interpretation, these deities and unseen forces are described as being an aspect of mind. From a Western perspective, this is often reduced to *my* mind, an isolated experience within myself. Each person having their own mind.

In Tibetan Buddhism, the mind is typically something larger, something more than just our experience. Within many contemplative traditions, everything is mind. Everything is made of mind – you, me, everything you are seeing, hearing, experiencing – all mind.

This makes room for the possibility of genuine encounters with powers that are not "human," something more than we are able to understand from our limited perspective within consciousness. Powers capture the unknown, the unknown forces potentially impacting all of us day in and day out.

Once again, I do not want to make the case that experiencing madness makes you more divinely connected or touched than "sane" folks. Edward does not romanticize the powers within his writing. He highlights that encounters with powers often end in confusion and self-aggrandizement, which I can personally attest to. Whatever experiences I may have had, they did not leave me in a healthier mindset or experiencing greater harmony in my life.

For a clinician who does not identify with having lived experience with madness, only decades of experience working with folks in extreme states, Edward is humble enough to acknowledge the deep unknown occurring within it. Something is happening. It is not just in someone's head, but what it is, it is hard to say. Edward says power.

This perspective of the mad individual potentially connecting to aspects of reality seen and unseen (typically not perceived) allows for humbleness from those around them. While a mad person's delusions and communication may sound absurd and easy to dismiss, who are the "sane" people to say that how they perceive reality is the only way? Maybe there are other faculties, other ways of sensing the world around us which would lead to very different views.

Even as I talk about Tibetan Buddhism, a pre-modern religion heavily rooted in connections to spirits, demons, and non-human forces, it is both acknowledged and praised by the modern west. Tibetan Buddhism's connection to more "primitive" ways of viewing the world is often ignored or interpreted away. But who's to say whose worldview is the right worldview?

I've lived in multiple worldviews throughout my life. I spent time as a fundamentalist Christian, believing the only way to salvation was through accepting Jesus Christ into my heart, also believing anyone who did not accept Jesus as their savior was going to hell. I've spent time as an agnostic materialist, identified with the scientific worldview.

I've spent time as a committed Zen student believing in the possibility of enlightenment, liberation, and awakening from the human dream. I've been psychotic, living in a dream-like reality of unseen forces becoming seen and being as real as anything else.

I've also spent time in an in-between trapped place: not quite human, not quite dead. And I am here still. Not sure what is "real" and what is "delusion." From a contemplative perspective, this is the human condition. Continually living within the unknowns of our limited perspective of consciousness and life.

Currently, I see my worldview as an opinion and probably an ill-informed one at that. It is an attempt to understand the world around me from my limited perspective. When encountering someone in madness, it can be helpful to not assume you are "right" or "accurate" in your story about the world around you. This will often allow for a possibility of greater connection with the person you are with and can lead to an increased understanding of what is really being communicated through the often-distorted language of those suffering in extreme states.

It is a way of honoring the person in front of you. It allows for both of your opinions to be "possibilities." So, please do not correct someone's "wrong" ideas while in madness. Just help them stay safe and supported.

Within the notion of power, Edward repeatedly highlights the fundamental impact mania and psychosis have on a person's experience. It impacts our senses and the way our mind operates, also potentially impacting human faculties we do not acknowledge in everyday waking consciousness. Acknowledging these fundamental changes continues to allow for the possibility of more fully connecting with someone in madness.

Imagine a person is living in their "other world," hardly able to connect to the world around you. You try to reach out, try to connect, and are continuously pushed away. When this happens, there can be a tendency to respond with anger, dismissing the person for not receiving your help.

But what if their senses are operating in a way yours are not? What if they are perceiving and experiencing the world in ways you cannot imagine? While what they are saying does not make sense to you, you can guarantee that someone in madness is having genuine experiences that would cause *you* to be confused, overwhelmed, and in need of a story to make sense of it all.

History of Sanity

> *The patient has a history of sanity as well as a history of illness. It is made up of landmark events in his life that describe a developmental yearning for health. On one hand they are historical moments, but also they can presently be cultivated.*
>
> *Edward M. Podvoll, MD.*
> *Recovering Sanity*

Following the acute phase of my psychotic break, as I started to descend into the depths of depression that would consume me for almost two years, I completely lost sight of the me who was present before my break. I was only the depression.

I was only the wasting away of a life. Only the shame. Only the embarrassment. Only the fear of starting over again. There was no tactile memory left of the me who rode bikes, rock climbed, enjoyed backpacking, loved to cook, enjoyed connecting with friends, loved to read, and – above all else – was interested in living.

I became defined by my period of madness, defined by my life falling apart in such a dramatic and catastrophic way. All I could think was, "How did I let this happen?" "I was supposed to do more with my life than this." As I would sit in my father's basement, watching another episode of television to keep my mind from the self-repulsion dominating my experience, I was only my history of madness.

On one hand, this repulsion was the source of my suffering, the barrier to me moving forward with my life. It was the constant onslaught of suicidal thinking defining me as broken, a failure, and not able to have a "normal" life.

On the other hand, the repulsion was an accurate reflection of my life. I was in a dark place. Struggling. Disconnected from everyone and everything. I was living as a Shade: part human, alone, and trapped in the cocoon of my shame and suffering.

I needed the repulsion to recognize a drastic need for change, for getting my life back in order. The disgust helped clarify a direction of change toward meaning and connection again. Yet the repulsion was too large for me to hold. It dominated me, primarily due to me being defined by my history of madness, forgetting my history of sanity.

No matter how far "gone" someone is, we all have histories of madness and histories of sanity. But in the medical model's understanding of madness, our history of illness is highlighted. Often, our unique histories of sanity are ignored or even dismissed. Many times, what is actually a hallmark of health, discipline, clear thinking, and compassionate action can be reduced to an expression of one's illness.

When a therapist engages in an assessment, they are typically searching to understand one's history of madness. You see it on the forms therapists fill out when they are providing intakes. Only at the end is there a small section for SNAP: strengths, needs, accomplishments, and preferences.

For me, the only mirror I was able to hold up to see myself was my history of illness. I had become defined by my "failing." As if having a psychotic break is a personal failing, a mark of my character.

So often in the recovery journey, we get defined by our illness, our shortcomings, and our lost potential. This is why community and healing relationships are essential and the bedrock of the Windhorse Approach. We need someone to hold up a mirror, to reflect something other than our brokenness.

My mirror came in the form of a gift from my mother. For what felt like an eternity, I only knew a punishing self-hate as I was disconnected from the world around me. No other influences found their way in. The cocoon I had created was so impenetrable, the only thing I was with was my own thinking, which was a singular thought of self-hate.

There were no counter-voices, no alternate opinions, no kindness. So, when I received the gift from my mother, something broke through the self-hate. It was kindness. I mattered to someone else. I was a participant in life.

All these recognitions and feelings surfaced again. I glimpsed all of me under my history of illness. All of the me's I had been before my madness: student, athlete, friend, adventurer, partner, and contemplative. For a moment, I could remember I was more than my self-hate.

Within this recognition, I was able to connect to my history of sanity. To my history of being a son. Of having lived a life before my psychotic break. This was my doorway. The support I needed to break out of being defined by illness and, instead, remember possibility again.

With the arising energy of possibility, I moved toward the activities that had given me meaning, joy, and connection. By reconnecting to these activities, the list I had created – yoga, rock climbing, cooking food, being in a spiritual community, riding my bicycle, swimming, and reading – I was able to tap into my history of sanity. Tap into the activities of self, storing my sanity for me.

The first time I did yoga again, I knew how to do it. I knew the movements. I knew the breath pattern. I knew the discipline of maintaining concentration throughout. I knew the state of mind that allowed me to finish the strenuous hot yoga class. I was tapping into my sanity. Into my discipline. Into my willingness to suffer in the present moment for growth and healing.

It is paramount, if you are on a journey of recovery, to acknowledge the many you's you've been through this life. There have been moments of struggle, moments of joy, moments of connection, and moments of alienation. We all move through this human experience. As Buddhists say, "Ten thousand joys and ten thousand sorrows."

Within our human journey, there are periods where we honor sanity, our health, and our desire to grow and become the person we feel ourselves to be within our core. We need to remember these times. Remember the times when we felt possibility, when we felt connected, when we felt we were honoring the seed of our life wanting to bloom.

In our memories, can we recall what we were doing with our time? How were we spending our days when our lives felt possible? It is time to reclaim a history of sanity and bring forth the activities that allow us to know ourselves as sane, as kind, as a valuable part of this thing we call life.

I think we see sanity and insanity as givens. You are either one or the other. From this perspective, this understanding of history, sanity is a practice. Sanity is how you live your life. It is the choices you make. It is how you relate to your mind. How you relate to your heart. How you relate to your loved ones. How you relate to your goals, hopes, and dreams for your life.

Practicing sanity can be a slow process. For many of us, like myself, you can drift far from the foundations of sanity you've built through your life. You can lose touch with aspects of living that allow you to know yourself as "sane."

This is the practice. Reconnecting to the activities, interests, and communities where our sanity lives. By stepping into the practices of sanity, even when we are far from it, we are inviting sanity back into our lives. We are making offerings to our sanity. Going to shoot hoops each day because when you played basketball regularly, you were your healthiest and happiest. So you shoot. Maybe your mind is wild. Maybe there is fear. Maybe you are overwhelmed. But you shoot baskets. Your body knows how to do it. The rhythm of basketball pulls you back, brings you back into yourself.

Maybe it's not basketball for you, but something. Something where you can let yourself be in your struggle while honoring your sanity. The more we step into our sanity, into the practices of sanity, the more anchored we become in ourselves. The more rooted we are in our lives.

While engaging in one of your hallmarks of sanity, you might start to feel like yourself again and get a glimpse of the self you were before. Maybe you've been on edge for a long time, raw, exposed, and the world too much. Yet, while riding your bike, you are able to open up. You're able to appreciate the trees, to see the people moving through their days. And you appreciate, appreciate this gift of being alive for a moment, which only happens when you feel open and relaxed. In this grounded state of taking in the world, you can be grateful for your life, and for life in general.

If you've been on edge for a long time, barely holding on, to have a taste of appreciation for life can be monumental. You remember you can be grateful. You can weather the challenges for small moments of joy and connection.

I had a small moment on my bike. It must have been the first couple of weeks of me trying out living again. I was riding to the library or yoga, I can't remember. I do remember that at this time, I felt flat. Like I was going through the motions. Much like I am suggesting you try. Going through the motions of sanity.

While in this sea of pervasive flatness, I caught a glimmer on the side of my eye. I looked down and saw the shadow of myself riding my bike. In the white-painted stripe of the bike lane, a circular rainbow was staring back at me, radiating from my heart in the shadow. I just kept riding, looking down, seeing this rainbow heart being reflected back to me.

It was a beautiful small moment just for me. It reminded me of beauty, of wonder, of the amazing surprises life has around the corner. I felt my flatness melting and excitement for my life started to grow. Excitement for what was possible now that I was living again. An island of clarity.

Islands of Clarity

> *You must understand that working with the mind of recovery ultimately means recognizing, appreciating, and directly relating to what have been called "islands of clarity." They are moments of spaciousness and relaxation, when things can be understood and life can be enjoyed. They can be sudden or gradual. If one is not attuned to their occurrence, they may be easily missed; and when they are missed, frustrated, or inhibited, things become worse.*
>
> *Edward M. Podvoll, MD.*
> *Recovering Sanity*

For me, islands of clarity are a central tenant to the recovery process from psychosis and directly linked to one's history of sanity. An island of clarity is a moment of slowing, of entering one's senses, of letting go of the "other world" for a moment to remember this tactile shared world we also inhabit. To remember who you are in this world. Who you are now, and who you were before the mind became out of control.

By making islands of clarity a central tenant to his therapeutic model, EdwardPodvoll returned humanity to those who've experienced madness. Instead of seeing someone as "crazy" – a permanent condition of confusion, delusion, and hallucination – Edward defines "illness" as he calls it an out-of-control positive feedback loop. Where our "secondary processes" take over and we are lost to the "microoperations" of the mind. An area of consciousness or awareness that has great power while also being out of control, unpredictable, and often completely overwhelming.

When walking down the highway leaving Stockton, before being picked up by a police officer, I became lost to the secondary processes as my mind made meaning of the spray-painted construction symbols on the ground of the freeway at an alarmingly rapid rate. My mind took in the images and started to build a story out of each. The story occurred so fast that I was just a witness to the ever-changing nature of the meaning I was making without ever being able to comprehend it.

This is a moment of madness. Of being taken over by the machinations of the mind and becoming entranced in their processes. Edward would call this "mindlessness." But this is just one story, one facet of madness.

For Edward, there are also islands of clarity, moments when we are not lost to the other world. When we reenter our senses, our environment, and can have moments of rest and clarity. Edward has even described enjoying the taste and experience of smoking a cigar as an island of clarity. A return to simple pleasures outside of the speed of the secondary processes.

Throughout my journey of madness, I would have flashes of islands of clarity, which is often how they are described. Flashes interspersed between being lost to the other world. Like the moment I saw myself making art on my friend's wall and thought, "This is what crazy people do."

When riding the bus, in a moment of quiet and trying to appear "normal," I would often reflect on how far my life had drifted. How quickly it had changed. How far I had let it go. These moments would linger, but I wouldn't be in the space either internally or within the circumstances of my life to act on my islands of clarity.

Later, when I first landed at my father's house, I was able to honor a moment of clarity. I was able to see how far my life had drifted and how much I had let go of. I was in an island of clarity. In a more stable home environment, I was able to sit down and write out my list. The things I needed to get my life back on track. To return to a stable foundation to begin the process of becoming, of building a life for myself again.

Yet this moment of clarity could not be sustained. The list was not ambitious. And I had no money or capacity to work at the moment. My father was barely getting by financially and I had lost touch with family members with more means. I was stuck. I didn't know how to activate the list without resources, and I became despondent.

Instead of my island being a catalyzing point, the list became a source of shame and self-hatred. I would remind myself how "fucked up I was" because I couldn't move toward my goal of rebuilding my life. The list became a reminder of my failure. A weapon of my ongoing, relentless self-hate.

I would not have another island of clarity for some time. I would get lost to the avoidant world of television and sleeping I created to protect myself from the intensity of my inner hatred. Not the other world of madness, but the inner world of judgment and shame. Paralyzing me to remain in my barely human state of just getting by. By blocking myself from my inner experience through the mindlessness of television, I was protecting myself from my inner hatred while, at the same time, blocking off any possibility of the emergence of an island of clarity.

Then came the package, the gift my mom sent me, the one I avoided for months. Something in me emerged, some willingness to face my fear presented itself. When I opened the package, I was reminded of kindness, of being loved, of family, of my life before madness. I was able to reconnect for a moment to my history of sanity. I remembered I would not be "restarting" or "rebuilding" my life, but reconnecting to the activities and connections that once gave me meaning and supported my wellness.

It was this island of clarity that allowed me to honor the previous island of the list. I was able to recall the list and, this time, move forward with activating the activities that would allow me to remember myself outside of my history of madness. Allow me to reclaim the history of sanity covered over by my self-hate.

To activate my list, I had to turn off the TV. I had to shower. I needed money, so I had to work. At first with my father, washing windows for hours at a time. I had to learn to center myself enough to complete the work day. Once I started riding my bike again, I had to remember to be present enough to pay attention to my surroundings. I had to give up the speed of my thinking, the intensity of my shame, to pay attention to what was in front of me.

With yoga, I had to remember discipline. I had to remember my will to endure painful moments. Remembering this allowed me to face my mind. When my mind was wild, when I was scared of what was emerging from it, I could face it with a knowing. Knowing I could face difficult moments and make it through them.

After rebuilding the foundations of my life, I was able to step into the world. To move out of my father's home. To make friends. To date. To work. To explore who I am now, after everything I've been through. I was still just an early twenties kid trying to make sense of my life and find some meaning and connection to something more.

In order to move into the world, I had to have faith. Faith it was possible for me to be me. Possible to have a life as myself. A life that would continue, evolve, and become something.

My life had fallen apart so thoroughly that I knew what was possible in the reverse, how far my life could drift. Yet I was staking a claim to having a meaningful life by choosing to enter the world again. I was honoring my history of sanity over my history of madness. By putting on my shoes and riding my bike to yoga class, I was also stating, "This act of yoga is an expression of the possibility of my life being more then it was at that point." By saying yes to the list, I was saying yes to a foundation from which my life would begin again.

Islands of clarity are the moments that allow us to see ourselves. Sometimes we remember our goodness, we remember kindness. Sometimes we are repulsed by what we see. Those moments on the bus, when my madness first started to take hold, are when I would see how far I had drifted from the life I knew just weeks before.

Whether the island is "positive" or "negative" does not matter. The island is simply a moment of clear seeing, of acknowledging what is. In the Windhorse language, it is the synchronization of body-mind-environment that allows for clear recognition.

When I wrote the list that would allow me to rebuild my foundations, I was in a moment of repulsion. I saw my life and I knew I needed to rebuild. I couldn't go on living like I had. I was able to tap into my history of sanity and reclaim the activities and practices that would allow me to feel like a person again. A person living in the world.

It was due to seeing how far I had drifted from myself and my life that, in the clarity, I could recognize the need to rebuild my life. But the pressure, the recognition of how far I had gone, became too much. I collapsed by the weight of having to "start over." My repulsion transformed into shame and self-hate. A positive recognition of what my life had become was co-opted and used against myself. It is the positive feedback loop Edward refers to when describing madness.

This is the danger of islands of clarity. They can be used against ourselves. Either by inflation and grandiosity or by shame. We might use an island of clarity to build up a perfected image of ourselves. If I saw my list as an opportunity to become special, to reclaim the "potential" of my previous life, this would have been grandiosity grabbing hold of my island of clarity. It would have created the conditions for another positive feedback loop into madness. If the list was co-opted by shame, like it was during my year and a half of depression, I could use the list to put myself down, making the island of clarity a weapon of my self-hate.

This is why community is so essential in the recovery process. Communities can recognize our islands of clarity and help protect them. Later in my life, when I decided I wanted to write about my experience of recovery, I would feel overwhelmed. Overwhelmed at the thought of conveying my story. Overwhelmed by the thought of outing myself as "crazy" in our culture of pathologizing and dismissing differences.

My wife would hold my intention for me. She would occasionally prod me toward writing. "When are you going to start the book?" Sometimes I would complain about feeling a lack of meaning or direction with my life and she would say, "I bet if you wrote, you would feel like you were moving towards the life you want." For years, I would hear her remind me of the clarity I felt when I decided to write about my experience. She held my island for me, even when it was too overwhelming for me to hold myself.

This is the gift of community. Holding our tender shoots not yet ready to blossom.

Synchronizing Body, Mind, and Environment

> *Simply put, body-mind-synchronization is being mindful of body, mind, and one's activity all at the same time. This kind of "tuning" and being present is a key point in mindfulness-awareness meditation practice.*
>
> *Synchronization can happen just now, in any activity, in this present moment. Because of this, because of this real life actions are the basis for any anchor within the emotional tide of the thought-world. For the patient is involves an engagement of all the senses to help ground his thinking and provides natural "brakes" to the system of mental speed in which the patient is caught.*
>
> *Edward M. Podvoll, MD.*
> *Recovering Sanity*

Synchronizing body-mind-environment is a core tenant of the Windhorse Approach. From my understanding, it is rooted in the teachings of Tibetan Buddhism, specifically the Shambhala Lineage founded by Edward Podvoll's meditation teacher, Trungpa Rinpoche.

With most of my contemplative training being in the Zen tradition, I was not familiar with the concept of synchronization prior to working at Windhorse. At the same time, when I look back on my early experiences, so much of what I did to support my recovery journey was rooted in synchronizing body-mind-environment.

So often in madness, the speed of our mind is mismatched to the world and people around us. Often, if someone in active psychosis opens up to another and shares what is on their mind, the experience can be extremely overwhelming and destabilizing to the recipient. Folks in madness typically do not realize how quickly their minds are moving compared to those around them.

The act of learning to anchor the mind and steady its speed can be a lifelong journey. One I am still walking. I feel I have come a long way and yet, at times, my mind accelerates at speeds that feel unstable and counter to living the healthy grounded life I desire.

Along with the speed of mind, folks in madness can experience significant emotional upheaval due to events imperceptible to those around them. A person's relation to their other world will generate significant emotional states, from the sublime to the disturbed. While these emotional experiences can feel important and "real," they can be barriers to connecting to the world around them.

For me, any experience we have is "real." The question is, is it real to others or only real to me? If we are deeply immersed in our "other world" and significantly impacted by that connection, the experience may not be "real" to those who do not share or have knowledge of our particular "other world" experiences. So, these experiences are real but not grounded in consensual reality. This can create a barrier to recovering one's capacity to participate in consensus-based reality.

In a way, this is what recovery is about. It is not about healing or fixing our tendency to participate in our "other worlds." It is about having a firm connection to consensus-based reality with a capacity to distinguish those experiences rooted in our other world and experiences shared by those around us.

Synchronizing body-mind-environment is essential to reconnecting and regrounding within the everyday world of consensus reality. It is the root function that allows us to slow our minds, stabilize our emotions, and connect to those around us. When I first started my recovery journey, almost all of my activities were rooted in this principle of synchronization.

Riding my bike was synchronizing movement with the environment, forcing me to pay attention to the world around me and not be so lost in my shame and self-hatred following my psychotic break. Reconnecting to intense yoga practice is inherently yoking body and mind together. The practice, for me, is about rooting my attention within the movement of my body, allowing for the movement to be the most important thing in my attention.

Due to having practiced yoga before my break, I had a built-in capacity to "let go" of what I was thinking about and redirect my attention to my body. This is a valuable skill within the recovery process, to let go of the almost complete focus on the mechanizations of our other world. When we can do this, we move our attention back to a more grounded reality, with the body being one of the surest pathways to grounding and letting go of the speed of mind.

At times, the body can feel overwhelming and intense. Where do you go when the body is not a refuge? Walking, moving, and taking in the world around us can be an anecdote to the intensities of our emotional life. To see the world continuing, people living, trees being trees. All of this can remind us of the impermanence of our emotional intensity.

Whatever the felt urgency is in the moment, it is not rooted in the movement of the city or the lives of those around us. It exists within us, even though we might think there is something happening in the world that warrants the urgency and intensity of the body that can be so prevalent in altered states.

It is of vital importance to understand that the urgency is rooted in our other world experiences and may not correlate to the world around us. By anchoring ourselves in the world around us, we are able to live in two worlds. We live in the world of intensity while also acknowledging the different pace, rhythm, and feeling of the world around us.

On many occasions, I have witnessed a homeless individual shouting on the streets. When this occurs, I can feel others around me reacting to the person shouting by moving away from them, changing the speed of their walk, or holding off on conversations until passing the individual in distress. This person is engaging in their "other world" and not attuned to the world around them.

When I get into a conflict with my wife in a public space, there is intensity in my reactivity. I immediately feel how out of tune I am to the world around me. Our conflict doesn't fit in the setting we are in.

The process of synchronizing to our environment can be such an anchor in reducing the speed and intensity of our minds and bodies into something grounded and slower. This anchor can allow us to settle and let go of the intensity for a moment. This is why Windhorse is often referred to as "environmental healing." The approach utilizes healing environments as a grounding anchor to the intensity of the mind, much like a tuning fork harmonizing another tuning fork.

Unfortunately for me, while homeless, I was living in an environment of intensity, uncertainty, and hostility. The world around me mirrored my other world experiences. I was not able to rely on an environment to support my healing journey. While living at my father's, the basement I was in was more stable and safer than the world of the city streets I was in. At the same time, it was not uplifting. It was sad and depressing, so it did not help bring me out of my depressive loop.

As I moved forward in my recovery journey, while I worked cleaning windows with my father, I was forced to synchronize my movements with my visual field. I had to notice if I actually cleaned the window. I was not able to slip into my inner reverie, getting lost in my thinking. Instead, over and over again, I had to see if the window was clean and, if it wasn't, I had to reclean it. This was such a blessing. To have this anchor of attention forcing me to connect to the environment around me, in this case, the cleanness of the window in front of me.

I was drawn to activities I had engaged in the past. I searched through my history of sanity and identified the activities that would support me in synchronizing body-mind-environment. Activities that would help me in this synchronization emerged from my islands of clarity, providing clear recognition of what I needed to build a solid foundation for living again.

I remember even getting a skateboard again. Something I had done as a teenager. Just needing some activity to connect to. Something from my past that was familiar to me. I would bring it to the nearby school by my dad's and just mess around. It never really clicked for me again. But I was trying. Trying to remember what felt good. What felt like me again. Alive.

I imagine we all have a history of activities supporting synchronization. We all walk, run, and ride bikes. We have played sports and enjoyed activities rooted in the senses. And if you can't think of activities to support this grounding and connecting process of synchronization, there are always chores.

Windhorse loves the healing power of chores, what they might call, domesticity. So much of my work there was about supporting a client to anchor into the domesticity of their lives: cleaning, doing laundry, grocery shopping. We would call it "uplifting the environment." It is a powerful practice of stepping out of the feeling of importance and intensity of our other world preoccupation and remembering the simple, humble acts of being human.

One example of synchronizing one's self to the environment is remembering that your clothes need to be washed. Engaging in the process of gathering and cleaning clothes. Remembering to transition wet items to the dryer. Taking the clothes out and eventually folding them. Noticing the difference in your home after doing the laundry. Appreciating the clean clothes you have to wear.

This is synchronizing body-mind-environment. For most folks lost to their other world, there is no interest in the everyday domestics of living. It can feel below oneself, not important, or even too difficult to attend to with the intensity of extreme states.

To honor the domestics of laundry, dishes, grocery shopping, and arranging your living space so you feel supported and loved is the act of uplifting your environment. Of creating an environment you want to synchronize with.

All these activities can be the heart of recovery. If you attend to your space with love and attention, you are supporting the settling of your mind. You are pivoting attention away from your altered states and toward the state of your life. This is the pregnant ground that allows you to let go. Let go of the stories of madness. Let go of the preoccupations and, instead, just be a person doing laundry. Nothing special. Nothing important. Just like anyone else. Doing laundry.

This act of humbling while uplifting is a wicked recipe to support recovery and often helps you become the person you want to be in your life. The person who can attend to their needs, follow through with commitments, and care about the world around them. By working with your home, working with your environment, you are cultivating qualities that will help you as you expand your life outward.

Another Reality

I think back to my recovery story. During a turbulent period in my life, as I was transitioning out of college and stepping into the next phase of my adulting journey, I went to a house party, took some psychedelics, and had an acute psychotic break.

While in my heightened state of overwhelm, living in a psychedelic-like reality, I became homeless and wandered the streets for months, unable to put my life together from the state of mind I was locked in.

I finally gave up trying and let my father take me in, for the first time since I was five years old. After a couple of initial "failed" attempts to get back on the functional living train, I descended into a profound depression, lasting a year and a half, where I didn't engage with human contact.

Somehow, after all this, I was able to step back into living and build a life for myself. A life I still live to this day.

Many times during my years at Windhorse, I wondered what my recovery journey would have looked like if I had been provided the healing conditions contained within the Windhorse Approach. Healing relationships, a team-based community of support, lack of pressure to "put things back together," and encouragement to reconnect to prior activities of meaning and vitality.

I would have also had access to a community that understands healing from extreme state crises is an everyday thing. If my family had the resources to cover the expenses of a Windhorse treatment, I imagine my journey would have looked different in many ways, but maybe not different in others.

Like most folks receiving care for psychotic breaks, it is often when the extreme states begin to fade that people enter treatment. Someone in a heightened state of madness is doing their own thing, generally hard to redirect, and hard to contain within a treatment program. After the extreme states begin to fade and some grounding emerges, folks typically see the destruction of their period of madness and are more open to receiving support.

Most clients I've worked with who are recovering from a psychotic break enter treatment either after they have settled in with family or been released from an acute stay at a hospital. I imagine my story wouldn't be any different.

Around the time I decided to go live with my father, a different version of my life, an alternate timeline of my recovery journey, might have started. Instead of settling with my father and descending into a severe isolating depression, I would have entered a Windhorse program.

I would arrive at Still Point, Windhorse's landing home. It is a nice house, near shops, restaurants, and city parks. Everything is walkable. One staff member lives there full-time and their job is to help new clients land. There is no rotating staff, just a reliable, steady person there to support you with your basic needs as you settle into the Windhorse program.

Unlike many other treatment facilities, I wouldn't be landing in a group home with others in extreme states. I wouldn't have to navigate the many overlapping dream realities playing out, like the group home I previously worked in. Instead, Still Point is meant to be what it describes: a still point to settle and land after the tumultuousness of a psychotic break or equally devastating catastrophic mental health crisis.

The fridge would be stocked with food. Right away, the house manager would ask if there was any food I would want purchased. I would be invited to go to the grocery store with the house manager and pick out my own food. None of it is locked up. Within a day or two of landing, I would meet with my team leader. They would provide context for the treatment, explain their role in my life.

Having been a team leader, I imagine my fictitious team leader would acknowledge the strangeness of the situation, going from a period of homelessness to living in a nice, well-furnished, home. They would then explain the basic expectations of being at WIndhorse.

Once a day, a team member will come by for Basic Attendance, where I will have an opportunity to connect and discover how we want to spend our time together. It will be explained that this is the one expectation of being at Windhorse, participating in the Basic Attendance shifts.

That day or the following, the whole team would gather and introduce themselves. The client, in this case me, will be overwhelmed by all the new places, the new expectations, and often not know what to make of the experience of having seven new people sitting in a room for my care.

The first four months are crucial at Windhorse. In more technical language, the Windhorse Treatment Approach is considered "environmental healing." The focus is on creating and maintaining a healthy and supportive environment for healing to occur, with human relationships being a core part of this healing.

What this means in the everyday living of Windhorse is that clients are not expected to make any progress, to "put their lives back together," for the first four months. I would tell this to the parents of clients I worked with. "Please, for the first four months, we do not put any pressure on your child." "If they are watching TV all day, isolating in their room, it is okay for the first four months." The goal was to help the parents take pressure off their kiddos "getting better."

Often, the burden of "being broken" and "getting better" is too much for someone to handle after a break. My role as a team leader was to help alleviate this pressure, with the family and team I would manage, and most importantly with the client.

When I was in my extreme states, I was trying to "put my life back together." But I was doing it with the intensity of mind I was experiencing in those states, a frame of mind that is not conducive to creating a grounded, balanced life. At Windhorse, we wanted to give clients time to settle from the extreme states. To allow for a more grounded version of themselves to emerge and let this version of themselves begin the process of putting their lives together again.

This serves a number of functions. First, after four months of being in a relatively uplifted, sane environment, you can get a better sense of where the client is at. Second, it allows the client to really understand that there is no fixed agenda. No program they have to get through to graduate. We are not trying to heal or fix them. We are truly here to support them in their healing journey.

Third, giving them time to settle provides a period where the parents or loved ones are not pressuring them to get better. Sometimes, this pressure can be too much for the client to take. Individuals who have experienced madness are generally already disappointed in the direction their lives have taken without the addition of the shame and judgment they feel for disappointing their families.

So, for the first four months, they have no expectations. This can even be hard for the team, letting go of the need to fix or know what is best for the client.

During this time, the client is acclimatizing themselves to the schedule, the routine, and the new relationships in their life. In the first four months, there is often one agenda and it isn't about fixing the client but about finding common ground in a relationship. This is finding a shared discipline.

Shared discipline is a phrase used to describe the intention of finding a common activity to engage in while on Basic Attendance shifts. Something for the client and staff to do together that supports health, connection, and vitality.

There's usually someone at Windhorse who skateboards a bit. I might have been skating with them at a park rather than alone, during those first few months of recovery.

One way of exploring shared discipline is understanding the client's history of sanity. The psychotherapist explores this with the client, trying to get a better sense of who they were before or outside of their history of madness. The idea is that we all have disciplines that help us work with our minds – whether sports, music, art, or other activities. Activities we have spent time mastering and learned to have a certain grounded, clear mindset to engage in.

Sometimes Basic Attendance isn't generated from past activities but comes from a desire for a future self. It comes from activities the patient has always wanted to do.

The act of discovering a shared discipline is an organic process emerging within the relationship. Sometimes it can be explicit, "Oh, you used to play soccer? I love soccer! Want to go kick the ball around during our shifts?" Other times, the shared discipline just emerges, like a client I would get tea with each week. It just became our routine, our way of connecting.

The beautiful thing about shared disciplines is there is no consequence or negative feedback if the client is not able to engage in it. This makes room for them to be in periods of struggle, when they want to isolate and disappear into their "other world." I spent many shifts sitting on the couch, allowing the client to take space from the relationship. With some space and time, the client would often be able to reconnect and we could explore what would be a good use of our time given their state of mind.

This is so valuable. To be able to struggle and be supported in struggling while, at other times, being supported in engaging in activities of health and reconnecting to their former lives. This perspective understands the non-linear process of recovery and prioritizes the relationship as more important than any progress. If my client isn't able to live up to our commitment, I am going to pivot and attempt to meet them where they are. I've had many patients tell me, "I just can't do this right now," take space, and then come back an hour later and we go get lunch together.

If I had been at Windhorse, I imagine my psychotherapist would have explored my history with me, learned about my connections to yoga, cooking food, playing basketball, riding my bike, etc. My team would explore integrating these activities into our Basic Attendance routines. Helping me, at my own pace, to connect to the activities that stored my pre-mad self. The activities that contained my history of sanity and natural ability to work with my mind.

We would continue like this for months. Engaging in these activities, exploring relationships, helping remind me of my functioning, reminding me of my prebuilt abilities stored within my history of sanity. Helping to capture again a more grounded, anchored self. A self-engaged in the world around us.

At some point, my aspirations would arise. Maybe I'd want to go back to school. Maybe I'd want to start working. Some desire to build a life would take precedence and the team would be there for me. Supporting me in moving my life forward. The basic idea being that as my life progresses, I have less and less time for the team. As I start to fill my schedule, fill my life, the team would begin to fade away. I could maintain working with a minimal team, seeing my therapist and team leader once a week, or I could move on to living my life outside of treatment.

I'd have a life that was built within the "walls" of the Windhorse community. This is one of the most beautiful things about the Windhorse Approach. It is not a facility somewhere, it is set in a city. I rent my own apartment (obviously with some family money) as I make progress on the journey and am ready to be discharged. I have built a life for myself. This is not like other treatment facilities, where you find some grounding, some healing, then are thrown back into your life, expected to put the pieces back together.

Sometimes when I imagine spending time with a Windhorse community, I wonder if anything would be that different. Maybe my recovery journey would take a similar arc, a six-month acute psychotic break followed by a year and a half of downtime until I was ready to start living again. If this is the case, I cannot imagine the relief.

I cannot imagine how it would feel to not be alone through my journey. To have support. To have community. To have human contact. To not be perpetually trapped in the mindset of self-hate and shame I had descended into.

I cannot imagine how it would feel to have a community to help pull me out of myself and remember the wider world around me. Help me to remember the me before my break. The me who loved to read, be in nature, and have connected conversations. The me who was interested in the mind, interested in living a healthy life, interested in finding a place for myself in the world. Maybe the team could have held these aspects of myself for me while subsumed by the inner struggle I was immersed in post-break.

I think a lot of the world knows now how vital human contact is. How essential it is to our health and well-being to be in a relationship with others. I would give anything to not have been alone for that year and a half. To have had ongoing human contact.

I imagine that with human contact, I would have felt more support, more willingness to try putting my life back together again. I would have had the security of knowing I had a team supporting me on my journey of recovery. I imagine I would have been able to move toward a functional, independent living much sooner, with more confidence and less doubt about whether it was possible to go on living after a period of madness.

And whether I recovered "quicker" doesn't matter. No one should be alone in their struggle. A struggle as immense as a psychotic break requires an equal amount of support. It requires human support.

Section Three:

Expertise by Experience

WHILE I AM indebted to the many thinkers within the psychological space who have contributed support to the healing and recovery from psychosis, psychology is not the realm of my experience. It is an aspect of it. My experience is rooted in a more contemplative framework.

I relate to the mind as a rich tapestry of experience, states, and ways of being. My mind is not individual to me. Mind is connected to Mind, one might say in Buddhism.

I remember listening to a talk by th well known buddhist scholar, Robert Thurman at a local Tibetan Buddhist Center. He told a story of wanting to meditate when he was young, while living in a monastery in Mongolia, but the abbot wouldn't let him. So Robert would sneak outside at night to secretly meditate and, like clockwork, his teacher would come out and interfere.

Eventually, Robert said in frustration, "Why won't you let me meditate? Aren't I here to meditate?" His teacher responded emphatically, "Robert, you think you have mind, but you don't realize you are a part of Mind," and then suggested they go have some yogurt.

From a contemplative framework, I am interested in the creation and maintenance of a separate sense of self or what is often called ego. This section will explore the formation of a madness-based ego to navigate the unique experiences that emerge when our sensory gating channels are abruptly opened. I will also offer some perspectives on how to support gating channels in closing their aperture to slow the speed of mind and allow folks to co-participate again in a more grounded consensus-based reality while maintaining connection to their personal reality.

Diagnosis

I have been at my father's for a few months and in the beginning of losing myself. Losing myself to the endless voice in my head telling me to kill myself. My voice.

My mother calls me. She is reaching out. We have not spoken in months. She lets me know she will help me get support. She can help pay for me to see a psychiatrist or a therapist.

I get angry, tell her I am not crazy, and hang up the phone. We will not speak for over a year.

I do not remember this story. It was told to me later. Years after my madness, once I was recovered.

Just today, I was with a young man. He is not "crazy." He does not have a formal diagnosis of psychosis. He is just a young man who struggles with pretty bad anxiety that has shaped and governed his life for years.

Years ago, my client went to his doctor to seek support. He has IBS (irritable bowel syndrome), expressed as pain in his stomach and diarrhea. The doctor placed him on a series of medications, including anti-anxiety medication. The doctor informed my client he has generalized anxiety disorder. IBS is often linked to anxiety.

This client had no idea what his new diagnosis meant. His doctor did not explain what a diagnosis was. He was not told why individuals are given a mental health diagnosis by the medical industry or what he could "do" about his diagnosis. He was provided the medication, the diagnosis, and sent on his way. As if the diagnosis and medication were one and the same.

This client had no idea a psychological diagnosis is not the same as a medical diagnosis. Typically, a medical diagnosis points to a known biologically-based medical condition that can be treated through Western medicine. This is not true of psychological diagnosis.

For years, my client thought his anxiety was "just something I have to deal with," his "illness." He had no idea that people recover from generalized anxiety. He did not know there were things he could do to help heal from the past that were impacting him presently through his anxiety symptoms.

The client wasn't aware of the plethora of "tools" like breathing techniques, mindfulness, and other re-emerging strategies to support downshifting the nervous system and addressing anxiety in the moment. Nor did he know there is the possibility of being free from crippling anxiety in the future. None of this was provided to him when he received his diagnosis from his primary care provider. He was told, this is what you have: generalized anxiety disorder. He was provided with no other option than to take this medication.

Although he just brought up his diagnosis with me today, we have been months into working together. He has started to see some progress, some change in his relationship to anxiety. He no longer experiences the severe stomach pain of IBS or some of the other extreme features of his anxiety. He is starting to have difficult conversations with people he has been anxiously avoiding. He is beginning to think about his future and the life he wants to live after years of being crippled by the limitations of his anxiety. He has started the often long journey of processing the traumatic past still significantly impacting his nervous system in the present.

Now the client feels less hostage to his anxiety. He is learning that his anxiety is a signal from his body, sometimes accurate but often misguided. He is starting to learn to calm himself, to talk himself off the ledge of anxiety.

Today in our session, he needed to process. He needed to process the anger he was feeling toward his doctor, the one who diagnosed him years before. His anger was rooted in receiving a diagnosis and medication without being provided a map, a way of navigating through his generalized anxiety disorder. He told me he did not want to be on medication for the rest of his life. Yet, he thought that is what he "needed" to do to "manage" his anxiety. As his anxiety improves, he is starting to question his assumption, the assumption he would be medicated for his entire life.

I started to tell him some of my views on diagnosis. I wanted to be careful, careful to not sway him to "my side" or "my view" of diagnosis, while also wanting to provide him an alternative to the lack of story he was provided when he was diagnosed. At the end of the day, psychological diagnoses are more stories than medical illnesses. Diagnosis is our attempt to understand the complicated and mysterious forms human suffering takes. We need stories to heal. Stories of possibility. Maps of the journey we are to go through on our unique healing path. Stories help us make sense of our experience and the world.

For millennia, we have told stories to understand the varieties of human suffering, particularly madness. The Greeks had stories about humors being off balance. Stories of satanic possession in the Dark Ages. Animal magnetism in the Victorian Era. The more recent story of libidinal energy. Now we have a story of chemical imbalances to make sense of madness.

For me, the story I needed was witnessing the life Paul had lived after his years of madness. He showed me, through being a living example, that there was a way to move beyond the limited story provided by the Western medical model. He was a testament to living a wholehearted life post-madness, a life that was grounded and connected to community. *He* became my story. A story of possibility. I had no other maps. Just a friend who had been there and lived through it. Paul also showed me it was possible to identify with an experience of madness while living outside the story of Western medicine.

I knew one thing when I left my father's basement: I was unwilling to start again, to put my life back together, if it was just going to fall apart due to some genetic condition I inherited. A condition that would inevitably lead to a future of psychotic breaks and the ongoing deterioration of my life and brain. This was the only story I knew. One of schizophrenia.

While in my father's basement, I had yet to do the research, to hear the stories of others who have recovered from psychotic breaks and gone on to live full, rich lives. These stories are not shared by our media or by the psychological industry. The only story is one of "maintenance," getting by until the next break.

This story terrified me. It most likely stalled me for months. When I was starting to feel "ready" and able to move forward, the fear of being condemned to a life of ongoing madness did not feel worth the effort of putting my life together again, after everything had so drastically collapsed. I could feel the years ahead of me, rebuilding my life. What would be the point if it was just going to fall apart due to another break?

When I finally gathered the courage to leave the basement, I knew I was going to have to leave behind a Western psychological understanding of madness to make it through the journey. I knew I could not rely on mainstream psychological services. I was unwilling to take on the story of "broken" and needing "maintenance." Or of having a life that could resemble "normal." I've never wanted "normal." I've always wanted to live fully.

I was interested in wholehearted living. Of expressing my life physically, relationally, and spiritually. Of growing, healing, and loving. Of seeing where this life might take me.

In order to do this, to go on living, I had to leave the basement without a map. Without a story of healing, of possibility. I knew the story I was provided through culture and my minimal undergraduate psychological training was not going to be sufficient for the journey I was going to take. I was unwilling to receive a diagnosis.

So, I stepped forward blindly. I started to "put my life back together." I ignored the suggestions not to meditate. I committed again to spiritual practice. I did the foolish thing of working in a group home for severe and persistent mental illness. I saw firsthand how the "mad" were treated.

And I began to read. To study. To look over the many stories of recovery living on the internet. I started to understand the Western medical model's story of schizophrenia was just one privileged story among many stories of recovery.

It was through meeting Paul, seeing someone who had lived fully into his 80s, that I knew I could go my own way and not end up lost in a sea of madness. I at least knew it was possible.

Paul showed me I could forgo the Western map as there was another possibility for healing. It was at Windhorse that I more fully learned the nuance of supporting recovery, even seeing some of the intuitive "steps" I took that helped me in my recovery.

Through my journey of trying to unwind myself from the medical model's stories of psychological illnesses concerning extreme states, I've had to make sense of diagnosis. I've had to understand the thing I wanted to leave behind. How could I understand the depth of impact diagnosis implicitly has without understanding the thing itself?

Through my attempts to understand diagnosis, I came to the conclusion that the history of diagnosis is rooted in a fundamental confusion around mental health. Mental health symptoms are not illnesses. They are often corrective mechanisms of the mind, an attempt to bring about healing to restore balance.

As I began to share my views of diagnosis with my client, I also started to tell him what he wasn't told. That he could recover from his generalized anxiety disorder. That it is possible. I let him know I have witnessed people learn to heal from their past and restore their present-day nervous system.

He looked at me and said, "Really? I can do something about this?" I told him with honesty, "Yes." I did qualify that not everyone can heal. Not everyone grows in ways where they move past their diagnosis. But it is possible and many do.

I saw in him the beginnings of hope, of possibility, of something to work toward. He now has the growing motivation to heal. To face the difficulties of his past. To learn to meet his anxiety and to learn the most difficult thing for him, being honest with the people in his life.

This client's experience is not unique. Most people are provided a diagnosis without any understanding of what a diagnosis is. Without an understanding of the scientific evidence that allows medical providers to give a mental health diagnosis, or when there is a lack of this evidence.

Mental health diagnoses are not "illnesses" in our traditional sense of the word. We cannot test for a mental health diagnosis like we can for a viral infection. We cannot do blood work and determine someone's mental health "illness." Instead, mental health diagnoses are referred to as symptom categories. They are clusters of symptoms, grouped together without a biological or underlying physiological reason for this grouping.

The only supplied reasoning in the grouping of symptoms is because they are often seen together in other patients. Usually, mental health diagnosis comes with the qualifier of having 4 of 7 of that diagnosis' symptoms. If you meet the minimum number of symptoms, you meet the criteria for a diagnosis. Symptoms allow us to make sense of human suffering by categorizing the suffering into diagnostic categories.

If you look at the criteria for a diagnosis of schizophrenia, one of the more relevant diagnoses to a conversation about madness, an individual must display two or more of the following symptoms: delusions, hallucinations, disorganized speech, grossly disorganized or catatonic behavior, or negative symptoms. For the diagnosis, these symptoms must be present with a marked decrease in functioning in areas such as work, interpersonal relationships, or self-care.

This is the crux of most mental health diagnoses. The symptoms themselves do not matter. What matters is the functional impact of the symptoms. If an individual is able to meaningfully navigate their lives, having hallucinations, delusions, or disorganized speech does not warrant a diagnosis of schizophrenia.

Originally, diagnoses were only used by therapists to talk to other therapists. Individuals were rarely provided their diagnosis. It was a shorthand way for therapists to describe the "type" of client they were working with without needing to go into elaborate detail when consulting with colleagues.

The roots are not even "biological" or "scientific." Many of our common diagnoses have roots in Freudian psychoanalysis, which sees mental health symptoms as expressions of pathology in the development of early childhood sexuality. Before chemical imbalances were the main explanation of depression, there was castration anxiety and oedipal complexes. Essentially, if you were depressed, you had complicated sexual feelings toward your parents or sometimes siblings.

Eventually, therapy started to be integrated into the medical model. Integrated into insurance benefits. Therapists were able to be reimbursed for their services. This is not inherently a bad thing as it made therapy more affordable for those who had insurance. But it had its downfalls.

In order to enter into the medical model, into the world of insurance, therapists were required to provide a medical diagnosis to the insurance company to prove that the therapeutic services met medical necessity. Through medical necessity, therapists were able to "justify" to insurance companies the continued reimbursement of therapy for their clients.

As time went on and the pharmacological industry gained power and impact over the medical industry, the use of medications was often linked to a mental health disorder. This drug helps with this diagnosis. (Think antidepressants for depression.) Pharmacological companies began to need to prove that their medications were helpful for the "clusters" of symptoms. That they allowed for symptom reduction and improved functioning for the client.

From here, you can start to see the "destigmatization" of mental health disorders. Making it normal for people to have mental health challenges and to receive treatment for those "illnesses." Treatments were often directly tied to pharmacological products.

In one way, this is incredibly helpful. By normalizing mental health diagnoses and symptoms, you are letting people know it is okay to receive treatment and to seek the help you need. Humans need help. It is hard to be human. Sometimes we need pharmacological help.

What is not understood so well is the underlying stories embedded within mental health diagnoses. Most biological or medical illnesses have symptoms, with the symptoms pointing to an illness that can be healed through medical intervention. Mental health diagnoses are symptoms without illnesses.

We do not know why people demonstrate the symptoms they do from a physiological perspective, especially madness. Occasionally, a medical illness can impact mental health. For example, a thyroid disorder and certain infections like Lyme disease can affect the personality. But these illnesses can be tested for, and then one's depression can be ruled out as a symptom of the disease or disorder.

When there is not an underlying medical reason for the mental health symptoms, we really don't know why they happen. Our current theories are rooted in chemical imbalances in the brain, which are often inherited through the genetics of a parent who also struggles with mental health symptoms. I like to think of this as our current myth of madness.

We've had countless myths of madness. Madness has been with us since there have been humans. Humans love to privilege their myths above other people's myths. Joseph Cambell, the late mythologist who informs a lot of my thinking on mythology, has a famous saying, "Myths are other people's religion."

A lot of people think our culture has "moved past" religion. We are in an era of science, post-religion, where rationality and observable reality are the dominant ways of understanding the world. To me, this is just another religion. It is a worldview that orients people to themselves, others, and the world at large. Unfortunately for mental health "illnesses," there is little evidence of a "chemical" imbalance theory of madness.

Upon leaving his position, Thomas Insel, the former head of the National Institute of Mental Health and the current head of the United States' research around mental health, called into question the theory of chemical imbalance:

> *"Whatever we've been doing for five decades, it ain't working... When I look at the numbers - the number of suicides, the number of disabilities, the mortality data - it's abysmal, and it's not getting any better. Maybe we just need to rethink this whole approach."*[15]

When our own head of research is challenging the current privileged myth of chemical imbalance, you know something is up.

He argues that we should begin to explore electrical signaling in the brain, which seems smart in a way. The brain is built as an electrical system, moving

15 Greenberg G. The Rats of N.I.M.H. May 2013.

information through the currents of electrical flow. If you're going to "help" the brain, this is probably another place to look.[16]

But it completely misses the point for me. Instead of trying to find the "right" myth of madness, it is time we start to understand the underlying function of myth, especially a myth of madness. This should be the real function of a diagnosis. Mental health diagnoses do not need to be "medical illnesses." Instead, they are stories that help us understand our unique flavor of human suffering and how to navigate through that suffering.

After studying the world's mythologies for his career, Joseph Campbell beautifully articulated the four functions of myth. He broke it down this way.

> *The first function is to evoke a sense of grateful, affirmative awe before the mystery that is existence.*

What if we were to imagine our symptoms as an expression of the mystery that is existence? For most people, symptoms are something to be overcome, a barrier to living. From my view, symptoms originate in health. They are our body/heart/mind's way of letting us know something is off. There is an imbalance in our lives.

In depression, people usually begin to feel flat, dead inside, when they are not able to make a change they know will be best for them. So often, with help, building the courage and growth needed to make life changes lifts their depression.

Could it be possible that depression is trying to help us make the changes we need to live a more fulfilling life? Is it possible that symptoms are really health emerging, attempting to support us in change? In that mysterious way life often works, could the symptoms be worthy of our awe and appreciation for their function in helping us heal?

---

16 Thomas R. Incel. Faulty Circuits. Scientific American. April 2010.

The second function of myth is to provide an image of the mystery of existence that will help you maintain connection with the mystery of life.

How might we understand our human struggle as an expression of life's generative healing capacity? Our current image of mental health illness is a chemical imbalance in the brain. It is an image that captures a worldview of separate selves, isolated, who have limited agency to affect their experience.

According to this view, our psychological foundations are laid out by our genetics or early childhood experiences. They are so foundational that they become concretized into a set of chemicals in our brains that determine our ability to function, find meaning, and lead fulfilling lives.

Our current images of mental health disorders are of "brokenness" or "weakness." What if we saw mental health struggles as opportunities instead? As signs of needed healing and an opportunity to attend to our lives? To give attention to facets of our experience, our life, and our world in need of support and growth? What image might capture this story?

Currently, we have a broken brain as the image. And for me, I do not know that this image of mental health captures the complexity and beauty of symptoms and their role in supporting healing. A new image is needed.

The third function is to provide, validate and maintain a certain sociological system, a shared set of understanding.

So much of our current understanding of mental illness is rooted in maintaining a certain worldview. A medically oriented, materialist worldview that sees the brain as chemicals and consciousness living inside its neural firing. This just isn't my worldview. This worldview of brain-based disorders has done little to move forward the healing of mental health struggles. Even currently, much of the "advancement" in mental health is a return to ritualistic psychedelic use.

If a myth is not generative, if it does not support culture, what is its value? Myths are not true. They are helpful. Our current myth of madness is not helpful. We have not received a return on our investment. The billions of dollars spent in research hunting chemical theories of the origins of madness have been wasted.

Why not put the same money into developing healing communities? We know community is one of the primary curative agents when supporting recovery.

> *The fourth function is to help an individual move through the stages of life, to move through the healing and growth that is required in their life.*

Currently, our mythological structure of providing diagnoses only honors the third function, to validate a certain sociological system. The system of the medical model and its understanding of how to treat illness. A reductive approach that sees the brain as the root cause of most mental health illnesses. A view that does not take into account a person's history, the culture they grew up in, or their unique temperament.

What if we were to start to see diagnosis as a holistic myth? A myth that connected us to the greater mystery of life, that placed us in a meaningful and rich mystery, that allowed us to maintain meaningful engagement with our culture and society, and – most importantly – provided a map of moving through the healing journey?

What if we started to include the many stories of recovery that exist outside of the medical model's worldview? What if we became curious about all the ways people move through recovery, widening our understanding of what's possible and what stories support this possibility of recovery?

I never allowed myself to be formally diagnosed during my healing journey. I hung up the phone on my mom at the prospect of having to receive a diagnosis. Our current diagnoses of madness are not diagnoses of illness. They are more akin to curses.

Remember that the first significant movement toward our modern conceptualization of disorders like schizophrenia, bipolar disorder, and schizoaffective disorder was the publication of *The English Malady*. In the 1700s, an English "nobleman" declared that some of the mental health struggles in Victorian England were actually the product of being "civilized." They were signs of being a part of the "in group," the privileged elite. Illnesses and symptoms that were not part of *The English Malady* were considered primitive illnesses, reflective of a person's poor upbringing and family history. Madness fell into this category.

Do you notice how in the process of de-stigmatizing mental health, of normalizing mental health symptoms and diagnosis, it is commonplace now to admit to depression and anxiety? It is a safe thing to say. People might say, "Everyone suffers from those at some point in time." For me, this is rooted in the history of *The English Malady*.

You do not hear people normalizing "hearing voices" or auditory hallucinations as a typical part of the human experience. Yet, upwards of 60 percent of people report hearing voices in their lifetime, one of the primary symptoms of schizophrenia.[17] Almost the same number of people will report having "mystical" experiences, being connected to a larger universe, to God, losing the boundaries of self and becoming part of all that is.[18] They experience a common quality of madness, feelings of specialness, of being connected to a larger order in the universe. These experiences are rarely talked about.

Remember also the research project from the 70s, the Rosenhan experiment, where people voluntarily entered a psychiatric hospital reportedly hearing a

17 Jim Van Os. "New Visions for Psychiatry". Madness Radio. March 21st, 2016.

18 Russell Heimlich. Mystical Experiences. Pew Research Center. December 29, 2009.

voice saying their name. They were often hospitalized for months. It's an experience that happened to me early in my recovery journey, hearing an auditory hallucination say my name.

Imagine if I went to the hospital at this time and told them I was scared after hearing an inner voice that was not my own say my name throughout the day. Especially if I told them I had recently recovered from an acute psychotic break. I would most definitely be given the diagnosis of schizophrenia and placed on medication. Much like the client I described earlier, I would be provided a diagnosis that had no road map of healing built into it.

When you look at the history of schizophrenia, you see something far darker than the stories around generalized anxiety disorder. I think this is one of the most important things to take in if you are on a recovery journey. To know the damning effects of any of the madness-based diagnoses.

As I mentioned, in the late 1800s, Emil Kraepelin was the first to separate out multiple diagnoses of madness, or lunacy as it was called at the time. He distinguished dementia praecox, the precursor to schizophrenia, and manic depressive disorder, the precursor to bipolar disorder.

With the separation of these illnesses, Kraepelin designated dementia praecox as the no-way-back illness. For him, to have this diagnosis meant you would never heal. You were destined to deteriorate further and further. Similar to an illness like Alzheimer's, there is no way back.

Just think about this. If looking at this as a story, a type of myth, Emil made a category of illness without having any biological indicators of a brain-based disorder. He decided that schizophrenia is a brain-based disorder rooted in the ongoing deterioration of the brain.

In a horrible twist of faith, the way life is so often ironic, this is what schizophrenia has become. This is mostly due to the ongoing use of antipsychotic medication which slowly deteriorates the brain over long time usage, leading to increases in schizophrenia symptoms and more frequent psychotic breaks in the long run. And it's coupled with a lack of supportive care to navigate recovering from extreme states. No one questions this because it is the expectation of the illness. A historical expectation, to deteriorate over time.

We know this is not true. In Finland's Open Dialogue program, over 70 percent of people recover.[19] In non-western countries, you are far more likely to recover from a psychotic break than if living in a western country like the United States. There is even evidence that if an individual does not receive any treatment, they will recover at a rate of 30 percent.[20] This makes no treatment the better treatment for madness-based disorders in America.

This is why I say "it's not worth it" to modern diagnoses. They serve no purpose. They do more harm than good. Even if they are helpful in the way of helping someone find meaning through their symptoms, they do not help the person recover. They do not point to the possibility of healing.

I am going to tell you something, something I often don't share with others, something I keep to myself. I think "diagnoses" are utterly full of shit. Our human struggles – our depressions, our anxieties, our compulsions, our madnesses – are the ground from which we transform.

Our diagnoses are how we become the people we are meant to be. Not our diagnoses so much, but our symptoms. We like to categorize our suffering into diagnoses to create distance from them. "I have this." "I have that." What we all have is suffering. It is through our suffering that we grow. Human suffering sometimes falls into typical patterns, maybe as simple as depression, anxiety, and psychosis. It's probably more complicated than that, but not by much.

In my view, it is through struggle that we heal and become who we are meant to be in this world. Our struggle is our gift. It is what allows us to heal. To find our unique place in the cosmos. My struggle brought me here to you through writing this book. I am grateful for my struggle.

To me, our symptoms are angels, our helpers sent here to support us in becoming the people we need to be in the world. The world needs humans who

---

19 Seikkula, J., Alakare, B. & Aaltonen, J. (2011). The comprehensive open-dialogue approach (II). Long-term stability of acute psychosis outcomes in advanced community care: The Western Lapland Project

20 Warner, R. (2004). Recovery from schizophrenia: Psychiatry and political economy. Brunner-Routledge.

have healed. Who have gained compassion and wisdom. Who understand suffering and the resiliency at the core of human beings.

We need to understand the deep possibility of transformation that is inherent to all human beings because there is a lot of transformation needed to begin to heal the state of our world, of our planet. And we need deep-seated confidence in knowing that people do heal. There is a path forward from the suffering, from the crushing depression, from the madness. There is a way toward harmony, connection, and joy. We are the ones who lay the groundwork for what is possible.

Until there is a formal medical diagnosis where madness is considered a normal human experience that some of us go through, a journey where most people heal and where it is acknowledged that human connection and decency are the best "medications," I will not subscribe to diagnosis.

Our diagnosis needs to be updated, to move beyond Kraepelin's basic and flawed understanding of madness. Madness is not an ongoing deterioration of the brain. It is something else. Something more mysterious and confusing than our limited stories of science can capture. Not to romanticize madness, but to honor it. Madness does not make sense. How can we go about making sense of something that is inherently rooted in senselessness?

Our diagnoses have to acknowledge that human suffering is normal. To suffer is to be human. We must start to see our "symptoms" as guides in transforming our lives to become healthier and fuller expressions of who we are.

We also need a shared understanding of suffering and how to be there for others when they are in acute phases of human suffering. To not see our catastrophic mental health struggles as failure of the "person," but see them as opportunities to come together to support a loved one who needs to find their way home. We might all need that support at some point in our lives.

If you find your diagnosis helpful, I hear you. Having a story can be so grounding and clarifying. I just hope that it holds the possibility of full recovery, of living wholeheartedly.

Sensitivity

I had a friend who was also a mentor. My first spiritual mentor. He helped me after an "opening" in college. Helped me adjust to living in a vibrant universe, not the dead universe I had been living in since leaving Christianity.

When he was in his twenties, somehow – he never shared the details – he ended up "carrying medicine" for a traditionally trained Native American. He was asked to help his native mentor when traveling and assist in healings and clearings.

My friend would describe how his teacher prepared him for his role. The teacher would take him into the forest and "doctor" him into an intense, overwhelming state of mind. A state that felt like overwhelming fear. This would prepare him to not be afraid while doing clearing work.

My friend told me how after those trips with his teacher, he would go into the hardware store or be in line to get groceries and "feel" everyone's stories around him. He said he would know the depth of their lives, "while I was just trying to buy nails."

It would take my friend years to learn to turn down the sensitivity required to help his teacher with his healing practices. Where he could go from a heightened awareness to a more mundane awareness when needed. Where he could learn to just "buy nails."

People who suffer from periods of madness are often described as being sensitive, typically overly sensitive. After a child has a severe mental health crisis, parents often reflect on how especially sensitive the child was while growing up. They give examples of their child having intense emotional reactions, feeling overwhelmed by the world, and being strongly impacted by those around them. Where their kid was not able to be consoled by their parents in a "normal" way.

This anecdotal information doesn't come from psychological assessments or brain scans, but from family members who've watched their children grow up. Parents with multiple children will report that the child who struggles with madness has been more sensitive than their other kids. Like my friend and mentor described above. He was sensitive.

This is probably why he was asked by his teacher to help him "carry medicine." He had a type of innate sensitivity. Maybe it is part of his temperament, a word used to describe our template when we are born.

Some people are high energy, some are low energy. Some people are extroverted, some are introverted. Some people are impulsive, others are hesitant. It is thought that these traits are part of the temperament we are provided when born. Some folks have a sensitive temperament.

It is also clear that people's sensitivities are impacted by their life experiences. They become more sensitive from what they go through in life. This might be early childhood events or even later in life near-death experiences. Or engaging in intensive spiritual practice.

My mother struggled with depression when I was younger. My parents separated at a young age and she was left to provide for both of us while putting herself through law school. I most likely became extra sensitive to other people's moods and inner emotional life due to my mom's depressive tendencies and the amount of burden she took on as a single mother. I was sensitive to being "too much" for her, so I would learn to track how she was impacted by my presence. This wasn't conscious learning on my part, but more of a survival mechanism. Like how a child will learn to make their depressed father laugh and go on to be a comedian.

My learning serves me well now as a therapist, having an almost hyper-attention to individuals' underlying emotional landscapes. It was often a struggle growing up, being hyper-aware of others' emotional landscapes, what others sometimes call an empath.

I don't identify with the label of empath personally. At younger ages, I didn't know how to interpret the underlying emotional information I was picking up from others. I often assumed anyone's negative mood or reaction was about me, making my awareness of others self-centered. Because I learned this "skill" as a child, it was rooted in a self-centered protective function, scanning others to make sure I was safe.

Even after growing up, I would still assume others' reactions are due to my actions. Over time, I learned to suspend assumptions about why someone feels the way they do. I learned to either check in with them or allow them to have their feelings in private. It took a while, but I can be aware of others' underlying experiences now and not assume it is directly correlated with me.

I am probably a combo of having an innate sensitive temperament and my sensitivity being amplified by the environment I grew up in as a child. I used my sensitivity to track other people's emotions and inner landscapes. In a way, training myself to be attuned to others' inner lives for my own safety. This is not uncommon.

In my mentor's case, his sensitivity wasn't trained from a young age like his teacher's was. His teacher was "traditionally trained." This is a term used to describe someone who is trained in a lineage or tradition that has a long history and training method – in this case, with indigenous roots – particularly around learning to work with sensitivity or altered state experiences for healing, divination, and other spiritual functions.

From my White, Western interpretation, I see indigenous or traditional societies as having long known that some individuals are born more sensitive than others. These individuals are often recognized at a young age, just as parents today recognize their children's sensitivities at a young age.

Within traditional societies, I imagine longstanding lineages of healing and working with sensitivity which allow individuals to learn to use their sensitivities and become a benefit to others through work as healers. For many, this is an arduous training, like the one my friend went through.

In our modern world, we often send our sensitive children to receive mental health and psychiatric treatment, where they are defined as "pathological" and provided therapeutic and medical interventions to "adjust" to their home and school life with less disruption. Most providers in the medical industry are not "sensitive" themselves and have never had to learn to live with the sensitivities their clients struggle with. They do not know how to teach these kids to navigate their sensitivities, like my mentor's teacher was able to guide him to learn to work with his.

For as long as it seems humans have been around, there are those of us who are more sensitive. When I say sensitive, I do not mean emotional or easily damaged by others. This is one of the common definitions of sensitive: easily damaged, injured, or distressed by slight changes. When parents are referring to their children as sensitive, they are often pulling from this definition.

I am referring to a more basic definition of sensitive: quick to detect or respond to slight changes, signals, or influences. Both of these definitions include the same phenomenon of being able to detect slight changes. The easily damaged definition refers to how someone is impacted by their sensitivity. The second definition refers to the basic phenomenon which is sensitivity: able to detect subtleties.

I imagine that being sensitive in pre-modern cultures was seen as a blessing and a curse, an innate capacity that one needed to learn to work with to navigate life coherently without being overwhelmed by their sensitivities. It often caused people who were sensitive to be different, to be a sort of outsider who perceived and experienced life differently than others. But this wasn't seen as a pathology as it is seen today.

I bet many people feel that homeless individuals clearly lost to their other world perceive and experience life differently than others. Yet, in more traditional societies, individuals who were taught to work with their sensitivities provide a valuable offering to their communities. They are the ones who can help community members navigate difficult periods in life, help with transitions, and understand struggle in an intimate way. They are the counselors, healers, and diviners.

Modern neuroscience understands the challenge of managing this sensitivity when experiencing psychosis:

> *"A fundamental feature of information processing dysfunctions in psychosis is the inability of these patients to screen out, inhibit, filter and gate extraneous stimuli and to attend selectively to salient features of the environment. Gating deficits may cause these subjects to become overloaded with excessive exteroceptive and interoceptive stimuli, which in turn could lead to a breakdown in cognitive integrity and difficulty in distinguishing self from nonself"*[21]

One of the keywords to focus on is gating. When family members refer to their children as sensitive, most likely they are referring to the child's sensory gating capacities. Sensory gating refers to an individual's ability to filter out "unnecessary" stimuli in order to maintain focus on the necessary tasks of living. Think of tuning out the noise at a coffee shop to focus on reading or the work you are doing.

We are constantly gating the world around us, filtering the amount of "information" we receive from the environment. When we deem a stimulus to not be "salient" or of value to us, we start to habitually tune it out. Most people go through their lives tuned out to the world around them, only focusing on the aspects of their experience or environment they deem "worthy" of their attention.

Sensitive kiddos often don't have this choice of gating sensory information that is not needed. In my case, instead of tuning out my mom's subtler depressive tendencies, I was hyper-focused on them. I focused my gating on an aspect of my environment, in this case, the underlying emotional field. With this focus, I "trained" myself to perceive aspects of the environment most people tune out. I think it is safe to say that many people in my life would say I have an uncanny ability to perceive subtle emotional currents.

---

21 Franz X. Vollenweider, MD. Brain mechanisms of hallucinogens and entactogens Dialogues Clin Neurosci. 2001 Dec; 3(4): 265–279.

Sensitive individuals often adapt to their sensitives over their lifetime, refining their ability to be with their unique gating system. Psychosis is often different. Due to whatever cocktail or incident that invokes the psychotic break, an individual's gating system will be blasted open, fundamentally altering the way they perceive and make sense of the informational reality they are swimming in. Essentially overnight.

One way to think of psychosis is a flooding of this sensory gating system, where the ability to filter out stimuli – or as I refer to it, information from the environment – is severely impacted. People in psychosis often experience their gating system being blasted open.

I know for myself, that in my psychosis, I was overwhelmed by the amount of information I was able to perceive moment to moment. Much like my mentor, I would "feel" everything around me.

Whether I was accurately feeling is a different question. But I was perceiving layer upon layer of extra information from the environment. I was often unable to make sense of the flood of sensory information. I struggled to make meaning out of the sea of experience I was continuously drifting through, like an astronaut hurdled into space, unable to direct myself, continually in motion with no way of stopping.

Within my psychosis, the gating moved beyond the subtle emotional tones of the environment. I started to perceive aspects of the environment I had never imagined perceiving.

When modern neuroscience refers to the challenges of sensory gating for individuals experiencing psychosis, it is perceived as a "deficit," with a normal person's ability to filter out information being praised. It is one of the few biological indicators the Western medical model has for an individual who has either become psychotic or has the potential of doing so. An inability to filter out unnecessary information from the environment.

This is verified through a simple hearing test, where an individual is played two clicks in quick succession. A "normal" individual will tune out the second click and only hear one. Someone with a "deficit" in sensory gating will hear both clicks.

It is a totally silly example but I cannot wear glasses. I need them. My eyesight is shit. But when I wear glasses, I cannot "tune out" the glasses. I always see them on my face and they continuously distract me. So I don't wear glasses.

When people train in mindfulness, in practicing meditation – which is so valued by our culture currently as evidenced by the degree of funding for research and the number of magazines promoting mindfulness at grocery stores – these individuals decrease their sensory gating through the process of learning meditation. They are actually training to intentionally create a "deficit" in sensory gating.

Meditation studies from the 70s would try to measure meditators' increased capacity to "pay attention," one of the primary goals of meditation. They had this study where subjects would listen to clicks through headphones. The clicks were subtle and faint.

The "average" person, through sensory gating, learns to block out the clicks after they realize they are not helpful to listen to. A meditator, on the other hand, particularly Zen meditators, will continue to hear the clicks. Essentially, through their meditation practices, they have learned to open their sensory gating to allow more information to flow into their experience. And to tune out less, in this case, the clicks that are normally tuned out. [22]

When scientists are trying to determine if someone has schizophrenia, they use a similar test called the auditory paired-click paradigm. This involves playing clicking sounds close together. If the individual is able to hear both clicks, they are considered to have a sensory gating deficit that correlates to a potential for schizophrenia.

The interesting thing to consider here is the limitation of what is being measured. The way scientists can externally observe an individual's sensitivity is through this basic sound test. It is currently one of the only tests to determine someone's likelihood of having a psychotic break.

---

22 David E Becker, David Shapiro. Journal of Psychophysiology. Volume 18, Issue 6. November 1981.

If you read or listen to firsthand accounts of people experiencing madness, they report a wide phenomenon of sensory information impacting them, not just increased noise from the environment. Scientists and the Western medical model do not like to admit the possibility that individuals with "sensitivities" might be detecting information from the environment that they are not able to measure or understand.

In the contemplative tradition of Buddhism, we are thought to have six senses, not five. They believe that we have the typical senses of sight, hearing, touch, taste, and smell. But they also see the mind, our ability to be cognizant of ourselves, as our sixth sense, though they are not necessarily referring to extrasensory perception.

Currently, modern neuroscience is not able to measure one's interior, to measure a person's mind. It does not know what others feel, think, and sense. The only way to measure a person's interior experience is through self-report. However, as I have mentioned, individuals who are experiencing madness and given a diagnostic label are often denied subjectivity. Their inner world is denied. It is not considered a valid experience.

Yet, the individuals who have sensory "deficits" are actually more accurately experiencing reality by not tuning out the unnecessary second click. So, we try to have it both ways as a culture. We point out a "deficit" of picking up too much information from the environment while at the same time denying the "reality" of the interior lives of those experiencing madness.

I remember many incidents of clients of mine "picking up" on things in an uncanny way. One time, I had just come from a meeting to see a client. This client was struggling with alcohol, recently drinking more, and being noticeably drunk around others. Trouble was, he lived in a community space where other clients lived.

As I walked up to the client, he looked me square in the eye and asked, "Are you kicking me out of the house?" In the meeting I had just come from, we had discussed the client's housing situation not being sustainable in the long run. How he picked up on this information I do not know. This is a common experience when working with folks experiencing psychosis. They often have a subtle sense of things happening around them that is uncanny.

This doesn't only happen to those with "deficits" in sensory gating, like my patient. My mentor, who I described as sensitive, could sense uncanny things. I remember the first time I drove to his house, I was unable to find it. He called saying, "I felt you outside. You seemed lost." These little examples are easy to explain away, but they add up over time and make it harder to dismiss the information individuals who are "sensitive" are picking up on.

My mentor was not just sensitive in his abilities of sensing. He was also highly skilled at navigating altered states of consciousness. The first time I learned about some of his capacity was from his son, my roommate.

We were sitting around our table having breakfast and my friend started to tell me about his dad being a shaman. I had not heard the word up until this point. I didn't know the history around the word "shaman" and its connection to White academia attempting to understand healing through altered states. My friend didn't believe his dad was a shaman or that a shaman was a real thing. So, my mentor asked his son if he wanted him to prove it. My friend said yes.

The next day, while they were sitting at their breakfast table, my mentor asked his son why he was dreaming about a Catholic church when he was Jewish. At that moment, my friend flashed back to his dream from the night before and remembered seeing his father sitting at the church pews during his dream. With training, this is some of what my mentor learned to do with his sensitivities. Entering others' dreams. Far beyond hearing two clicks.

I know for myself, in my madness, I experienced countless moments of uncanny experiences that would not be validated by the Western medical model. Yet I experienced them. Were they true? It's hard to say. They did happen to me.

My mentor was taught to work with his sensitivities. My sensitive client was not trained. My client entered treatment in his teens. He was medicated from a young age and lost to the other world more than he was able to relationally connect in consensus reality with those around him. In his early twenties, a medical provider even suggested he receive a lobotomy to decrease his sensitivity.

When you look at the meditation studies demonstrating a decrease in sensory gating, it is clear that people have the capacity to train their sensory gating. This capacity is now called neuroplasticity. Shout out again to William James, who first used the term plasticity.

There is little acknowledgment of the reverse process being a possibility, of learning to intentionally increase sensory gating to decrease the information impacting an individual. There is even less acknowledgment of the possibility of opening and closing our sensory gating intentionally, like my mentor who could enter heightened states to do healing work and "come back down" to get groceries and shoot the shit.

I imagine this is entailed in traditional training for individuals who are sensitive. Our culture, our Western dominant culture, has almost negated any possibility of working with consciousness up until recently in modern history. We have lost our ability to support others in navigating sensitives and instead rely on a medical intervention, antipsychotic medication, that traumatizes the brain to reduce sensitivity. An intervention with long-term impacts on individuals' abilities to live full and vibrant lives.

So on one hand, having an innate capacity to attend to stimuli typically gated by "normal" individuals is seen as a deficit. But individuals who are suffering from depression and anxiety are provided specific interventions that decrease their ability to gate out "unwanted" stimuli.

Much modern research looking at the healing and curative effects of psychedelic therapy is rooted in a similar understanding. Researchers are finding strange phenomena. They imagined that live brain scans of individuals on psychedelics like psilocybin mushrooms would show explosions of activity. This was based on reports of intense positive life-changing experiences of participants.

What they are finding instead is a reduction in brain activity. It seems, in a basic way, brains are designed to gate reality from us. When we decrease the activity of our brain, we experience an increase in sensory experience. This is considered healing for those who undergo psychedelic-assisted therapy. Yet for the individual experiencing psychosis or another "information processing dysfunction," it is seen as pathological.

One way to relate to this dichotomy of valuing decreasing sensory gating for healing through meditation and psychedelics while devaluing the same process or "deficit" when referring to individuals experiencing madness is to think of the "wrong medicine at the wrong time." When someone is suffering from madness, it is often time to support the closing of the aperture of their neural gating.

Think of it as a gate that got locked open and needs help in closing. This is the flooding of experience in extreme states, an open gate unable to close, often due to heightened distress. Think of open gating while in fight-or-flight.

We think we are helping individuals by providing antipsychotic medication, which does increase sensory gating. But we are robbing individuals of the opportunity to learn to work with their sensory gating system, like my mentor was able to do when he could "just go get groceries."

In the initial stages of recovery, it is often paramount to close the aperture of gating, to reduce the amount of sensory information entering the system. One of the things that is hard to understand is the rate or processing of information. People in madness are typically processing a flood of information entering their system. To the outside, this processing appears fast and jumbled. Which it often is.

When we slow the information entering our bodily systems, we actually slow our experience. Our thoughts slow, our emotions steady, and we start to feel more in touch with our bodies and environment.

A way to think about this is learning to anchor ourselves into the present-moment sensory experiences happening around us – the sights, sounds, and physical sensations present in the moment. When we learn to anchor our attention in these primary sensory experiences, we are providing ourselves the much-needed time to slow down and begin to process at a slower and steadier rate.

This will be one of the main focuses going forward in this book, learning to slow and anchor our experience into the lived moment. This allows for a letting go of the speed, intensity, and overwhelm of the flood of experience in extreme states.

For me, psychosis is not an "illness" like it is often thought of. It is a gating system blasted open, unable to close. A dam that is locked up. "Healing" comes from supporting the person experiencing psychosis to gradually close the aperture of their gating system in a kind and supportive way. Allowing them to return to a more grounded and consensus-based consciousness not as some end goal, but as the medicine that is helpful for the moment.

Beginning to explore more open expansive gating might be really important to someone's life journey, maybe down the road. Even learning to move between states of open and more closed gating might be part of someone's path.

Unfortunately for many people who experience psychosis, while in blasted-open sensory gating, they begin to make meaning out of the experiences they are having. Experiences that are not rooted in consensus-based reality.

Making Meaning of Experience

> *I am in a Windhorse meeting. So many meetings. This is a large one. A seasonal review. The whole team is there with the client. His parents are calling in from out of state. We are reviewing his last few months in the program.*
>
> *At some point, the client becomes angry, telling the team leader with force that he is "chewing on sticks." The team leader does not know what the client is talking about.*
>
> *The client gets bigger, starting to forcibly repeat that the team leader is "always chewing on sticks." The client has a tendency toward anger, often getting upset during meetings.*
>
> *The team leader looks at another team member and kind of shrugs, moving on, dismissing the statement from the client.*
>
> *I step in, asking the client if he was alluding to the team leader talking about things that are not relevant to the client's treatment. The client affirms, stating something about the team leader "just goin on about nothing."*
>
> *Another team counselor steps in and helps him further express his frustration. We are able to identify the rupture in the meeting and support the team and client in coming together on the same page.*

In the previous chapter, I made a rather radical statement, *individuals who experience psychosis more accurately perceive reality*. This is based on the double-click studies determining sensory gating deficits among individuals provided the psychiatric diagnosis of schizophrenia.

I think this is an inflammatory statement. If taken literally, it would dismiss the deep confusion and suffering of those experiencing psychosis. Yet there is a truth to the statement if you look at the evidence. "Deficits" in sensory gating point to sensitive individuals' ability to perceive phenomena that are filtered out by "sane" or "normal" people's sensory gating process.

Earlier, I stated my intention to avoid the trap of romanticizing madness as an expression of some divinity or to reduce it to brain-based brokenness. My statement that *individuals experiencing psychosis more accurately perceive reality* should be filtered through this polarity.

On one extreme, we could take a divine madness stance, stating that individuals who experience psychosis are more connected to a higher plane of existence. That they can better connect to spiritual dimensions. Those who take this stance, and there are many, often negate the significant suffering, confusion, and disorientation experienced by those in active psychosis. All psychosis is a spiritual emergency, an awakening not fully supported. This is the romantic view. And there is truth in it.

I had numerous experiences I would call "genuine" spiritual experiences while in my state of acute psychosis. Experiences that I still hold today, reflect upon, and continue to make meaning from. At the same time, there was something off. I was unable to stand on both feet during these experiences. I could not integrate the genuine spiritual experiences into my everyday life as my everyday life had fallen away.

There are many ways to hold the value of spiritual experiences. One of the primary ways I relate to the function of spiritual experience is to imbue everyday life with more vitality and meaning while inspiring internal and external changes that often change our everyday reality. Many spiritual experiences are moments of insight and inspiration that support the changing of our everyday habits, perspectives, and ways of relating to ourselves, others, and the world around us.

There is a Hasidic saying, "A spiritual experience is only real when another person hears it." This is where I think the crux of the challenge of the divine madness paradigm misses the essential breakdown of communication in psychosis. Where those who may be genuinely perceiving and participating in a spiritual reality are not able to share that reality with those around them, often leaving these individuals stranded and lost within their unique personal experience.

If someone had not clarified with the client his statement of "chewing on sticks," as a team, we would have dismissed his statement and anger as an expression of his psychosis not as our failure to understand what the client was highlighting about our team dynamics.

On the other hand, we could dismiss evidence from the double-click study, much like dismissing "chewing on sticks." Deny that individuals who suffer from psychotic-like experiences are accurately perceiving reality when they hear both clicks. Dismiss this sensitivity as a "deficit."

By denying the implication of this evidence, we can maintain the collective story of people experiencing madness as not being "connected to reality" and "living in their own world." Yet, people who are "sane" are shaping *their* own worlds, filtering out aspects of reality to make it easier to navigate through life.

We are all deluding ourselves to maintain our story of reality, the delusion being the belief that our perceived reality is itself reality. Not just a cultural consensus that varies through time, culture, and sensory awareness. The only difference between folks who are deemed sane is that others share in their story of reality, hence the phrase consensus reality.

The scientific materialist paradigm is saying that consensus reality is reality. That the reality science can measure, the materialist paradigm, is the only reality that matters. And those who are perceiving outside of the confines of consensus-based reality are wrong. They are not accurately perceiving the constructed reality based on consensus.

Imagine the double-click test from a neutral stance, not thinking about schizophrenia or psychosis. Just a simple test, where you are asked how many clicks you hear and most people hear one click but some hear the actual number of clicks: two. Then imagine that those people who accurately perceived the sound were told they have a deficit and the people who unintentionally blocked out the second click are "right" for not hearing it. It's almost like the people who failed the test were told they passed it.

The whole premise is predicated on "sane" people being the hallmarks of healthy consciousness. Scientists fail to consider the limitations of their sensory gating, what it does to individuals to deny reality around them, consolidating reality to appear to be a certain way to make it easier to navigate. It's like saying that seeing in too many colors is overwhelming so it is better to see in black and white.

I've heard that people who have their sight restored struggle at first. They struggle to make sense of the flood of visual information they are now perceiving. They have not yet been able to make sense of it.

Would we ever tell a person it is better to not see? That seeing is overwhelming and scary so you should go back to being blind? No, we typically try to restore sight at any cost. We help folks who have their vision restored through their transition. Help them make sense of the overwhelming visual field they are now swimming in.

Most people who experience psychotic breaks are being flooded in the same way with a heightened reality they cannot make sense of. They are experiencing things they have never experienced before. They see brighter colors, have a new sense that "picks up" on everything around them, hear voices that are not physically present, and see the world beyond just the physical world, knowing things about others they couldn't know.

For me, the newfound sensory world I was living in during my psychosis was nothing like the world I was living in pre-break.

The walls of my personal self were fairly intact before the break. I did struggle and engaged in spiritual practice to help me open up so I would taste expanded, heightened states of consciousness periodically. But those tastes of expanded consciousness were nothing compared to the kaleidoscopic reality of extreme states.

I could go from being expanded to the size of the cosmos to a small, insignificant void of nothingness in a matter of seconds. I was floating between dream-like realities that were constantly changing and shifting on me. Never solid. Never anything to hold onto. I desperately desired some stability to stand on, some stability of meaning I could hold to make sense of what was happening to me.

What lies between these two polarities, between a romantic fetishizing of divine madness and the dismissal of the interior lives of those who are psychotic? I do not know. A modern Western vision does not yet exist, a story that can capture the reality of sensitivity and the struggle in navigating one's sensitivity.

I imagine traditional cultures have a middle-ground story. A story that allows folks who struggle with their sensitivity to make meaning of their experience while being able to move toward a more grounded functional expression of their sensitivity. Feet on the ground, head in the sky.

If *we* take a more middle-ground approach, acknowledging the apparent truth of the depths of confusion, disorientation, and fear pervading the experience of someone in madness while acknowledging the reality of their sensitivities, what is the middle way forward?

It might be a good time to take a detour into the function of our ego or our "self." Ego is a loaded word. It's actually a mistranslation of Freud. When Freud was being translated from German to English by James Strachey, Strachey thought the original version should be spruced up a bit, made to sound more scientific for the American audience. So, he translated Freud's chosen word "ich" into ego. Ich translates as "I." The ego becomes the "I." There are many ways of conceiving what an ego is, of what it means to be an "I" in this world.

I have a preferred understanding of the term ego. I think there are many interpretations of the term but, for me, ego is the equivalent of a life buoy. You know, those innertubes people hold onto when stranded at sea, holding on for dear life until they are rescued. This is the closet image I know to capture ego as I understand and relate to it.

The "I" is a story we tell ourselves. It is the rhythms and routines of our daily lives and how we consolidate reality through our sensory gating. In a way, most folks are shaping reality, i.e. limiting sensory gating, to conform to their story of it. We saliently shape the perception of our environment to match our needs.

When someone has to go to the bathroom, they only notice bathrooms. When someone is thirsty, they are consolidating reality to fulfill their thirst. When someone feels they are hated, they perceive the world as hating them. All these filterings often occur within "normal" consciousness.

Most folks within the Western medical model conceptualize ego as a separate self apart from the world we perceive, and we work to uphold this story of reality. There is a subjective me and an objective reality separate from me. Most anyone who has experienced psychosis experiences a breakdown in this story of a me separate from the world around me, an ego apart from the world.

Those with lived experience of madness often see how intimately interwoven we are in all experiences. Mystics talk about this and are valued for their ability to communicate subtle spiritual dimensions. When individuals who are struggling in their sensitivities communicate the blurred boundary between self and other, they are dismissed as crazy. "Chewing on sticks" is not a description of the reality of the client's team. It is an expression of a client's illness.

Our ego is our safety mechanism allowing us to feel contained and safe while moving through an uncertain and unknowable reality. In a way, our ego is a limiting factor, the sensory gate that limits our lives and how we perceive reality. Limiting allows reality to be navigable and manageable. Our sensory gating allows us to maintain the stories we tell about ourselves and the ways we habitually relate to the world around us.

Western approaches like psychotherapy and science see the "I" as a thing that exists in the world. To most mystical traditions and what I imagine of indigenous views, the "I" is just a story we tell ourselves to help us feel safe when swimming in the sea of meaning we are continuously surrounded by.

For those who have the ever-illusive "healthy ego," the ego functions in the background. The individual is able to move toward what they desire in life. They can create connections and relationships that are fulfilling and feel a part of the larger world in a meaningful way. Their "self" works in its ability to help them navigate through life. In a way, they don't notice the self so much because it's not interfering with their ability to live the life they desire. They are "well adjusted."

When egos struggle, I am usually called. As a psychotherapist, I help people understand how their safety mechanism, their ego, is harming them by trying to keep them safe in the sea of life. There are many ways the ego chooses to attack itself to support safety. This is often the underlying work in psychotherapy, helping people move past destructive ways of relating to themselves and move toward "healthier" ways of relating that allow the life they desire. A kinder, more open, and generative life.

The ego's job is to limit reality. It shapes an image of oneself and the world around to benefit its function: keeping the person safe and moving their life forward. Often, when we think of the limiting function of the ego, people think of limiting beliefs. I am not good enough. I am too much. There is something wrong with me at the core. These limiting beliefs can be punishing to any individual who lives with them, but they only scratch the surface of the ego's function in limiting reality around us.

Just look at the double-click study. "Sane" people do not hear the second click. That is amazing. Our brain, our ego, or whatever you want to call the aspect of our experience that regulates and shapes our perceived reality before we perceive it, is doing a lot of work behind the scenes. Like stagehands in a theater, making the stage look organized and coherent when, behind the stage, it is often utter chaos.

We cannot handle the chaos of reality. We cannot take in the sea of information we are swimming in. So we limit it to be able to navigate and make sense of our lives. And somehow, Western materialism has praised this limiting as the real "reality." Where the single click is real and the double click is a "deficit." It's amazing that a truth-seeking discipline, a discipline desiring empirical truth, is advocating for limiting perceived reality, for dulling our instruments so we deny the depth of experience we are living in.

I once heard a story about the Dalai Lama's physician. He was joining a group of doctors doing rounds at a prestigious teaching hospital. The Western physicians decided to test the Tibetan physicians' ability to assess illness, so they took away the patient's chart and asked the Tibetan doctor to do an assessment. The doctor walked up to the patient and sat on the bed with him, taking his pulse, touching his skin, and listening to the rhythm of his heart.

After about twenty minutes of sitting with the patient and just listening to his body, the Tibetan doctor said something to the effect that he was suffering from a damned river on the left side of his heart. The Western doctors checked the chart and the patient had a blocked left artery in his heart. With his trained sensitivity, the Tibetan physician was able to diagnose the patient without Western medical technology.

By identifying with our current consensus-based reality of individualistic material selves living in an objective world, we may be denying our human capacity to utilize our sensitivities for healing, creativity, and cultural advancement.

When I was younger, before my break, I worked at a "spiritual" research institute, the Institute of Noetic Sciences. Fancy name. I was transcribing interviews with spiritual teachers from around the world and working on one particular transcript "If you could actually perceive the world around you, you would not even be able to walk across your lawn." You would be too awed by the reality of the grass, too aware of your impact on the grass, to actually step on it.

Instead, we tune out. We tune out our impact on the world around us. We tune out our impact on loved ones. On our communities. On the planet. The ego helps us tune out so we can keep making the choices we make.

An ego is typically created. It is developed in childhood. When a kiddo is given the support they need and is relatively safe, they can develop an ego that supports their life. Yet when a kiddo grows up in a challenging environment, an environment in which they are not safe, they develop an ego that keeps them safe in their unsafe environment.

For instance, when my environment contained my mother's depression and my hyper-attunement to those around me, my ego internalized that my own emotions were "too much" for those around me. So, I created a story that contained limited beliefs of being "too much." This story had a function. It helped me to push down my emotions and learn to hide my feelings from those around me. When I was younger, this was incredibly helpful. My mother wouldn't be overwhelmed by me and I could have a more regulated mother.

Yet as I aged, this did not serve me. I started to see how I broke off my emotions for others, which left me feeling cut off from myself and, in turn, unable to really connect to others around me. My ego did not serve my adult life, it only served my childhood. Hence the years of psychotherapy I went through to help me learn to reanimate my emotions into my voice, into my face, and into my words and expressions. Becoming a feeling with others again. I'm still on the journey and I've come a long way.

Modern neuroscience points to one of the primary functions of our brains as organizing our perceived reality. In a way, the harder the brain works, the more it organizes reality into a stable, perceivable phenomenon.

We know from modern physics that reality is much more nebulous and complex than we can perceive. The world is less solid and more dreamlike than we like to acknowledge. The real world is most likely nothing like the world we consolidate through our sensory gating.

Our brains are working to stabilize our experience of reality, limiting the amount of information we are tuning into so we can more functionally navigate our lives. Too much information overloads our systems. It negates our capacity to functionally navigate our world. Wake up, go to work, and let off some steam before doing it again.

Over time, we learn to "filter" out reality, to limit the information we take in. This is the creation of consensus reality. By taking in the narratives of the world around us, we limit what we experience so our experience conforms to the consensus reality we are embedded in. Anytime we have an experience outside of the norm of consensus reality, an anomalous experience, we threaten the foundations of consensus reality. We explain away anomalous experiences through the dominant narratives of the consensus reality we are participating in.

Currently, our main collective story is one of scientific materialism. Science is "real" and all other understandings of reality are not scientific and dismissed. Through this story of consensus reality, anything that is unexplainable to material science is not permitted. It is dismissed and most likely ridiculed. Just like someone experiencing madness is denied interior subjectivity because it does not adhere to the consensus world around them. They are outcasted and seen as "broken."

Like with the client picking up on something in the communication of his team leader, there was an avoidance of directly addressing the concerns of the client. The client "saw" this but was not able to articulate it in a way that made sense to the team leader and other team members. So it was initially dismissed. But when he was taken seriously and assumed to be communicating something of importance, he was able to translate what he was seeing into a digestible language for the team to understand. He didn't feel like the time was being used to address what mattered to *him*.

From my side of things, the client was picking up something the team leader was unaware of. The leader was performing the role while not addressing what really mattered. The team leader was parroting what the meeting should look like and the client was picking up on this.

So here you have a dreamlike otherworld expression of "chewing on sticks." It alludes to the phenomenon the client was experiencing without the statement being clear for the community members to understand. Through support from the team, he was able to translate what he was perceiving into a more consensus-based communication that enabled his statement to be understood and taken into consideration when running future meetings.

As the team initially dismissed the client's communication, scientists dismiss open sensory gating as a "deficit." The single click is real and the double click is an inaccurate way of perceiving reality. I use the double-click study as an example to highlight the limits of science. After billions of dollars of research, this is one of our best biological indicators of schizophrenia. This also highlights how limited Western science is in measuring an individual's sensitivity. If we know folks can perceive sounds that others can't, what other aspects of reality can sensitive individuals perceive?

I hope my disdain for science is clear when addressing issues of madness. It is through science that we have experienced a decrease in care, loss of recovery rates, and a general decrease in compassion toward those suffering from madness.

In public journals, we have seen physicians proclaim the great advancement of lobotomy technology. Yet, according to one physician's personal notes, this Nobel Prize-winning procedure leaves people "no better than a house pet." [23]

We've seen a pharmaceutical industry take hold of the narratives of madness, determining that individuals need lifelong antipsychotic medications when this has been clearly demonstrated to cause long-term brain damage and damage to other essential organs, at the same time increasing symptoms and the number of psychotic breaks over a client's lifetime. Not to mention, antipsychotics are the most profitable class of drugs in all of pharmaceuticals, most likely due to the clinical recommendation of lifetime use. [24]

For me, this is science. So when I use the double-click study to highlight a point, I am in a way trying to make fun of the scientific perspective. They are able to measure the double-click difference and gain empirical evidence between "sane" and "insane" individuals or, as I've alluded, to the impact of being a sensitive individual.

This to me is the fundamental limitation of empirical evidence. This evidence is only alluding to a small fraction of the capacity of a sensitive individual to take in information from the world around them. Like a canary in a coal mine, the double-click study highlights how little science understands about the inner life of being human.

If one of the few biological indicators known, the double-click study, is the primary way of proving biological deficit in individuals experiencing madness, yet the test determines that individuals are more accurately perceiving stimuli, what is happening in madness?

If you've ever encountered someone in the throes of a psychotic break or passed someone on the street lost to their otherworld, it does not seem they are more accurately sensing reality. It seems they are lost and unable to be contacted

23 Kuroski, John. "The Twisted History Of The Widely Misunderstood Lobotomy." AllThatsInteresting.com, April 6, 2017, https://allthatsinteresting.com/lobotomy-walter-freeman. Accessed May 3, 2024.

24 Field R. I. (2010). Antipsychotic medications are spelling legal trouble for drugmakers. P & T : a peer-reviewed journal for formulary management, 35(11), 621–622.

in their other world. I know for myself that when I was processing information from the world around me at an alarming rate, I was not living.

This is where one of our basic human functions comes in. Meaning-making. It is thought that humans are primarily meaning-making creatures. We make meaning from our experiences. This is how we develop relationships, identify patterns, create technology, make art, and develop culture. Through our capacity to make meaning.

When you look at the process of meaning-making, there is often a gap between the stimulus, like the "extra" click, and the meaning made from the stimulus. I've stated this many times throughout the book. Madness is not due to the experiences one is having but is rooted in the meaning made from the experiences.

I still believe that if I were in a different head space, given different supports, and had a better understanding of what I was going through, I could have had the same experiences I was having while mad and made different meanings of those experiences. Meanings that would have allowed me to maintain contact with my life, maintain friendship, and have a sense of continuity.

I've met folks along the way who have drifted far into madness but had the anchor of relationship and community to help tether them back to their lives. Where the transition from mad to sane was smoother, with less loss along the way. This is where treatment is deeply flawed. One of the primary ways people try to help the mad is through pointing out mad people are wrong. The reality they are experiencing is not accurate.

It is deeply disturbing for many people to see the delusions of madness and not need to correct them as "wrong." Yet, the deficits of sensory gating which allow people to attune to what is real with greater precision is the very foundation that leads to the generation of delusions. It is not a matter of perceiving reality but making sense of the reality that is perceived.

In classical Buddhism, there is the parable of the second arrow. You are walking through the forest and hit with an arrow, then immediately hit in the exact same spot with another arrow. Sensory experience is the first arrow.

There is this raw moment happening right now that is filled with sensation, a sea of sensation. We usually limit the sea of sensory information we are continuously swimming in. We do not want to tune in to ourselves and the world around us. It is often too much to truly bare. Like the grass. Hence the reason so many people always have TV, podcasts, or music on. People don't want to know what they are experiencing moment to moment. It terrifies them.

Sensory information is the ground from which we make meaning out of our experience. It usually happens on a subtle level, out of awareness. We are typically good at distinguishing interoceptive awareness, awareness of our inner sensations, and external awareness, or awareness of our environment. However, these are nominal distinctions.

When one truly connects to the present moment and relaxes their habitual holding patterns of perceiving reality, there is often a breakdown in inner and outer awareness. Both merge into a continuous stream of sensory experience. This is captured in the Mahayana Buddhist text of the Paramita Heart Sutra:

No eye, no ear, no nose, no tongue, no body, no mind.

No seeing, no hearing, no tasting, no smelling, no imagining.

These lines from the seminal Buddhist text capture what is understood to be a non-dual realization of self. Inner and outer awareness are just stories we tell ourselves to help us navigate and make meaning of our experiences.

Typically we are caught in our thinking, in our sense-making of our sensory experiences. Maybe we notice a tightness in the chest. We feel it and tell ourselves we are anxious, then scan our lives to identify what is "causing" the anxiety. "Oh, it must be the test I have later in the week."

We then think about what we need to do to manage the anxiety. "I guess I need to study this week, but I can't study. I have to work at night." Our thought process actually compounds the tightness in our chest, but we usually never circle back and notice the impact of our meaning-making on our sensory experience. Did thinking through the tightness in the chest alleviate the distress? Often not. Typically it compounds the distress.

Most folks are not aware of their subtle sensory experience. They just say they are anxious without connecting to the bodily signals of anxiety. When I work with folks who say they are anxious, I will often ask about what is happening right now which allows them to know they are anxious. This will often orient them to the present-moment sensations of anxiety in the body – the racing heart, tightness in the chest, the feeling of pressure in the body.

An amazing thing happens when I ask folks to "stay with" or "just notice" their distress. It starts to relax and settle. This is a typical process of identifying a subtle interoceptive experience and providing support for it to settle.

Now imagine someone whose gating channels are blasted open. Someone who is picking up information they do not understand, information they do not have a name for. They scramble, trying to make sense of the flood of sensory information bombarding their system. To make sense and order of their experience, they create meaning. When someone who is psychotic creates meaning, we typically call it delusion. It is an unacceptable meaning-making of experience.

Just like a "normal" person calling tightness in the chest anxiety, a psychotic individual calls the expanded state of awareness they are in "special." They see themselves as special, unique, or different. Hell, they might be Jesus Christ because this must have been what he was talking about. Maybe I am Jesus Christ because what else can explain this expanded heightened reality I am now participating in?

It is not different than calling tightness in the chest anxiety. The psychotic person is attempting to make meaning of their experience, to communicate their experience to others. But the experience does not lie in the realm of the "known," it is outside of consolidated consensus reality. How do you communicate what is beyond the allowed known? You are "chewing on sticks."

Like the anxious person, the meaning-making is typically rooted in trying to alleviate suffering, to make things better. But just like anxiety, the meaning of madness often compounds the distress. If the world is out to get you, what are you supposed to do? Freak out.

What if we were able to help people step back from their meaning-making and connect to the root sensory experience the delusional meaning derives from? Like the client who could easily be dismissed for getting angry about "nothing," who was rambling about "chewing on sticks." When in reality, he was sensing something of the relational field he was a part of without being able to name what was happening. When he was supported in his experience, he could communicate it in a way that was understood.

Unfortunately, as people drift further and further into their personal realities, they need to create a cohesive meaning structure to navigate the newfound gating they are living in. So they create a new ego, an ego to make sense of the sea of meaning.

Madness-Based Ego

My sensory gating is wide open. I am trying to make sense of the world around me. I am failing.

I have a flood of experiences I have never known. An expanded energy field that extends beyond my understanding. Sensations I have never tasted. "Knowing" things I've never known. Seeing "beyond" what is in front of me.

I cannot tell what is "real" and what is madness.

In my flood of experience, I desperately try to make sense of what is happening to me. A story eventually emerges. A story of my spiritual importance. I grab onto it like a floatation device, to keep me buoyant in the sea of experience I am drowning in.

My story becomes more solid with time, more "true." The further my life falls apart, the tighter I hold onto some meaning to help me make sense.

I take on my story of importance and assume it is true. Waiting for the world, for others to acknowledge it. I am left alone waiting for the acknowledgment.

I am ashamed of the delusions that emerged to make sense of the new experiences I was having in my blasted open sensory gating. I feel deep shame. This is probably reflected in the vagueness with which I describe my "stories of spiritual importance." I wish I could say I thought I was Jesus, that would be easier in a way.

As I've described earlier, my story of importance was shaped by my past experiences, the cultural frameworks I was raised in and the ones I adopted as I aged. The story I created was shaped within these narratives. It was a desperate attempt to create some meaning, some stability amidst the sea of experience I was drowning in. Some footing as the world kept changing around me.

I know I use this phrase a lot. "Drowning in a sea of experience." I use it because I think it is appropriate. It is the closest I can come to conveying what it was like for me to be lost to my other world. Drowning. Trying desperately to hold on to something to make sense of what was happening within my experience. What had happened to my life.

I remember a dream from around the time I was homeless:

> *I am falling into a well. I try to grab something to hold on and stop the fall, but there is nothing I can hold, nothing I can grab onto. I just keep falling.*

Early in my recovery journey, I had another dream, a dream of drowning. That dream has become one of my guiding metaphors for recovery from madness, a map of the process I am still on.

This dream reflected the healing arc I was to go through in recovering from my descent into madness. I am going to share it with you in full as I think it is relevant to what I am talking about, the building of a madness-based ego to make sense of the intensity of ungrounded open sensory gating.

> *I am floating in a river. It is a sunny day and the water is a comfortable temperature. Two work friends float by in innertubes. I wonder where they got the tubes. I am in the water without support, working slightly to stay afloat. They seem much more comfortable.*
>
> *I find myself being pulled into a different branch of the river than my friends are floating in. While being pulled, I am sucked into a*

whirlpool. I desperately try to swim my way out. The harder I fight, the further I am pulled in.

I am so overwhelmed that I lose my orientation to space. I am in panic as I am being pulled further and further under the water, desperately trying to free myself without knowing which way is up.

I know I am drowning and must do something to save myself.

At some point, I remember that I have on a backpack. I fight the disorientation to take my backpack off. Once freed, I am able to drag myself from the whirlpool, out of the water and onto the nearby rocks on the river's edge.

I stand on the rocks, watching the river from the shore. I am grounded, anchored in the earth. I feel more solid and connected than I ever have.

Clear in my connection to my life, I have a sense of solidness and security I have never known. As if I am clear on my purpose in life and confident in my ability to honor my purpose. It is a simultaneous feeling of relaxation and power, hard to describe and the most nourishing experience I have known.

I see my friends floating by on their tubes and ask if they know where the whirlpool exits, as at some point, I will have to go get my backpack and make sense of what I've been through. I also know it is not yet time and I can enjoy the grounded connection I feel standing on the rocks. Finally on solid ground.

I had this dream early in my recovery process. It has been one of the guides I've used in navigating my recovery journey. There is a lot here I could unpack about the recovery process but I want to focus on the letting go of the backpack. I want to address the letting go that I found necessary in finding my way out of the whirlpool to stand on the rocks, on stable ground.

My backpack was symbolic of the "stories of spiritual importance" I created to make sense of what was happening in my openness. While I was homeless, I would write, interview people, and create art. I thought I was creating something of value, something of importance that would be of benefit to others. Something that might change the world, hence the grandiosity of the delusions. I thought my sketchbook would change the world.

I held on tightly to my backpack in real life. It was the only thing I brought with me into homelessness. If you remember, I gave away most of my belongings. I gave away my wilderness survival gear. I gave away nearly everything I owned. But I held onto my everyday backpack and my laptop.

In the dream, this is what I needed to let go of to finally step out of the overwhelm of the whirlpool. The whirlpool represented the real-life drowning I experienced in my wide-open sensory gating. Openness without the appropriate groundedness and inner support to navigate my gating aperture blasted open.

I had to let go of the backpack, of the stories I created in my madness to make sense of it. The story of someone on a mission, someone creating something that would be of benefit to others. Someone important.

I do not think the "ambition" I held was inherently wrong, to want to be of benefit to others. But it denies where I was in my life. Homeless, without community. No longer anchored in a purpose or meaning tangibly connected to those around me.

It was only in my head, in my story, that I was going to save people, the world, the spiritual plane of existence. It's hard to say now what I thought then. But I know I felt like I was on a mission and it was important.

I've spoken about ego and the appropriate translation of the "I." I see the "I" as a type of floatation device, like my friends with their innertubes as they floated downriver together. This is the hope, that our "I" can be built in such a way that it allows us to navigate the river of life with some ease and relaxation, connecting to others and acting on our meaning.

The innertube represents their floatation device for life, the "I" created to help navigate the complicated and messy journey of being a person. A device used to stay on the surface of the river and not sink too deeply into the water.

As I've shared, sensory gating limits one's experience of "reality." People reduce their sensory experience into a consolidated way to make sense of the "sea of meaning" we are all swimming in. Limiting the amount of water they must swim in to move through life.

In my dream, I not only didn't have an innertube but I was pulled deep into the water in a chaotic and overwhelming fashion, completely lost in a whirlpool. This is my story. When you're in the tube, you only get so wet. You are protected from being totally submerged. Without an innertube, I was working to stay afloat, wondering why it was easier for other people. People with innertubes, just floating by.

The innertube itself is the limiting factor, the sensory gating that keeps people dry and afloat through their journey. On one level, it is so valuable, our "ego." It is the conditions by which we limit our experience of the world so we can stay focused and able to navigate through life.

On another level, the tube is a limiting factor, another "story" we tell ourselves to support navigating life. In this way, a madness-based ego and an everyday consensus reality ego are not that different. They are just different inner tubes for different rivers, one for the other world and one for consensus-based reality.

With the everyday ego, a person limits their perception of the world around them. Through this sensory gating, they are able to comfortably navigate their lives. Unfortunately, folks who live primarily in an everyday ego do not realize they are "gating" reality around them to find comfort. They assume their gating is the reality.

People who experience madness have gating that is blown open, creating a flooding of sensory information from the world. These people are possibly experiencing "more" of reality, but the experience is so intense and overwhelming that they have to create a story, another ego, to make sense of the flooding of experience. They create a madness-based ego.

As I've reflected on the dream, I didn't have the best floatation device. Actually, I didn't have any floatation device. I was swimming without the inner support required to navigate life in a coherent and relaxed way. I didn't have an

"I" that was built to navigate consensus reality with ease. This is most likely rooted in my childhood wounding of abandonment.

Hence the necessity of some disruptive experience that would allow me to address the lack of structural support within myself, the inability of my "I" to support me through life. This disruptive experience came as my psychotic break. In the falling apart of my "I," deeper structural needs within myself were addressed, needs that were covered up as I walked through the world with an "I" intact.

I'm getting ahead of myself, talking about the healing function of psychotic breaks. Right now, I simply want to orient around the creation of the madness-based ego, the "I" that evolves to make sense of the experiences happening in madness.

If we take the premise that some individuals experience more open sensory gating than others – even expanding the premise to acknowledge those who get abruptly dropped into the open gating, as I did through my use of psychedelics at an inopportune time in my life – this abrupt introduction is often referred to in the medical model as a psychotic break. It is a break in our gating channels.

When this break happens, we often get flooded with the new experiences unleashed when gating channels open. In the flood of experience, the drowning, there is a desire to make sense of the new experiences. This is a natural human function we all have, making sense of the experiences we have. Most of us are nearly always interpreting our experiences within our frameworks of understanding.

"I am crying because I am sad about *this*." "I am feeling *this* because of *that*." "*This* happened to me because of *that*." "The pain in my stomach is because of *this*."

We are always interpreting our experiences through some lens of understanding. This is the "I" for me. It is how we interpret the experiences we are having moment to moment. It is the sense we make that consolidates our experience into reliable narratives about who we are and how the world is.

Most see the "I" as a collection of experiences and beliefs. They see it as our past experiences and beliefs being shaped together to create our ego, our way of making sense. For me, this interpretation does not factor into account our sensory gating. Our gating channels are key determinants of the experiences we have that our "I" makes sense of.

Typically throughout life, we have a stable experience of sensory gating. There is little fluctuation, only some anomalous experiences here and there. Typically when these happen, we either explain them away through our sense-making or update our sense-making to account for the anomalous experiences. This expands our "I," a process that is typically gradual and allows for a grounded maintenance of our everyday life, of our participation in consensus reality.

When I was in high school, I had an experience of open sensory gating that surprised me. I was sitting downstairs in my house, stoned, and watching television – a common activity of mine – when I "felt" my phone ringing. This was hard to comprehend because my phone was on vibrate and upstairs in my bedroom.

I wanted to dismiss the feeling, but it nagged at me. So, I went upstairs and checked. My phone had just rung. What blew me away was how often I missed calls when my phone was right next to me, yet here I could "feel" it vibrate on another floor of my house. At that moment, I realized the limitations of my sensory gating and the possibility of more expanded gating. This was aided by cannabis, which is known to open sensory gating. [25]

On a side note, this is why people with a predisposition to open sensory gating should be careful with cannabis. It can blast those gating channels open in a way that is hard to navigate and make sense of. This is why I believe there is a "story" around folks who have a predisposition to psychosis having breaks on cannabis. Yes, the person has a predisposition to open gating, but this does not mean they are forever destined to be "psychotic" unless properly medicated. This just reflects the need to work with their gating channels, to heal their nervous system and learn to work with their unique experience.

---

25 Samantha J. Broyd, Lisa-marie Greenwood, Rodney J. Croft, Anna Dalecki, Juanita Todd, Patricia T. Michie, Stuart J. Johnstone, Nadia Solowij, "Chronic effects of cannabis on sensory gating," *International Journal of Psychophysiology*, Volume 89, Issue 3, 2013.

Some of my clients want to experiment with cannabis again after a psychotic break. I tell them that certain people are more porous than other people. Often, people are drawn to cannabis because of their lack of porousness, of being locked into consensus reality and needing a taste of open gating to feel refreshed and less trapped.

For those of us with more open gating, this is not the case. Cannabis can be an overwhelming and intense experience. If you're struggling with your gating, feeling too open or too porous, maybe give cannabis a break until you feel more consolidated within yourself. Even then, continue to be careful. Any substance that opens has a tendency to drift us too far into our other world, especially when abused, but sometimes with just one use.

Most of us walk through the world with semi-consistent sensory gating. We do not think about it or notice much change. This is why most people don't even know there is such a thing as sensory gating. Their experience of "reality" is so consistent, that they assume everyone's reality is consistent.

Yet when someone has a psychotic break, there is an abrupt change in their sensory gating. They are often experiencing the basic sensory experience of being human in a radically new way. They are having experiences they have never had before. And they are trying to make sense of those experiences, often drowning, like I was.

This sense-making is what we often refer to as "crazy." It is the stories we create to manage our newfound experiences. The stories we tell to help us navigate through our sensory gating.

Since these stories are based on experiences others have not had and therefore do not use the shared language of consensus-based reality, they do not make sense to those hearing them. Unless the other person is trained or has a natural faculty in hearing the deeper meaning conveyed through consensus-based language, stories of anomalous experiences sound "crazy."

It is normal and natural to create meaning of our experience. I know that I needed some "story of importance" to get me through my period of madness. I needed some way to stay afloat. My grandiose delusions served a function, as my friends' innertubes served them in the water. My grandiosity and delusion allowed me to navigate the flood of experience I was having. To feel some center, in this case, a center of importance, helped me to stay connected to myself without becoming completely lost to the sea of experience I was in.

The problem is that this did not help me navigate life very well. It did not support grounding or being able to connect with others, which was something I desperately needed. I needed some support through the intensity of experience I was continuously in.

It was a catch-22. The madness-based ego I generated to stay afloat through my experience made it almost impossible to communicate and participate in a consensus-based reality with others, and I desperately needed to make some sense of my experiences to not completely drown in them.

The new "I" created to navigate my experience was rooted in wide-open sensory gating. It was created to make sense of the new experiences I was having, replacing my previous "I." This is why it is often called a "break." It is a break in one "I" toward another "I" that is not recognizable to family and friends and often disruptive to those moving through consensus reality.

Prior to my madness, I had a story of my life, a story of my place within the cosmos. Like Joseph Campbell's four functions of mythology, the idea is we all have a personal mythology we are living out. My story before madness was based on what I was doing and where I was going with my life.

I was entering a PhD program. I was building a life for myself in the new town I was living in. I wanted to be of benefit to others and have enriching experiences. I wanted to pick up surfing again. I wanted to create communities around positive connections.

It was not so different from my grandiose stories in madness, but more grounded or less grand, for lack of a better explanation. I was a cog in the wheel of change. I was not the wheel.

When my break happened, all that fell away. I was no longer on the same trajectory as before. I was navigating a new "reality" and creating a new story to help in my navigation. In this story, I became a more important player in the cosmic game. I had more meaning and significance than I had previously accounted for.

As I was having more intense experiences, experiences beyond my comprehension now but incredibly real to me at the time, I shaped a story based on their extremes. My story, my madness-based ego, was shaped within the extremes of experience I was having. It lived in those extremes.

This is the problem. The new story I began to tell about myself was dependent upon the wide-open sensory gating experiences I was having, which was not good. My experiences were too much for me to hold. Remember, I was drowning.

In a way, I created an "I" that was dependent upon drowning, that only lived within the overwhelm and confusion of the open experiences I was having. The new madness-based "I" was now required to live in this state of overwhelm to exist for its story to make sense. It's only in the "grand" experiences I was having that the grandiosity was reflected back to me.

So while the madness-based "I" serves a purpose in helping someone navigate their new experiences, it also traps them into those experiences, as most of us need an "I" to feel safe in the world. This is me trapped in the whirlpool and still holding onto my backpack, the very thing causing me to drown.

There is a sad irony here. The backpack, my madness-based "I," was to help me get out of the madness. I truly wanted to get back into functional living, to community, to engagement, to connection, to meaning, and to sharing in life with others. Yet the madness-based "I" was driving me further and further away from the things I loved and wanted back. I needed to let go of it in order to actually find my way back.

Many people get attached to the stories they tell themselves while in madness. They are Jesus. They are going to create a new world. They are persecuted. The FBI is out to get them. These are just some stories we tell to navigate madness.

The thing is, continuous extreme states are hard to sustain. The degree of open gating required to be "swimming in the sea of meaning" takes a toll on the body. Eventually, everyone needs to "come down," to return to a more regulated gating channel. This doesn't mean the person comes back to "normal," just a more grounded state than the intensity of the "break." This is the post-break depression I experienced.

When this coming down happens, there can be a desire to find our way back into the extreme states, back into the place where our newfound madness-based "I" exists. This is because the madness-based ego only exists in those heightened states of experience, as it was formed to navigate those experiences.

Unfortunately for many people, they develop practices and ways to find their way back into the extreme states where their madness-based ego lived. Others use spiritual practice for the same purposes. A lot of the methods of finding our way back into madness are the same practices deployed for millennia to enter spiritual states of openness. Fasting. Staying up for days at a time. Taking substances to expand our state of awareness. Isolation. Breath practices. Thinking ourselves into a frenzy.

When I started to "come down" or "come back together," I missed the expanded state I had felt, the feeling of extending far beyond my physical body. There was something about the experience that was nourishing to me. I wanted it back. When it started to fade, I tried to figure out how to get it back, with no luck.

My wife's friend recently had a descent into madness. To manage and work with the new energies flooding her body, she became a poet, staying up for days at a time writing poetry. I hung out with her a few months after her experience. She was in a more grounded place and also sad she couldn't write poetry anymore. I got scared for her, scared she would try to recreate the conditions of her madness to create the state of mind she needed to become a poet again.

Her poetry was a strategy to manage the extreme states she was in. It was how she made sense and moved through the experiences she was having. Becoming a poet allowed her to stay afloat in her madness. The gravity, the desire to be who we were in madness, often pulls us back into madness. It is in the extremes of the wide-open sensory gating where our new "I" lives.

I am just going to say it directly. Whatever stories emerge in madness, stories created in open-gating experiences, they do not matter. The stories themselves make no difference. They are not helpful. Instead, it is important to see them for what they are, stories created to make sense of the experience of open gating. An innertube to navigate madness.

I am not saying the experiences themselves are not real. It is the sense we make of these experiences that traps us in a prison. Traps us in a whirlpool where we lose our orientation, our direction, and our ability to move toward a life of meaning and connection.

I would never tell someone in a break that their delusions are not real. I see no value in that. But after a break, as things begin to settle, it can be helpful to nudge people away from the madness-based stories and remember some of the stories before the madness took hold. Some of the ways of being in the world that are rooted in narrower sensory gating, a more manageable sensory gating.

In a way, it is the giving up of our specialness that is most important. To give up the story of being the center of the universe, the chosen one, the persecuted one. There is a reality to these stories for we are cosmically important, all of us. At the same time, it is helpful to ground oneself back into humility, not self-punishment for being delusional. That is where I drifted to, punishing myself for the stories I told in my madness and the actions in the world generated from those stories.

No, it is more simple. There is nothing wrong with creating stories to manage our experience. But when the experience ends, can you let go of the story? This applies as equally to spiritual practice as it does to recovering from madness.

The Buddha once famously said, "When you cross the river, let go of the boat. You don't need to carry it with you." He was talking about Buddhism. Being a good Buddhist isn't the goal, but getting enlightened is. After you are enlightened, do you need to hold onto the story of someone trying to get enlightened? No. You let it go.

Letting go of the madness-based ego is the same function, to let go of the you that supported you through your madness. Like a boat, it served its purpose and it is important to say goodbye. It is in the letting go that something new can emerge, something beyond what you know now. The new you who has gone through madness and stepped on your rocks, stepped into your "functioning" and your place in the cosmos.

I can see some people interpreting what I am saying as returning to "normal" sensory gating. This is not what I want to convey. I am suggesting letting go of the story that requires you to be in wide-open sensory gating.

By letting this story go, there is a possibility of having a more fluid relationship with sensory gating. Maybe spending a period of time learning to be grounded, to be slower, and more connected to earth and community. To be able to slow our thinking, reduce the speed of our perceptions, and allow our sensory gating to open and close in a more organic, fluid fashion. A sensory gating that brings heaven and earth together, the other world and consensus reality impacting each other.

One of the primary tasks of folks like myself who experienced extreme states as a crisis is to cultivate safety in the body when in open gating. When there is more safety, there is less need to create a "story" to make sense of the gating. Typically, the more grounded and connected we feel to ourselves, the less we need to tell ourselves a story to feel safe. We can let the experience be without needing to interpret it.

Maybe over time, we can learn to open our gating more gently and deliberately, slowly opening it over time to learn to be in a more open gating with relaxation and ease. Without the need for an elaborate story to make sense of the experiences. Where the experience can be the experience.

This is often the way in spiritual communities. There is a gradual support of opening, where the opening can be integrated into the consensual self. Unfortunately, many of us do not get this opportunity. We have experiences of abruptly being thrown into open gating. Our learning is often different. It is about healing and grounding, relaxing and allowing for the open gating to return of its own accord versus "forcing it open."

The thing is, I think all of our stories, all the narratives of the "I," are as delusional as the madness-based ego. By this, I mean that I believe they are tools to help us feel safe within our experience. They are not "real."

This is reflected in many contemplative traditions. In Buddhism, it is referred to as Anatta, one of the three marks of existence. Anatta means "no self." For Buddhists, the self, the "I," is not a real thing, but a flimsy creation emerging to create a sense of safety within the sea of experience. Much of Buddhist practice is about learning to recognize this mark of existence, really being able to see the flimsy nature of the self so that when it begins to flare, when our reactivity is strong, we don't necessarily need to act on it. It is not real.

There is a researcher out of Brown University, Willoughby Britton, who studies "the varieties of contemplative experience." She found that many people who casually started meditating 15 to 20 years ago, when mindfulness started to be taught in the West, more recently started to have experiences of depersonalization. Another DSM category of mental illness, in depersonalization, you lose the sense of having a self.

Britton found that these casual meditators also were never told this is the end goal of many meditations: depersonalization. Depersonalization is often the experience of letting go of the ego, of no longer filtering one's experience through an "I."

I am not suggesting people who've had an abrupt descent into madness should give up their egos and live in a depersonalized state. The idea within many contemplative traditions is that it takes a tremendous amount of time and training to learn to be relaxed in a depersonalized state. To not fight it. To not freak out, like those of us who freak out when drowning in madness. The more we freak, the more we need a story to ground ourselves.

I am instead suggesting that the madness-based ego needs to loosen its grip on the narrative. The best way I've found to help this ego relax its grip is to reconnect to what I call "the body of activity," the activities where our pre-mad self still lives. This calls back our previous sensory gating and sense of self, through reconnecting to the activities of self. The rhythms and routines of our lives before madness.

It is not sexy. It is not glamorous. It is often as simple as doing the dishes again, folding our laundry, and anchoring ourselves back into the mundane existence of consensual tasks. Consensual tasks that support a more grounded, steady sensory gating.

The Body of Activity

I am sitting in my dad's oversized leather computer chair, in front of his built-in desk. I have a pen in hand and am starting a list on a legal pad. I have only been at his house for a short time after spending months on the streets.

As I start the list, I write out the things I need to "get back." I need to find a therapist and a local yoga studio. Price used road bikes. Find listings for part-time work in food. Find a local Zen Center. Look up graduate school education. The list isn't extensive but it is what I feel I need to jump-start living again.

Once the list is written, I feel defeated. Unable to move forward and activate the items on it. I am overwhelmed by the thought of "starting over," of "rebuilding" my life after it fell apart so thoroughly.

I am still coming down from the extreme states I resided in for the last few months. Finally coming "back together." Remembering how to be slow, be present, and have a "normal" conversation. Just settling.

In the settling, the list feels like too much. It's still hard to just be. So I put it away. For a year and a half. I stay cut off from the world, wishing myself dead and yet not able to follow through with killing myself. Trapped in a bardo between living and dying.

I find my new rhythm and routine. My life support of television and sleep. Falling asleep in the same spot. Waking up. Turning on the television, just to get a break from the tormentor in my mind demanding my death. A chance to consolidate the wide-open channeling from before. The narrow band of watching TV.

I am lost for what feels like an eternity. Then, almost out of nowhere, I am ready. Energy is available to start again. Windhorse has descended, breathed life into my stagnated body and mind. Giving me hope of weathering the storm of renewal.

I activate the list. I get a bike. I ride to yoga multiple times a week. I ride to the next city to connect to the Zen community I had first found over a year ago. I meet my future therapist. I am just starting to move through the world again, being human.

I am living again. I still fade in and out. Watching TV for a full day, in my lost in-between world. And I come out. I find my way back to my bike. Back in the yoga studio doing the same 26 yoga postures I've done for years. I walk through the local Whole Foods, remembering the food I used to cook.

Thanksgiving comes. I cook my father a Thanksgiving meal.

Soon, I am more fully in the world than not. My life still feels small. The beginnings of rebuilding. Making friends. Living with roommates.

My life is moving again. I am in movement with life again. Living.

I cannot get over the list. More than ten years removed I can still see the legal pad, still see myself Googling the different providers, the different studios and places I thought would help reconstitute my life. The spaces, activities, and community that would help me re-remember how to live again.

When the energy to "start again" emerged, a year and a half after the depression, I didn't look at the list. I didn't remember the things I had written. I just started to do the things I thought would help me find my way back into myself, back into wholehearted living. In the year and a half in my father's basement, the activities I would need to find my way back were waiting for me the whole time. They were in stasis, ready to be activated. When I was ready.

It was only later that I remembered the list, remembered the things I wrote. At this point, I was already living the list, living the *body of activity* that would help me heal. To find structure, rhythm, and routine again. Really remember who I was by engaging in the activities and spaces I used to occupy before my break.

The activities were simple: riding my bike, going to yoga, working with my dad, grocery shopping, and going to a Zen Center once a week. It wasn't a full return, taking on everything I used to do. Before my break, I was a pretty engaged human. This was a slow stepping back into engaging with life and the world.

I wasn't meditating for hours like I used to. I would meditate for ten minutes and that was enough. Enough to remind me that I do meditate. I know how to work with my mind and I have training in being with my experience in a relaxed way.

Early on in this process, there was a catalyst I've mentioned, my mother sending me the gift of an e-reader. This act of kindness and generosity helped me break through the prison of shame I had constructed to hold myself in, away from life. With the boost of loving kindness from my family, I felt some ability to venture out of my prison. To move into trying.

The first thing I did was go to a local bookstore to activate the e-reader so I could use it. I remember it was so strange to be in public again. Doing an everyday task. I had difficulty establishing the Wi-Fi required to set it up. I remember a sinking feeling, this nagging voice telling me, "Who are you kidding? You can't just start over." I felt so out of place, with all the people just moving through their daily lives.

For me, the act of going to a bookstore and engaging in a task of meaning and importance, reconnecting to reading, was a revolutionary act. It was my first stand, the first moment I decided to challenge this voice in my head.

Sitting on the bench activating my e-reader was a symbolic gesture of activating my life. A renunciation of the story of brokenness, brain disorders, and deepening madness over time. I did not know I could start over. I did not know it was possible to come back into living after such a radical departure from the normal markers we consider being human.

And I did. I did start over. Although, it wasn't totally starting over. I already had templates. I already had activities and ways of supporting health and meaningful connection in my life. My history of sanity already lived inside of me. It was more about remembering those activities, spending time in nature, meditating, moving my body through yoga and dance, working, riding my bicycle, joking with people, and being interested and curious about others.

Once I was settled enough to put myself back into these contexts, a fully formed part of me was waiting. A part that almost said, "I got this. This is easy for me." I really thought I had lost myself and was unable to find my way back. By self, I mean being able to connect with others and move through the world.

I wanted to remind myself of the ways I was still me, see that I hadn't "disappeared" or "lost myself." I had not accessed certain parts of myself in a long time. They weren't needed. The part of me who made small talk with people was not necessary; I didn't talk to anyone for over a year.

Yet here I am, a few days after setting up the e-reader, in a grocery store during the day. Buying food I will actually cook and not just reheat. Thinking about nutrition again. Eating food that will help me have energy and be able to engage with my life.

I'm standing in line and I have a conversation with the woman next to me. I don't remember the conversation. I am a Libra and have been told I am naturally a "flirty" person. This conversation wasn't sexual or anything, just a playful back-and-forth that left a smile on both of our faces.

And I could tell the interaction was positive. It was a positive interaction for me and the woman I was talking to. It lasted no more than 30 seconds and I can still remember it. I was able to interact with the world in a grounded and connected way. The relief in knowing I could just be a person with another person was monumental. It broke through so much of my shame and fear around being "crazy." Even if I am "crazy," I just had a relaxed and playful conversation with a stranger.

In the madness, living in that heightened reality made it hard to engage my everyday rhythm and routine. I was just trying to manage the experience I was having, not moving my life forward in any way. I had to give up so much of myself to manage the moment-to-moment experience I was having. There wasn't enough "me" left to hold my life together, to keep the container of my life functioning.

Then the depression, where I gave up any hope I could "live," "start over," or "function" again. I remember how often the spell of endless television would be disrupted. Whether I needed to go get groceries late at night when no one would see me. Or reheating a prepared meal at home. Even taking a break to go to the bathroom.

I would see myself in the mirror and not know how I had arrived this far from living. When the haze I created to manage the punishing shame would lift. I would ask myself how it is possible to give up so many tangible aspects of being human and still be alive. Not living in a meaningful way but continuing to exist. I think this is a dirty secret of existence, it just keeps on going.

I could see how far I had drifted from the ways of living that supported me being alive and functioning in a basic way. It felt like it was impossible to come back, to go as far toward non-existence as I had and somehow return to functional everyday consensual reality and pretend like nothing had happened. This felt absurd. It felt like a lie.

I didn't realize in the absurdity that the list lived inside of me. I didn't "create it." It emerged from the history of sanity living alongside my recent history of madness. In my depression, in the negative interjective thoughts I cycled through – thoughts of being a failure, of ruining my life, of being crazy – as I lived those thoughts on repeat for almost two years, I never recalled the stories of my sanity. The stories of my discipline, of my kindness and consideration for others, of my desire to be of benefit. I never recalled the part of me who cared about living and was willing to work to live, was willing to work at living.

There was a period where I worked hard at living, though not in the crushing it, making money sense. I was a couple years into college. I realized the life direction I was going in was not for me, that it would only lead me to depression and meaninglessness. So I broke off, broke off the path the river of my life was taking me.

I took time to live alone. To work in nature. To cook all of my meals. To learn about nutrition. It was during this time I first started to do yoga regularly. To meditate morning and evening. To write out my dreams. When I started to "work" on myself. I am not a big fan of this phrase, of "working on myself." For me, it is working at living, working at loving, and working at engaging with life. Not fixing myself.

In the tortuous depression following my madness, I could not remember this aspect of who I was. The one who was willing to work, to grow, to embrace challenges. I was only failure. Returning back into living would be too much for me. It would be too much work. Hurt too much.

And I didn't know it was possible. No one was there to help me understand what I went through. No one was there to let me know psychotic breaks are normal. Not normal in the sense of everyone having them, but a normal part of the human experience for millennia. An incredibly painful and difficult experience for anyone to go through and still part of the human experience.

And I was through it. I had "come down," "settled" from the extreme states. I had let go of the narratives of delusion keeping me attached to those states. I was at a place where I could start living again.

If someone could tell me it was possible, that countless people over history have stepped over the cliff of madness and found their way back, I might feel less of the crushing impossibility I felt. Part of my fear in "putting my life back together" was not knowing if I could keep my life after I put it back. Would it just come crashing down again because I am destined to live a rollercoaster life of being in and out of madness?

This was the only understanding living inside of me. The only way of relating to madness I had been unconsciously indoctrinated in by our culture. It was only when the energy of possibility returned, the spark of belief that I could live again, that I first confronted my fear. The fear that I was destined to live a life in and out of madness. No one was there to remind me of my history of my sanity, my courage, or my willingness to endure.

I remember the first time I was in the 102-degree heated yoga studio again, going through a sequence of postures I had known for years. I could feel how out of shape I was. How much my body had changed in the two years. Yet I sat through the class, made it to the end, and reconnected to discipline. I moved beyond the voice in my head who said I couldn't make it through.

I remember the countless bike rides. I would often ride over an hour to get to work. The way back was mostly uphill. I hated every moment of it. I'm not a cyclist by nature, I just prefer riding my bike to driving a car. Plus at this stage, I wasn't ready for a car, car insurance, repairs, and all that is entailed in owning a vehicle. I wouldn't have a car for years into my recovery.

Anyway, I was on the bike, pedaling uphill, coming home from work. I was so tired, wishing I could be done. I just wanted to be done with the day, yet I would finish the ride. I was remembering my will. My ability to persevere through pain.

While "starting over," I lived with this latent anxiety in my body, the anxiety softly humming day in and day out and occasionally shouting at me, "You will have another break! You are only fooling yourself!" Still, I kept going. I kept reconnecting. Reconnecting to the aspects of living, of being. The parts of my life reminding me how to be me. The rhythms and routines that held "Brandon" embedded within them. The way I preferred a more explosive, intense movement when rock climbing.

I've always admired folks who have a more static, steady movement while climbing. My climbing nature is to explode, to push myself in an exaggerated and exuberant way to the next climbing hold. When I started to climb again, I remembered aspects of my spirit, the spirit that lives in the consensual reality of everyone else. My climbing spirit.

I started to sit again, bearing witness to the movements of my mind as I meditated. In Zen, we call meditation sitting, to just sit there. I had to learn how to be with my mind again. How to be with it when it was afraid, wild, sleepy, inflated, deflated, angry, and sad. I had to learn how to sit and let my mind be my mind again. No longer controlling it through watching television. No longer dampening it to manage the shame.

This is the most important thing I want to convey. Everyone has a history of sanity. Everyone has rhythm, routine, and activity supporting health, connection, and meaning. In these activities, a living memory of who we are is stored. This memory is also tied to our sensory gating.

Different activities require different sensory gating to function. When someone is hunting, I imagine they notice subtle movements around them more than someone who is just hiking through the same space. When we engage in sports, we often alter time, slowing it to notice minute details that support the activity of the sport. While playing tennis, we see the serve almost in slow motion, slowly hitting it back, even though everything is actually happening quickly.

For me to enjoy riding a bike, I can't be spinning in my head, thinking too much. It is just not enjoyable. I need to slow my mind down, anchor myself into my surroundings, and enjoy the movement in my body as I ride. This is a type of sensory gating that supports bike riding for me.

This sensory gating preference has a type of gravitation to it. When I ride, I naturally activate it. It is not a conscious choice. So when I started getting on my bike again, I saw my mind slowing. I saw myself coming out of myself and noticing the environment around me. I didn't have to "try" to do it.

I remember one day when riding to a yoga class, a few weeks into living again, catching the shadow of my reflector. In the shadow, it emitted a beautiful rainbow, following me as I rode, living in my shadow.

When I saw the rainbow out of the corner of my eye, I melted. Melted into beauty, into hope, into the grace of being alive. It was a moment of letting go of my story of "reclaiming my life" and appreciating the natural beauty of being alive. This was my first moment of freedom, the first moment I didn't have to be defined by "me" and my recent history. A moment I could appreciate the beauty of being.

Being on my bike, slowing my mind, and noticing my environment all allowed for this moment of grounded "opening." I was opening to the beauty of the world without creating some story of my importance or other delusional processes. I was just having a cool out-of-time moment of beauty before returning to my everyday consciousness of riding my bike to a yoga class. I was able to open and close in a more organic and functional manner again.

This moment was probably one of the most important moments for me. To know I could still taste the sublime and go on living. Not being swept away by the intensities of extreme states, but allowing altered state experiences to enhance the fabric of my everyday life.

When connecting with new people, I would be able to slow down and attempt to read their tempo, so we could match well for the engagement. I wouldn't just bring out the speed and intensity of my own inner experience, blasting them with it. No, I would slow down, see where they were, and explore connections. This ability was naturally inside of me. It only needed to be remembered.

If we can grab enough of these exercises, these activities, and commit to engaging them, there will often be enough of a connection to a more consensual reality mode. A more consolidated sensory gating that is appropriate to the contexts we are in, and a momentum starts to build.

We can start to feel life take hold again, guiding us through our healing journey. This time, in a grounded and steady way. Gently pushing toward increased connection, engagement, and meaning.

I had a dream around this time. My grandfather was haunting me in our family home. I kept trying to run from him, to get away. He was a ghoul-like figure. Then I went to shoot him with the pistol I somehow had and saw that written on his forehead was a Bible verse. It wasn't a real Bible verse but a verse for me from my Grandpa.

With effort, two years can be seven.

Slowly and sometimes quickly, people feel themselves returning. As they feel this return, they start to take on more, being able to reclaim more aspects of their daily life until they are similarly engaged and connected to their world. Then the work of continuing to grow and develop takes hold again. People move beyond the life they held before, exploring further and further dimensions of their growth, development, and engagement with the world.

People return to their growth edges and challenge themselves in a way that helps to build and grow their capacities further. Not just "remembering" who they were forever, but actually living at the edge again. Coming home.

For me, home is not a place. It is not a destination. Home is living on the edge of our growth. "Living our dharma," as the Buddhist in me would say.

Home is knowing the challenges you face now are bringing you toward a more kind and liberated future self. This is home to me. This is the home I came home to. The home that allowed me to feel alive again. It wasn't coming back to my life before. It was coming back to living and growing, to living in the challenge of this human existence.

This takes a certain time and space to happen. It requires a commitment to engaging in the rhythms, routines, and activities embedded within your history of sanity until you feel enough of a tether anchoring in consensus reality to begin to explore where your life wants to go now. Because it is often different than before the madness.

When I started to really engage my life, to honor it, I was surprised at the direction it went. It wasn't the same template or the same values and goals as before my break. I was moving in a new direction and can thank the experience of madness for that. In a way, my madness helped me align with a new direction, to let go of old structural wounds limiting my ability to flow with life.

In my journey, I waited until my experience settled, until I was out of the extreme states, to re-engage *the body of activity*, to connect to my life again. I don't know if this is always the best approach. I lived through a horrific depression while cut off from doing the things I loved. Isolated, in a personal hell.

Earlier I mentioned a client at Windhorse that was so raw, hardly able to engage, to make conversation and connect. Within a few months, we would be getting tea, trying out restaurants, talking philosophy, movies, and life experiences. Through engaging in his shared disciplines, the activities of vitality and meaning he knew, he was able to support the settling period, helping to reset his sensory gating and living in the world.

He did not go through his settling period alone. He was supported in connecting to the activities that would allow him to ground and know himself within consensus reality again. There were days when it was really hard on him, where he seemed completely open and overwhelmed. And there were days when he was grounded and able to connect.

This is what we need: help in engaging these activities that feel hard in the wider-open sensory gating. We need people to go on walks with us. Go to the grocery store. Run errands. Play basketball. Giving us the motivation to "come back together" again, which is no easy task. We also need these same people to be okay when we are not up for reconnecting and need space to hide away, to be lost in our *other world*, with those folks being there and waiting for when we are ready to come back into living again.

My journey was one of radical alienation from the people around me, from the life I had known. When I was able to connect again, I quickly rebuilt and started moving my life forward. For some, the process is more back and forth, movements toward engaged living and pulling back. Building up the strength, skills, and capacity to step into sustained everyday engagement.

If you have experienced a period of madness or know a loved one who has, try to honor these activities you once knew, the activities where you felt most like yourself. Really give it a go. At first, it might be hard, hard to orient and connect. But over time, it often becomes easier, these activities becoming a time to anchor ourselves in our brilliant sanity.

By sanity, I do not mean our ability to engage in consensus reality. I mean the part of us that goes beyond consensus reality, beyond madness. I am talking about the unshakable wisdom living inside of all of us, waiting to be heard and acted on.

We all have our own unique list. We all know what we need to heal. It is a matter of being able to honor the soft voice of sanity calling you home, an environment that will welcome you once you are ready to step back into living.

Conclusion

THOSE WITH SIGNIFICANTLY open sensory gating channels are orienting themselves to sensory inputs that most other people do not notice and attributing importance to the meanings in the sensory inputs that other people do not.

Further they don't know how to interpret the sea of meanings they are experiencing. They tend to use the cultural metaphors (and standards of normalcy) they have internalized to explain what is happening, the majority of which are inaccurate maps of the metaphysical background of the world. Those metaphors just don't work at helping orient the person in time, space or meaning. Often they make things worse. It's a software problem that extends as well to clinicians. Few of those that treat the condition actually have access to the metaphysical background of the world themselves or even understand what access to that world means. In consequence, not only are the interpretations by "schizophrenics" of their meaning inflows "crazy", so are the informational interventions by their caretakers.

This behaviorally orients those with this kind of widely open sensory gating far outside the cultural norm. In cultures that recognize the importance of this capacity, this group of people are trained to use their enhanced perceptual capacities for the benefit of the group.

Stephen Harrod Buhner
Plant Intelligence and the Imaginal Realm

Reading the most poignant and clear statement on extreme states from an herbalist was a surprise, to say the least. It happened years into my recovery. After my own academic exploration of extreme states. After my time at Windhorse. After the period in my life when I was focused on my recovery journey.

At the time I found this description, I felt I'd already landed in my personal meaning and understanding of what I'd been through. I wasn't looking to adopt someone else's frame of reference around madness. Honestly, I was hoping to learn about plants.

I never really felt I understood madness. What I went through. In my recovery process, I really wasn't looking for a system to make sense of what had happened. I was more oriented toward the rebuilding, the establishing of my life after catastrophically losing touch with it.

For me, this is the work of recovery. And it informed my meaning around madness. My more theoretical and academic interest was oriented toward the history of madness and historical movements that have brought us to our current state of care and treatment in the United States.

When folks would ask me to share my understanding of what happened, I'd often say my experience of madness lived in a box on a shelf somewhere inside of me. Not that I couldn't look into the box, more so that it didn't feel helpful to peek inside. Trying to understand the contents of my madness box felt like missing the point. As I've said enough by now, It isn't about understanding madness for me. It is about returning. Integrating. Standing on the rocky shore.

Then I read Buhner's words. They made sense. *Some of us have experiences we don't have good words for.* Often, individuals are abandoned in overwhelming states, without the support of skilled guides. Without the help of language and support in navigating the recovery process.

Buhner's conceptual understanding of madness allowed me to feel understood in a language that was accessible and clear. If someone asks me about madness now, I can somewhat quickly explain sensory gating and meaning-making.

After all the years of reading theories and others' attempts to articulate madness, here was someone describing madness more closely to how I experienced it.

> *Those with significantly open sensory gating channels are orienting themselves to sensory inputs that most other people do not notice and attributing importance to those meanings in the sensory inputs that others do not.*

This is as close to an accurate definition of madness as I've read. When I sit with madness, my own and the wider field of madness that my life expressed in – my work, my personal study, my life experience – I think about the nervous system. My nervous system knowledge is limited. And it's easy to see the significant impact our nervous system has on our experience.

There's a popular cultural saying, "The mystic swims in the sea the mad drown in." I've heard multiple variations attributed to different people, with Joseph Campbell often getting credit.

Essentially, this phrase captures the similarity between extreme states and mystical states. On one level, there might not be much difference between the two experiences. It is more likely that they're different in how the experiences are held, in what nervous system the experiences are happening in. I sometimes wonder if it is as simple as mystics being relaxed in the sea of experience where the mad are in a more reactive fight-or-flight sympathetic state.

From a contemplative frame of thinking, when folks are using more "gentle" means of altering consciousness – meditation, yoga, and the such – they will periodically enter wider experiential states. And usually, especially in the beginning of contemplative practice, folks often have a fearful response to experiences like the boundaries of the body beginning to dissolve. A somewhat common experience in meditation.

This fear response will stop the altered state from taking hold, like a brake. It ends the movement into the altered state quickly, often frustrating the contemplative. All that training to have cool experiences that are thwarted by a moment of fear.

Yet in madness, in the breaking through into higher energy states and wider experiential fields that Edward Podvoll so clearly articulates, the same brakes aren't in place. It's like the brake line gets cut. The fearful response, the wanting the experiences to stop, loses its power. The extreme states continue even with the fear. Fight-or-flight plus wide-open sensory gating. Not a good combo.

This brings us to a fuller definition of madness: intense experiences with meaning-making that is not culturally acceptable. And the cure? At the end of the day, it might sound too simple. *Do the things you used to do.* It is that simple. And it isn't.

This core concept does not come from a logical, scientific perspective like sensory gating. No biological functions were measured through an experimental protocol. It is what has been done through the ages. Before science existed as a modern worldview or mythos.

Reconnect to the embodied physical activities that made you who you were before your break. Reconstitute yourself through reengaging with activities that make you who you are. Reclaim your rhythms and routines to support the settling of your mind, aka begin to close your gating channels.

Before asylums took over the care of the mad, there was another care model that competed side by side with the asylum system. It was the moral treatment model. Moral treatment wasn't perfect and it wasn't scientific. It was more closely connected to religion and caring for the soul of the patient. They advocated for the use of kindness and gentleness when working with folks in extremes.

One moral treatment center in the 19th century was a well-furnished building with a garden where clients and staff both wore regular clothes for the time. Walking outside, reading, and art were all encouraged. The center even put on plays for the local community. It was a space where you might not be able to distinguish staff from clients.

This center was supporting the connection to meaningful activity that restores the capacity for more grounded human connection. It was inviting its patients back into themselves, into their consensual selves who could relate to and connect with their wider communities.

It is this function that has the most potent impact. Engaging in the everyday tasks of being human with other humans. Yet so often, we isolate and separate individuals in extreme states. Or we medicate to the degree that folks can no longer connect with loved ones.

Why is it so simple? Just do the things that connect you to a past version of yourself.

I believe without any scientific evidence, within our activities of health, a pattern of sensory gating is encoded. Activities alter our sensory gating. This is why they often show sports in slow motion. The slow-mo lets you see what is happening. Because it often happens so quickly. The play, the wave, the decisive moment of activity. A blur.

Unless you are living it. Time is dilated in heightened moments of flow-based athletic activity. The ball moves slower. The athlete can see the whole field. The surfer perceives the wave as moving in slow motion. This is due to the augmenting of sensory gating.

A researcher, Ellen Langer, once studied typists. People who could type super fast. She found that, from their perspective, they felt they were typing at a "normal speed." [26]These anecdotes highlight how activities are connected to our sensory gating system, in these cases, often around time dilation.

---

26 Ellen Langer, Arthur Blank, Benzion Chanowitz. The Mindlessness of Ostensibly Thoughtful Action: The Role of "Placebic" Information in Interpersonal Interaction. Journal of Personality and Social Psychology. 1979. Vol. 36, No. 6, 635-642.

By our activities containing a living memory of our sensory gating, when we re-engage activities we have a strong connection to, like riding a bike, we are returning to a previous pattern of sensory gating. One that is more likely to allow an individual to participate more fully in consensus reality, which is where most loved ones, friends, communities, and meaningful activities in the world happen.

By restoring our activities of health, we are restoring a pattern of living that was more likely grounded, slower, and engaged with the wider world. This is what extreme states need.

Psychologist Eugen Bleuler, who changed the name of dementia praecox to our modern word of schizophrenia, liked to say that people suffering from schizophrenia need three things: meaningful activity, community, and relaxation. They need a restoration of sensory gating.

Bleuler hoped the change from dementia praecox to schizophrenia would result in a re-conceptualizing of the psychotic process. He understood the flaws in the original diagnosis:

> *"We had to pose the question whether we are not merely dealing with the effect of a particularly powerful psychological trauma on a very sensitive person rather than with a disease in the narrow sense of the word."*[27]

Bleuler understood that people recover from periods of madness and return to living healthy, engaged lives. His attempt to change the name did little to change the cultural assumptions associated with madness. It is still seen as a deterioration process with no cure. This just isn't true. Individuals who experience a psychotic break are not destined to deteriorate.

---

27 Bleuler E. , Dementia Praecox oder Gruppe der Schizophrenien, 1911 Leipzig, Germany Deuticke

It seems for decades, if not centuries, we have been attempting to understand the biological cause of madness. To pinpoint the pathway of genetic or chemical imbalance resulting in psychotic processes. This has brought us nowhere. We are no closer to understanding the biological mechanisms of schizophrenia. In the time we've been looking for a "cure," our capacity to support individuals in a psychotic process has gotten worse, year after year.

This is not due to some expression of the "illness." This is a limitation of thinking within the Western medical model. As William James notes, "medical materialism," a phenomenon he warned about in the early 1900s, has resulted in worse care of those in need a century later. This is alarming.

In the varieties of religious experience, James warns about what can happen if "medical materialism" is taken too far. If all states and experiences are reduced to chemical processes, we will lose the value of spiritual states. Of different ways of thinking and relating to life. We will lose the possibility of our personal realities impacting consensus reality. Of someone's novel, unique experience impacting the experience of others. The reductionism reduces the possibility that our inner lives can meaningfully impact the wider world.

It also limits a clinician. If the medical materialism view is in the context of psychology, it is much easier to dismiss experiences that don't make "sense" within consensus reality. But if there is value to spiritual states – not reality, but value – we may take more care in supporting those having experiences in which it is hard to understand the value in the moment.

We need to start thinking about madness differently. I laid out a simple paradigm. Shifting from an "Apollonian" view of madness to a "Dionysian" view of madness. By this, I mean moving away from identifying a cure to learning how to support the natural process of recovery from psychosis.

In this book, I have laid out a case for sensory gating being a key component of the psychotic process, which I borrowed from Stephen Buhner's thinking. Essentially, how individuals who experience psychosis often have a greater sensitivity to their environments (which includes their bodies). This sensitivity can be understood through the concept of sensory gating. With open sensory gating, individuals perceive more information from their environments. Information others are not perceiving nor able to articulate.

Often, individuals in a psychotic episode experience a "break" from a more "normal" or habitually familiar sensory gating to a flooding of their sensory system through the abrupt alteration in sensory gating that occurs in madness. This is often facilitated through their "cocktail" of factors, resulting in breaking through into the wide-open sensory gating we know as psychosis.

As sensory gating is a process akin to an aperture on a camera, it can be both opened and closed. This is often where antipsychotic medication comes into play. It is a biological means of impacting a person's sensory gating, essentially outsourcing sensory gating to a pill.

Modern neuroscience speaks to our capacity for neuroplasticity. Individuals can change the structures and processes of their brain. Our brain is not hardwired, but a more flexible system than we've historically acknowledged.

For millennia, individuals have understood how to alter sensory gating through spiritual practice. Think meditation, fasting, yoga, praying, chanting, solo time in the wilderness, and of course psychedelics. Nowadays, we are only really interested in opening sensory gating to create positive healthy changes through altered states. This includes mindfulness and psychedelic-assisted psychotherapy.

The reverse is just as possible: to increase sensory gating through mundane, everyday activities to support the grounding and slowing of the mind. Hence the call to reconnect to past activities of health. To restore a sensory gating that is more conducive to living in the world.

This is all wonderful. A different story to capture and begin to understand madness. It's not the neurochemicals, it's the sensory gating. Like how the former head of NIMH called for a transition away from understanding the impact of neurochemicals on mental illness to understanding the electrical system of brains to support healing.

And I did something here.

I made up a story.

Not for me.

But for the Western materialistic worldview.

Our culture needs new stories of madness. I tried to make a case for an alternative story to the present understanding of madness. From broken brains to culturally inadequate meaning-making structures.

My story is borrowed from Buhner. He did the scientific research and found a story that more fully captures the lived experience of madness. It is open sensory gating with inadequate meaning-making structures. His story has the potential to be accepted by materialist science. He's speaking the language, to a degree.

I highlight one aspect potentially outside Buhner's conceptualization, which is the formation of a madness-based ego structure. I tell a story of sensitivity and how sensitive individuals either gradually or abruptly enter into periods of wide-open sensory gating, essentially entering sensory overload.

In these periods of wide-open gating, the creation of a *madness-based ego* begins. Humans are meaning-making creatures and almost required to make meaning of experiences. Our habituated ways of making meaning get reified within our ego structure. They become the "I."

When individuals enter into a period of extreme states, they often make meaning of their extreme states through the "cultural metaphors" of Western materialism. This is a horrible system to use to make meaning of extreme states. The whole system of thought is rooted in an absence of spiritual reality. And so often, "crazy" individuals are attempting to explain their experiences through a language system that is in opposition to the very experiences they are trying to convey.

As folks make sense of their extreme states, a madness-based ego begins to form. A new story about the person emerges that allows for the new experiences they are having to make sense. In my case, I made up a story of spiritual importance to make sense of the heightened experiences I was living.

This story I made up of my significance became the new "me." While I was in my heightened states of overwhelm, it was required in a way. It was the flotation device that allowed me to stay alive in the sea of experience I was nearly drowning in. As my extreme states began to settle, I held onto my story of importance even though I was no longer having the experiences that correlated to the sense of importance I had created.

Experience first, meaning second.

In the case of madness-based egos, the experience fades but the meaning stays. This can often result in a vicious cycle where folks feel "called" back to their extreme states so the story of who they are makes sense. We all want to be able to make sense of our lives. Much of the healing in madness is rooted in the necessity of letting go of the madness-based ego to return to a more grounded consciousness that is able to integrate and impact the everyday world of consensus reality.

When you combine the surrendering of the madness-based ego with reconnecting to past activities of health, this is usually a beginning foundation to start the restoration process of recovery. Especially when one is in a supportive community or environment.

This allows for the re-grounding into everyday life with the possibility that one's sensitivities will become a source of meaning and vitality for themselves, possibly beneficially impacting others as well.

I don't tell this story of sensitivity due to open gating because I think my story is the "right" one and should replace the old one. Anyone who is scientifically trained can most likely poke holes in my untrained use of sensory gating. I am not an academic trained in research, neurology, or biology.

For the last century, contemplatives have been attempting to use science to validate and popularize their contemplative frames of understanding. As a contemplative, I have attempted to contribute an understanding of madness by introducing the function of the madness-based ego being dependent upon extreme states for continuity. Thus, this creates the impulse to return to extreme states through tried and true methods of altering consciousness. I did not use science to derive this understanding. It came from my study of contemplative traditions and my lived experience.

By packaging my contemplative understanding within a modern Western worldview of brain processes, I want to be heard. To be validated as someone who can contribute to thinking around madness. To contribute my meaning-making, I must make sense to our current worldview, i.e. science.

This is where "crazy" folks are dismissed. They are not adequately translating their experiences to be understood, like my client who used the phrase "chewing on sticks." He was accurately perceiving a dynamic in the team while not being able to communicate his perception in a way where he could be understood.

There are many ways to explain madness in other systems of thinking, especially contemplative systems. Just the other day, I was talking to an acupuncturist who described madness from his view and how practitioners of Chinese medicine treat madness. It was a totally different model than the Western medical model uses to make sense of and treat madness. And it doesn't really matter to me if it's accurate because, in his model, individuals can be treated. They recover!

It is possible to think differently about madness. It is possible to understand madness outside of a paradigm of pathology and degenerative brains. This is the important turn. We can think differently. We can understand a fundamental point. Individuals recover from periods of psychosis and can go on to lead healthy, meaningful, and generative lives.

Can we fund this, please? Can we direct the exorbitant amount of dollars spent on research trying to understand the cause of madness in a different direction? Toward one of healing, community, and actually supporting individuals who are struggling?

Or will we continue to attempt to maintain the flimsy foundations of our current biological understanding of mental health crises? Ignoring common facts we've known for millennia.

In the 1800s, the European medical establishment essentially purchased the right to treat the insane, taking that power away from the church. Moral treatment no longer exists. Through medical propaganda and lobbying, the medical establishment purchased the right to treat people like me. And more importantly, to define our value.

They still possess this right. Governments fund the medical establishment despite this establishment continually being unable to deliver on a cause or an effective treatment based on their research. It is time for the medical establishment to admit that they had no right to purchase madness. They had no right to claim it as their purview.

The medical establishment has failed as stewards. They are responsible for the care of individuals struggling with extreme states, and they've done almost nothing positive with that care. A care they profit from.

I hope we can begin to think differently about madness. Start to question assumed worldviews and begin to work backward. If people recover naturally, how do we support the process rather than just trying to prevent, cure, or dampen it?

The conceptual understanding I brought forth in this book is not my personal way of understanding madness. My understanding feels weirder than what fits within the sterilized thinking that often emerges from the materialist Western worldview. It's spiritual.

As much as this book is for individuals recovering from madness, it is for our culture which needs to recover from our broken understandings of madness.

Please think differently.

We need it.

All of us.

We do not know what we've lost by denying sensitive individuals the capacity to express their lives within culture. We do not know what sensitive individuals are capable of if they are not being defined as broken by the medical establishment. By placing a story of brokenness on sensitive individuals, we are likely alienating a group of people who have a radical potential to impact our world today.

Currently, we are not supporting those who may help us out of the mess we are in. Novelty does not emerge from staying in the lanes of consensus reality. Novelty emerges by braving into the sea of meaning and coming back with something to offer.

We need novelty to adapt to our world. We need those who see, feel, and think differently. This is not the time to support conformity and the adoption of consensus values and ways of being.

Clearly, at least to my eyes, consensus reality is breaking down. Not in the sense of it being seen through or anything. More in the sense that consensus reality is no longer supporting its people. People are struggling and the models of self, others, and the world we've created are not up to the challenges of today.

If consensus reality is not reality, but our construction of an agreed-upon reality, what value does it have when it is not serving those who are embedded within it?

Let those who create, create.

And stop telling them they are broken.

Acknowledgments

FIRST AND FOREMOST, I wish to thank all those who helped me when I needed it most. My father for taking me in. My family for supporting me after I stepped back into living again. All the strangers who provided me rides or would pull over to offer me money and allow me to eat another day. It is only with great kindness from many strangers that I am here today. Small kindnesses add up.

I wish to thank the communities who supported me as I rebuilt my life. Whether informal friend communities, roommates I shared space with, the Zen Center I was a part of, my therapist who supported me through my years of recovery, and the many natural spaces that allowed me to breathe and feel a part of something larger.

I am forever indebted to the work of Edward Podvoll and the Windhorse community. Thank you for keeping the spirit of Windhorse alive all these years. It is through the work of many clinicians that Windhorse thrives. Community knowledge begins with those who say yes to trying something new. Thanks to Edward's students who were willing to pioneer a new treatment modality and keep it going.

Special gratitude to Stephen Buhner. Sometimes I feel I expanded his three paragraphs on schizophrenia from *Plant Intelligence and the Imaginal Realm* into a book. I appreciate your healing journey that allowed you to so succinctly articulate what most struggle to describe. I regret not sending you this book before you passed.

And to all the psychologists and thinkers who continue to push the medical model to reconsider its foundational views and the impact those views have on the care provided to those suffering.

Particular gratitude to Andrew Scull for researching and dedicating his life to studying the history of madness. Thank you for placing our current myths and practices of madness into context.

And to Robert Whitaker, for gathering the history of madness in America and the research indicating how backward our treatment and understanding of madness is. Thank you for finding the scientific evidence amidst all the noise.

I would also like to thank William Dorey, for his album, Love and Life. The song, "take my time" became a running mantra as I exclusively listened to the album to write this book. Many years with Skinshape.

And to my friends, family, and loved ones who believed in me when I wasn't so sure I was going to make it through.

And of course, my wife. Without you what am I?

To all those struggling without a map,
may you find your way home.

About the Author

BRANDON HOUSTON, MA, LPCC has dedicated his life to individual and systemic transformation. His dedication expresses itself in his work as a Gestalt and Somatic psychotherapist. As a leadership coach in the business world. And most recently stewarding a grove of second growth redwoods in Northern California, where he and his wife raise their family. He enjoys being in the forest, in the waves and with the people he loves. In his heart he sees himself foremost as a healer and a steward of wholehearted living.

Anonymous Forest

Invest in an Unimaginable Future

Appendix:

A Guide for Families[28]

A guide for families who have a member suffering from a major mental disturbance.

Written by: Constance Packard, MSW, Sally Clay & Harold Raush

[28] *A Guide for Families* written by Constance Packard, MSW; Sally Clay; and Harold Raush, courtesy of Windhorse Integrative Medicine. www.WindhorseIMH.org
Also available online at https://www.windhorseimh.org/wp-content/uploads/2019/09/Guide-for-Families-EBook.pdf

Contents

About Windhorse and this Guide

Introduction: Family Guidelines

Attitude: Cultivate Acceptance and Raise Respect

Orientation: Choose Happiness

Boundaries: Set Limits, Give Space

Full Expressions: Show Appreciation, Be Honest

Social Environment: Find Community

Conclusion

About Windhorse and this Guide

This is a guide for families who have a member suffering from a major mental disturbance, such as schizophrenia, bipolar disorder or severe depression. Constance Packard, M.S.W, wrote the basic text. She is the mother of a son with a diagnosis of schizophrenia, a family therapist and a past member of the Windhorse Board of Directors.

Windhorse is a coalition of professional, consumer, and family members and we consider it very important that these three groups work together in a way that informs the whole. The clinical staff, therefore, went through a process of revising and refining the Guide, with special input from Sally Clay and Harold Raush. Sally is a consumer/survivor activist who was, at the time, both on the staff and a member of the Board of Directors. Harold was the father of a Windhorse graduate, a clinical psychologist and co-lead the family program. He also served as our Windhorse elder unGl he passed away. We offer the Guide as an introduction to the way we at Windhorse Integrative Mental Health work with the families of our clients. We also offer it to other families anywhere who may Ind it helpful.

Introduction: Family Guidelines

Mental health professionals used to tell us that parents caused mental disturbance in their children. Students of psychiatry, clinical psychology and social work learned about "schizophrenogenic mothers" and distant fathers.

Fortunately, that belief concerning the cause of mental illness no longer holds sway.

At present, the predominant view in the field is that mental disturbance is a physical illness in which thoughts and behaviors are symptoms of an imbalance in the brain. Mental illness is compared to a disease such as diabetes. We are told that something is defective and can only be "fixed" through medical technology such as drugs. This view is often called the "medical model."

The implication of this view is that if there is a defect in the brain, then there is no hope of recovery, and the best we can do is manage symptoms.

The medical model requires a constant vigilance for the reappearance of symptoms and encourages a tendency to Ind something "wrong" in the slightest change in attitude or behavior. In addition, if families and professionals rely solely on the medical model, we tend to give messages that disempower those who suffer from these conditions.

The Windhorse approach is quite different. We view mental affliction as essentially a human problem that can best be addressed through human means.

While there are many factors involved in mental disturbances, including brain function and heredity, we do not regard the person as an illness, or a bundle of symptoms. Instead we deal with the problems at hand with common sense -- with respect, discipline, kindness and lifestyle choices.

We work to create a physical and psychological environment that benefits everyone who lives within it -- both the person in difficulty and his or her family and friends.

We believe that recovery is possible, and that we can emerge from the suffering and confusion of mental disturbances with a depth of understanding that will stand us in good stead for the rest of our lives. We believe that it is possible to have a meaningful life, in spite of disability, all along the path of recovery and whether or not full recovery occurs.

We believe recovery IS possible.

> *We include families in our work because family dynamics, attitudes and communication do affect the recovery process, either giving impetus to recovery as part of creating a "sane environment" or impeding it. Family members are deeply and powerfully interconnected.*
>
> *If one member of a family is in an extreme state, all members of the family will most likely Ind that they are also in an extreme state of some kind in response to the difficult situation and the intense emotions associated with it. The ongoing disruption, grief and anxiety experienced by families, combined with negative cultural attitudes towards mental illness and a fragmented mental health system, constitute major and continuous stresses of many kinds on many fronts. We know that it is a difficult journey, and that all of you have at times been stretched to the limits of your endurance.*

We know that families, as well as clients, commonly Ind themselves in a dark labyrinth of grief, fear, conflict and confusion -- and that it is hard to know where to turn for guidance.

No matter how great the stress or turmoil, in our experience there are two basic concerns closest to the hearts of most family members:

1. How can I give my son or daughter, sister or brother, husband or wife what he or she needs from me.
2. How can I and the other members of our family survive and flourish in the midst of all this chaos and heartbreak.

These are the two basic concerns to be addressed in thinking about the family situation and how to help. They are completely interrelated and interdependent and cannot really be addressed separately, because the ability of family members to give their mentally disturbed relative what he or she needs from them will be greatly enhanced if they themselves have attained a degree of equanimity and are leading satisfying lives.

In fact, the interconnectedness of these two concerns is an important principle underlying all our work and also extends to the network of professionals and team members involved in the client's treatment.

Stated in another way, the first principle guiding our work is that the client, the professionals and significant family members are all inextricably and closely linked in the recovery process and that everything affects everything else, for be]er or for worse.

Consequently, it is of great importance that we all work together with a common purpose and a common vision of what promotes recovery.

Through our combined experience as professionals, family members and recovered consumers, we have learned some guiding principles for families that lead toward healing and recovery.

It is these five principles that we present here and which we believe enable us to give our family member the support and nurturing he or she needs, to set boundaries and limits to protect everybody in the family and to Ind the space to nurture ourselves -- all necessary requirements if the family is going to function for the benefit of all its members.

Attitude: Cultivate Acceptance And Raise Respect

Attitude is key in the healing process. It is impossible to overstress the importance of an accepting attitude on the part of family members. Mental disturbance almost always seems to bring with it crippling self---doubt and low self-esteem. These are all too often reinforced by the stigma encountered in many ways in our society.

An attitude of unconditional respect and acceptance, therefore, from those who are closest to the client is the ground from which recovery can begin. This means accepting our relative exactly as he or she is at present. It means seeing all of his or her beauty and strength and good qualifies. It means letting go of our expectations that our relative should be any different than he or she is right now.

Looking at the situation solely from the point of view of the medical model makes this extremely difficult, if not impossible, to achieve. For if we view our family member as "sick" and want him or her to "get well," which implies change, we must think about the message we will be giving. The message will be that our son, for example, is not okay the way he is and must become something different in order to get our acceptance.

The ability to trust oneself and others that are important to you is a key ingredient in recovery

If we relate to him as if his words and actions have li]le or no meaning because they are the result of a chemical imbalance, what message are we giving? We are giving the message that he cannot trust his own mind, thoughts and feelings, and that we do not trust them very much either. Though we don't intend it, these messages come across as critical and disrespectful.

This can only reinforce our family member's very painful feelings of despair, frustration, anger and self-doubt. If these subtle and not so subtle messages are coming from both families and professionals, it becomes much harder for people in these difficult states of mind to trust themselves or others.

The ability to trust oneself and others that are important to you is a key ingredient in recovery.

How is it possible to give up our dreams and expectations that our family member must have a "normal" life with "normal" achievements? This can be a painful process and can take years of being worn down by failures, disappointments and setbacks.

It is important to remember, however, that one's attitude is a matter of choice. One can choose to adopt an attitude of unconditional respect and acceptance -- yet to do so requires letting go of most of our cultural conditioning.

We are conditioned to see mental illness as pathology and as tragedy. Almost all of the literature and professional opinion describe it this way. Our society's emphasis on achievement and status reinforce this view.

To let go of all of this requires a radical shift to a very different way of seeing things. It requires seeing the person as whole and perfect as he or she is. It requires cultivation of a nonjudgmental stance in recognition of our inability to know the whole truth about anything.

It requires trust that our experience and the experience of mental illness have meaning, regardless of the outcome. It requires acknowledgment that we are each in charge of our own path in life. It is a point of view that chooses to see the gift hidden in each challenge.

For example, when we talk to our son or daughter, we address their inner quality of humanness rather than their outward appearance or diagnosis. Let us say my daughter exhibits some strange or disturbing behavior. My first reaction may be to ask her if she is getting sick again, and urge her to take her medication. If I say this to her, she will probably regard it as an accusation and withdraw further into mistrust.

Instead I listen respectfully to what she has to say, with my mind open to appreciate her intentions and to follow her thought processes. I may honestly say that I do not agree with her, or that I Ind what she says to be impossible. But if I have truly listened, my daughter will trust that I want to understand and that I do not reject her as an adult person. The process of listening itself may serve to open the doors of communication, and may lead to new avenues of thought that will make sense to both of us.

The byproduct of mutual respect is that nobody needs to feel under pressure to be anything other than who they are. My daughter will feel free to talk openly to me. She need not feel that she is not acceptable

unless she denies her feelings and beliefs. At the same time, I do not need to feel guilt that I have caused some terrible catastrophe. My daughter is not a catastrophe -- she is someone I love and respect for who she is.

The unconditional part of respect is the way we value the person behind the symptoms, in spite of the mistakes and along with the confusion. We do not need to ignore or deny the symptoms, the mistakes or the confusion. Our family member can work on symptoms at his or her own pace, with a sense of relaxation.

Unconditional respect provides a backdrop of hope and acceptance. This attitude of acceptance of our family member is, paradoxically, the attitude on the part of families and caregivers that is most conducive to promoting change. Just as it is a paradox that when we are able to accept ourselves as we are, we are freer to direct energy toward what we might want to change in our lives.

Yet this attitude is a very difficult balance to achieve, because of course we all would like to see our family member happier and having the life he or she desires. The attitude toward our clients we work to cultivate is an attitude of wanting change for them but of not needing them to change.

It combines respecting and accepting wherever they are at any given moment -- psychotic thinking, altered awareness, difficult behavior and all -- with holding out hope and the possibility of change, and at the same time nonattachment to the outcome. This requires humor, patience and a light-handed approach rather than a heavy one. A tall order! Yet we have everything to gain and nothing to lose in reaching for it.

Orientation: Choose Happiness

As stated above, having a relative who is suffering serious mental disturbance places a great strain on families. The cultural attitude, which we have inherited, views mental illness as a tragedy and stigma is still common. The normal tendency in such a situation is to focus on the "sick" member and to try somehow to bring about change in him or her.

The reality is, however, that we do not have the power to change anybody else we have only the power to change our own behavior and attitudes.

When we put pressure on someone else to change, the normal reaction for that person is to resist, retaining his or her autonomy. In such a situation, all the energy is bound up in an attempt to influence another's behavior and in resistance to that attempt. Efforts in this mode lead to increasing entrenchment in frustration and a sense of powerlessness. Thus if the focus is all on the "sick" person changing and not on ourselves and what is happening in the relationships surrounding the individual, it is almost impossible to avoid getting trapped in destructive, repetitive pa]erns and power struggles.

These unresolved struggles and repetitive pa]erns lead in a downward spiral to the labyrinth of frustration, fear, grief and guilt where we don't know how or where to set limits and where there is often family disagreement over how to proceed. There is a good chance that in this situation we are "running on empty" and that the whole family atmosphere is pervaded with the heaviness of tragedy and grief. The family's energy and resources are depleted. Everybody's health and welfare are adversely affected. In this atmosphere, it is impossible for the family to function in a way that benefits its members.

We all need the benefits of healing one area or another.

In order to get the focus of the "sick" person, it is immensely liberating and helpful to turn the focus inward to ourselves, because that is the terrain over which we do have control. One's own state of mind is crucial in any healing work.

> *We have found that the recovery of someone experiencing serious mental disturbance is most likely to happen when everyone in this small healing community is actively engaged in taking care of their own well-being and mental health. That is, they balance their concern for and efforts to help the client with concern for other members of the family and for their own growth and well-being.*
>
> *No matter where we are on the spectrum, we all need the benefits of healing in one area or another. There is always room to become clearer, happier, less fearful and less controlled by past negative conditioning.*

Thus your happiness is of concern to us both for your sake and for the client's sake. The happier and freer you are, the more you will give impetus to your family member's recovery, because the more you will be able to be truly present for him or her. The greatest gift we can give to those who love us is our own happiness.

Confidence and lightheartedness are contagious, and are always healing to those in trouble. It is important to remind ourselves that just as we can choose our attitude, we can choose an orientation towards happiness. In fact, the two go together. Finding the time and space to take care of yourselves in whatever ways possible is another of the key interconnected principles guiding out of the labyrinth of suffering.

Boundaries: Set Limits, Give Space

All healthy relationships require limits and clear boundaries, but for people experiencing psychosis or other disturbed states, clear limits are especially important. It is often difficult for them to distinguish reality from non-reality and to know where the boundaries of one's self or others are, so it is crucial that family members know how to set limits clearly and firmly for the protection and wellbeing of everyone in the family. Limits can be internalized, but must first be external. They are containers of excitement by saying "this is how far you can go." They give structure, rules, a sense of order and predictability. As acceptance and respect prepare the ground for recovery, clear limits stabilize the ground and help make the client's situation reliable and trustworthy .

Limit-setting skills have to do with respecting both our own autonomy and the autonomy of the client. They have to do with accepting and respecting our own feelings, and with taking our own personal needs as seriously as those of the client. They have to do with asserting our right to be comfortable in our own homes. They have to do with making clear "I statements" about what we need, want or expect, rather than blaming and judging statements (which usually start with "you.")

Limit-setting skills include being prepared to take action to enforce limits if necessary. These are not easy skills to acquire, so we must work on identifying where limits need to be set and on how to set them.

Setting limits also involves setting limits on oneself. For example, it is very common that siblings and spouses feel neglected and unheard because so much attention and intense concern are inevitably drawn to the family member who is disturbed. It is important therefore that parents set limits on themselves by not obsessing too much about one member of the family and by not allowing their lives to be dominated by crises or grief.

Full Expression: Show Appreciation, Be Honest

Our clients often have a hard time appreciating themselves, so it is very important that they hear your appreciation of them exactly as they are in the present moment, without need for them to be different. It is important to acknowledge their good qualities and to greet their accomplishments with enthusiasm. This engenders more respect on our part and is empowering. In addition, it is an excellent way to express love. Appreciation and love, warmly expressed by significant others, is the most potent of healing forces.

On the other hand, it is extremely important not to treat the family member with "kid gloves," or to become falsely cheerful, or to attempt to protect the person from everyday frustrations and challenges. To make the mistake of "coddling" the person or to give dishonest praise will only backfire and make the person feel "different" and like a stranger in his or her own home.

The Windhorse approach places great emphasis on honesty in all communication. People who suffer from serious mental disturbance are most often acutely sensitive to the emotional overtones of whatever is being communicated. It is often hard for them to distinguish the line between reality and delusion, so consequently they rely on their antennae to pick up the underlying emotional tone of a message.

It is the emotional tone which, after all, is the true message being communicated. Thus it is crucial that we are mindful of the emotional message we are giving, and that we are sure that the words and their emotional context are congruent.

Both positive and negative honest feedbacks are important in establishing a trustworthy environment. Appreciation is one aspect of honest feedback. Another aspect is the ability to be honest about one's negative feelings in a non--blaming, non—judgmental constructive manner. The key, again, is mutual respect, for even the bitterest truth is palatable when expressed with graciousness and dignity.

Social Environment: Find Community

Mental disturbance in a family member takes a heavy toll. It absorbs energy of not only the afflicted person but also of each family member, whether adult or child. Although each member will react in his or her individual way, the illness can readily consume all of the family space. The burdens and challenges of the situation can leave each person feeling isolated and with a sense that his or her own needs are unrecognized. Professional institutions, in their primary concern with the "sick" member, most often provide li]le or no support for other family members. It is not only within the family that isolation can occur. The stresses of care taking and often the sense of stigma that is still associated with mental illness may lead to withdrawal and isolation from the broader social community.

It is especially at this time that the family needs support. Because of the stigma that is sometimes a]ached to families of mental health clients it may be difficult to be open about the need for support. This need is not a matter of psychotherapy although that might be useful for some families or family members.

What we are referring to here is rather a matter of finding a sustaining environment. Such an environment could consist of other families with similar problems, an environment in which participants can explore and help one another with modes of coping and survival. Or, it could be simply the cultivation of friends who provide resources that reflect the guiding principles discussed above.

Families with a mentally ill member can also achieve gratification and enrich their own lives by helping others who are in the same boat. Families differ, and each must Ind the kind of community resources that will enhance its own capacity for individual and conjoint happiness.

Conclusion

We see our joint work as "tending" the network of relationships that surround the client the way one tends a garden -- carefully and regularly. How is it that tending relationships promotes recovery? Recovering from serious mental disturbance requires great courage and motivation. Love, acceptance, nurturing and respect all evoke motivation and courage. As the network of relationships surrounding the disturbed person is tended, more of the energy required for recovery is available. We have seen that the client's struggle to grow and recover is stimulated by the following: a cheerful and hopeful atmosphere; unconditional acceptance; real exchanges of friendship; honest feedback including expressed appreciation of who he or she is in the present moment; the maintenance of realistic limits for the protection of everyone; and social support.

These are the same things that everyone needs from significant others to grow and flourish, so we take these principles as the basis of our work at all levels within the Windhorse community. We see this as the challenge, as the gift that comes along with the suffering involved in these difficult states of mind. For in meeting this difficult challenge, family members (as well as professionals) have the opportunity to find the best in themselves and by expressing it, to live freer and happier lives.

We offer Support for families.

"Inherent in every person there is a natural healing impulse
toward health and wholeness."

– Edward M. Podvoll, M.D.
(founder of the Windhorse approach)

CONTACT US WITH QUESTIONS OR PLAN A VISIT

AdmissionsEast@windhorseimh.org

(877) 844-8181

413-586-0207 ext.333

www.WindhorseIMH.org

www.ingramcontent.com/pod-product-compliance
Lightning Source LLC
LaVergne TN
LVHW090313210926
848480LV00001B/229